★ ★

T H E
CELEBRITY
A L M A N A C

★ ★

Ed Lucaire

Prentice Hall

New York   **London**   **Toronto**   **Sydney**   **Tokyo**   **Singapore**

Prentice Hall General Reference
15 Columbus Circle
New York, NY 10023

PRENTICE HALL and colophon are registered trademarks
of Simon & Schuster, Inc.

Library of Congress Cataloging-in-Publication Data

Lucaire, Ed.
    The celebrity almanac / Ed Lucaire.
        p.   cm.
    Includes index.
    ISBN 0-13-122367-4
    1. Celebrities—Biography—Miscellanea.   I. Title.
CT105.L78   1991
920.02—dc20   91-15559
                                                   CIP

Design by Richard Oriolo

Manufactured in the United States of America

1 2 3 4 5 6 7 8 9 10

First Edition

To our public libraries, which are great sources of information and are in great need of funding.

Thanks

Kate Kelly, Susan Lauzau, Bowling Hall of Fame, International Tennis Hall of Fame, *Time* magazine, Steven Levitt, Marketing Evaluations, Inc., Sasa Assari, Madame Tussaud Wax Museum, *Playboy* magazine, Hollywood Memorial Park Cemetery, *People* magazine, Pierce Brothers Westwood Village Memorial Park, United Chapters of Phi Beta Kappa, Green-Wood Cemetery, George Cuttingham, Meg McSweeney, American Academy of Dramatic Arts, Hasty Pudding Institute, Alex Hoyt, Kent Laymon, and Liz Smith

C O N T E N T S

★   A Note to the Reader   ix   ★

★   Birth   1   ★

★   Names   51   ★

★   Family   81   ★

★   Education   99   ★

★   Love, Marriage, and Sex   119   ★

★   Physical Attributes   129   ★

★   Hollywood   145   ★

★   Awards and Honors   169   ★

★   Presidents, Politics, and History   201   ★

★   Sports   215   ★

★   Miscellany   235   ★

★   Wit and Wisdom   253   ★

★   Death   259   ★

★   Index   273   ★

A Note to the Reader

When I researched my earlier books about the famous and the infamous, I found many sources in the library that contained *some* information about famous people—annual almanacs, books of records, who's whos, sports almanacs, and the like—but there were no books that specialized in comparative data and interesting facts about celebrated people of the past and present. I found this omission to be surprising, especially since the public has an unending fascination with the lives of famous people and celebrity-oriented TV shows, magazines, and newspapers have such large and loyal audiences. Being an editor, writer, and researcher, however, I realized that this was an opportunity rather than a problem. Why not publish an almanac of facts about famous people?

As a voracious reader of biographies and an avid talk-show viewer, I have amassed in twelve years an impressive amount of facts about celebrities, from Hank Aaron to Frank Zappa, in my dossiers. I reorganized the information by categories, such as real names, places of birth, ancestry, schools attended, habits, former jobs, hobbies, and heights. Some of the lists became surprisingly long. My list of real names, for example, now contains more than 1,300 people and a surprising number of them are *not* movie stars (for example, the man born Leslie Lynch King, Jr., became the 38th President of the United States). My original list of famous preppies contained a few dozen names but now has more than 200, including the likes of dubiously preppy Danny De Vito, Abbie Hoffman, Huey Lewis, and John McEnroe. My list of long marriages originally contained the names of only a dozen couples but now contains 120. Marriages aren't getting longer—I just dug deeper and deeper to collect more facts.

For the most part, I concentrate on people who are well known by the general public, but I have also included those who earned fame, sometimes fleetingly, for winning such distinctions as a Miss America contest, a Tony award, or a Heisman trophy. Most of these award winners enjoyed at least a year of fame and glory and earned their places in celebritydom.

I think I have produced the definitive sourcebook of facts about famous people and hope that you find it fascinating, informative, and fun. If you agree, by all means, feel free to recommend it to your friends, your relatives, and your friendly librarian.

Ed Lucaire
New York City

BIRTH

Birthdates and Birth Signs
(Jan. 1 to Dec. 31)

★ ★

Capricorn

January 1
Paul Revere (1735)
Betsy Ross (1752)
E.M. Forster (1879)
Charles Bickford (1889)
J. Edgar Hoover (1895)
Xavier Cugat (1900)
Dana Andrews (1909)
Barry M. Goldwater (1909)
Hank Greenberg (1911)
Carole Landis (1919)
Terry Moore (1932)
Frank Langella (1940)
Don Novello (1943)

January 2
Sally Rand (1900)
Vera Zorina (1917)
Isaac Asimov (1920)
Daniel Rostenkowski (1922)
Julius La Rosa (1930)
Jim Bakker (1939)

January 3
J.R.R. Tolkien (1892)
Marion Davies (1897)
Zasu Pitts (1900)
Anna May Wong (1907)
Ray Milland (1908)
Victor Borge (1909)
Betty Furness (1916)
Dabney Coleman (1932)
Carla Hills (1934)
Bobby Hull (1939)
Victoria Principal (1944)

January 4
Louis Braille (1809)
Tom Thumb (1838)
Russ Columbo (1908)
Jane Wyman (1914)
Barbara Rush (1929)
Don Shula (1930)
Sorrell Booke (1931)
Floyd Patterson (1935)
Grace Bumbry (1937)
Dyan Cannon (1938)

January 5
George Washington Carver (1864)
Yves Tanguy (1900)
Jean-Pierre Aumont (1909)
Friedrich Durrenmatt (1921)
Walter F. Mondale (1928)
Alvin Ailey (1931)
Robert Duvall (1931)
Diane Keaton (1946)
Pamela Sue Martin (1954)

January 6
Carl Sandburg (1878)
Tom Mix (1880)
Loretta Young (1913)
Danny Thomas (1914)
Sung Myung Moon (1920)
Earl Scruggs (1924)
E.L. Doctorow (1931)
Capucine (1935)
Bonnie Franklin (1944)
Nancy Lopez (1957)

January 7
Butterfly McQueen (1911)
Charles Addams (1912)
Vince Gardenia (1922)
William Peter Blatty (1928)
Jann Wenner (1947)
Kenny Loggins (1948)

January 8
José Ferrer (1912)
Soupy Sales (1930)
Charles Osgood (1933)
Elvis Presley (1935)
Shirley Bassey (1937)
Yvette Mimieux (1939)
David Bowie (1947)

January 9
Vilma Banky (1903)
George Balanchine (1904)
Simone de Beauvoir (1908)
Richard M. Nixon (1913)
Lee Van Cleef (1925)
Judith Krantz (1928)
Joan Baez (1941)

Susannah York (1941)
Crystal Gayle (1951)

January 10
Francis X. Bushman (1883)
Ray Bolger (1904)
Gisele MacKenzie (1927)
Johnnie Ray (1927)
Sherrill Milnes (1935)
Sal Mineo (1939)
Rod Stewart (1945)
Pat Benatar (1952)

January 11
Eva La Gallienne (1899)
Grant Tinker (1926)
Rod Taylor (1930)
Ben Crenshaw (1952)

January 12
Jack London (1876)
Tex Ritter (1907)
Patsy Kelly (1910)
Luise Rainer (1912)
Kreskin (1935)
Howard Stern (1954)
Kirstie Alley (1955)

January 13
Horatio Alger (1832)
Sophie Tucker (1884)
Robert Stack (1919)
Gwen Verdon (1925)
Charles Nelson Reilly
  (1931)

January 14
Albert Schweitzer (1875)
Hal Roach (1892)
John Dos Passos (1896)
Bebe Daniels (1901)
Cecil Beaton (1904)
William Bendix (1906)
Andy Rooney (1919)
Tom Tryon (1926)
Faye Dunaway (1941)

January 15
Goodman Ace (1899)
Edward Teller (1908)
Lloyd Bridges (1913)
Chuck Berry (1926)
Martin Luther King, Jr. (1929)
Margaret O'Brien (1937)

January 16
Alexander Knox (1907)
Ethel Merman (1909)
Eartha Kitt (1928)
Francesco Scavullo (1929)
Marilyn Horne (1934)
A.J. Foyt (1935)
John Carpenter (1948)
Debbie Allen (1950)
Sade (1960)

January 17
Noah Beery (1884)
Mack Sennett (1884)
Jerome Kern (1885)
Al Capone (1899)
Betty White (1917)
Moira Shearer (1926)
Vidal Sassoon (1928)
James Earl Jones (1931)
Muhammad Ali (1942)
Joe Frazier (1944)

January 18
Peter Mark Roger (1779)
Daniel Webster (1782)
Oliver Hardy (1892)
Cary Grant (1904)
Jacob Bronowski (1908)
Danny Kaye (1913)
Kevin Costner (1955)

January 19
Edgar Allan Poe (1809)
John Raitt (1917)
J.D. Salinger (1919)
Guy Madison (1922)
Jean Stapleton (1923)
Fritz Weaver (1926)
Robert MacNeil (1931)
Tippi Hedren (1935)
Janis Joplin (1943)
Dolly Parton (1946)
Robert Palmer (1949)

January 20
George Burns (1896)
Joy Adamson (1910)
Federico Fellini (1920)
Patricia Neal (1926)
Edwin Aldrin (1930)

Aquarius

January 21
Stonewall Jackson (1824)
J. Carrol Naish (1900)
Christian Dior (1905)
Paul Scofield (1922)
Telly Savalas (1924)
Benny Hill (1925)
Wolfman Jack (1938)
Jack Nicklaus (1940)
Placido Domingo (1941)
Richie Havens (1941)
Mac Davis (1942)
Robby Benson (1957)

January 22
August Strindberg (1849)
Conrad Veidt (1893)
Ann Sothern (1909)
U Thant (1909)
Piper Laurie (1932)
Bill Bixby (1934)
Sam Cooke (1935)
Joseph Wambaugh (1937)
John Hurt (1940)

January 23
Edouard Manet (1832)
Franklin Pangborn (1893)
Sergei Eisenstein (1898)
Randolph Scott (1904)
Dan Duryea (1907)
Ernie Kovacs (1919)
Jeanne Moreau (1928)
Chita Rivera (1933)
Princess Caroline (1957)

January 24
Edith Wharton (1862)
Estelle Winwood (1883)
Mark Goodson (1915)
Ernest Borgnine (1917)
Oral Roberts (1918)
Desmond Morris (1928)
Neil Diamond (1941)
Bill Bradley (1947)
John Belushi (1949)
Nastassja Kinski (1960)
Mary Lou Retton (1968)

January 25
Somerset Maugham (1874)

Mildred Dunnock (1906)
Edwin Newman (1919)
Corazon Aquino (1933)
Dean Jones (1936)

January 26
Gen. Douglas MacArthur (1880)
Paul Newman (1925)
Roger Vadim (1928)
Jules Feiffer (1929)
Eugene Siskel (1946)
Eddie Van Halen (1957)

January 27
Lewis Carroll (1832)
Samuel Gompers (1850)
Hyman Rickover (1900)
Skitch Henderson (1918)
Donna Reed (1921)
Mordecai Richler (1931)
Troy Donahue (1937)

January 28
Jackson Pollock (1912)
Claes Oldenburg (1929)
Susan Sontag (1933)
Alan Alda (1936)
Mikhail Baryshnikov (1948)

January 29
W.C. Fields (1880)
Victor Mature (1916)
John Forsythe (1918)
Paddy Chayefsky (1923)
Katharine Ross (1943)
Tom Selleck (1945)
Ann Jillian (1951)
Greg Louganis (1960)

January 30
Franklin D. Roosevelt (1882)
Hugh Marlowe (1914)
David Wayne (1914)
John Ireland (1915)
Dorothy Malone (1925)
Hal Prince (1928)
Gene Hackman (1931)
Dick Martin (1932)
Louis Rukeyser (1933)
Tammy Grimes (1936)
Vanessa Redgrave (1937)
Boris Spassky (1937)
Phil Collins (1951)

January 31
Zane Grey (1875)
Eddie Cantor (1892)
Tallulah Bankhead (1903)
John O'Hara (1905)
Garry Moore (1915)
Jackie Robinson (1919)
Mario Lanza (1921)
Carol Channing (1923)
Joanne Dru (1923)
Norman Mailer (1923)
Jean Simmons (1929)
James Franciscus (1934)
Suzanne Pleshette (1937)
Nolan Ryan (1947)

February 1
John Ford (1895)
Anastasio Somoza (1896)
Clark Gable (1901)
Langston Hughes (1902)
S.J. Perelman (1904)
Renata Tebaldi (1922)
Stuart Whitman (1926)
Sherman Hemsley (1938)

February 2
S.Z. Sakall (1884)
Jascha Heifetz (1901)
Ayn Rand (1905)
Gale Gordon (1906)
Abba Eban (1915)
James Dickey (1923)
Liz Smith (1923)
Stan Getz (1927)
Elaine Stritch (1928)
Tommy Smothers (1937)
Farrah Fawcett (1947)
Christie Brinkley (1953)

February 3
Norman Rockwell (1894)
James Michener (1907)
Shelley Berman (1926)
Victor Buono (1938)
Blythe Danner (1943)
Morgan Fairchild (1950)

February 4
Nigel Bruce (1895)
Charles Lindbergh (1902)
Ida Lupino (1918)
Conrad Bain (1923)

David Brenner (1936)
Dan Quayle (1947)
Alice Cooper (1948)
Lisa Eichhorn (1952)

February 5
Adlai E. Stevenson, Jr.
  (1900)
John Carradine (1906)
Williams S. Burroughs (1914)
Tim Holt (1918)
Red Buttons (1919)
Arthur Ochs Sulzberger
  (1926)
Andrew Greeley (1928)
Hank Aaron (1934)
Roger Staubach (1942)
Charlotte Rampling (1946)
Christopher Guest (1948)
Barbara Hershey (1948)

February 6
Babe Ruth (1895)
Ramon Novarro (1899)
Louis Nizer (1902)
Ronald W. Reagan (1911)
Zsa Zsa Gabor (1919)
Rip Torn (1931)
François Truffaut (1932)
Mamie Van Doren (1933)
Mike Farrell (1939)
Tom Brokaw (1940)
Fabian (1943)
Gayle Hunnicutt (1943)
Natalie Cole (1949)
Molly Ringwald (1968)

February 7
Eubie Blake (1883)
Sinclair Lewis (1885)
Larry "Buster" Crabbe (1908)
Eddie Bracken (1920)
Gay Talese (1932)

February 8
Jules Verne (1828)
Dame Edith Evans (1888)
Adolphe Menjou (1890)
King Vidor (1894)
Lana Turner (1920)
Jack Lemmon (1925)
James Dean (1931)
Ted Koppel (1940)

Robert Klein (1942)
Nick Nolte (1942)
Brooke Adams (1949)
Gary Coleman (1968)

February 9
Ronald Colman (1891)
Peggy Wood (1892)
Brian Donlevy (1899)
Carmen Miranda (1909)
Dean Rusk (1909)
Gypsy Rose Lee (1914)
Brendan Behan (1923)
Kathryn Grayson (1923)
Roger Mudd (1928)
Carole King (1941)
Alice Walker (1944)
Mia Farrow (1945)

February 10
Alan Hale (1892)
Jimmy Durante (1893)
Bill Tilden (1893)
Dame Judith Anderson
  (1898)
Bertolt Brecht (1898)
Lon Chaney, Jr. (1905)
John Farrow (1906)
Larry Adler (1914)
Leontyne Price (1927)
Robert Wagner (1930)
Roberta Flack (1940)
Donovan (1946)
Mark Spitz (1950)
Greg Norman (1955)

February 11
Thomas Alva Edison (1847)
Boris Pasternak (1890)
Joseph L. Mankiewicz (1909)
Sidney Sheldon (1917)
Kim Stanley (1925)
Paul Bocuse (1926)
Leslie Nielsen (1926)
Burt Reynolds (1936)
Tina Louise (1937)
Sergio Mendes (1941)

February 12
Charles Darwin (1809)
Abraham Lincoln (1809)
Omar Bradley (1893)
Buckminster Fuller (1895)
Ted Mack (1904)

Tex Benecke (1914)
Lorne Greene (1915)
Franco Zeffirelli (1923)
Joe Garagiola (1926)
Judy Blume (1938)
Maud Adams (1945)
Arsenio Hall (1955)

February 13
Grant Wood (1892)
Georges Simenon (1903)
Tennessee Ernie Ford (1919)
Chuck Yeager (1923)
George Segal (1934)
Oliver Reed (1938)
Carol Lynley (1943)
Stockard Channing (1944)

February 14
Frank Harris (1856)
Jack Benny (1894)
Stu Erwin (1902)
Thelma Ritter (1905)
Mel Allen (1913)
Jimmy Hoffa (1913)
Hugh Downs (1921)
Vic Morrow (1932)
Florence Henderson (1934)
Gregory Hines (1946)

February 15
John Barrymore (1882)
Gale Sondergaard (1899)
Harold Arlen (1905)
Cesar Romero (1907)
Kevin McCarthy (1914)
Harvey Korman (1927)
Claire Bloom (1931)
Adolfo (1933)
Marisa Berenson (1948)
Melissa Manchester (1951)
Jane Seymour (1951)

February 16
Katharine Cornell (1898)
Chester Morris (1901)
Edgar Bergen (1903)
Patti Andrews (1920)
John Schlesinger (1926)
Vera-Ellen (1926)
Brian Bedford (1935)
Sonny Bono (1940)
LeVar Burton (1957)
John McEnroe (1959)

February 17
H.L. Hunt (1889)
Marian Anderson (1902)
Red Barber (1908)
Wayne Morris (1914)
Margaret Truman (1924)
Hal Holbrook (1925)
Tom Jones (1928)
Alan Bates (1934)
Jim Brown (1936)

February 18
Sholem Aleichem (1859)
Wendell Willkie (1892)
Andres Segovia (1894)
Billy De Wolfe (1907)
Dane Clark (1913)
Bill Cullen (1920)
Jack Palance (1920)
Helen Gurley Brown (1922)
George Kennedy (1925)
Len Deighton (1929)
Gahan Wilson (1930)
Toni Morrison (1931)
Milos Forman (1932)
Kim Novak (1933)
Yoko Ono (1933)
Jean Auel (1936)
Cybill Shepherd (1950)
John Travolta (1954)

February 19
Cedric Hardwicke (1893)
Louis Calhern (1895)
Merle Oberon (1911)
Stan Kenton (1912)
Eddie Arcaro (1916)
Carson McCullers (1917)
Lee Marvin (1924)
John Frankenheimer (1930)
Smokey Robinson (1940)
Cass Elliott (1943)
Justine Bateman (1966)

Pisces

February 20
Ansel Adams (1902)
Sidney Poitier (1924)
Gloria Vanderbilt (1924)
Robert Altman (1925)
Amanda Blake (1931)
Buffy Sainte-Marie (1941)

Sandy Duncan (1946)
Peter Strauss (1947)
Jennifer O'Neill (1949)
Edward Albert (1951)
Patty Hearst (1954)

February 21
Anaïs Nin (1903)
W.H. Auden (1907)
Ann Sheridan (1915)
Sam Peckinpah (1925)
Erma Bombeck (1927)
Hubert de Givenchy (1927)
Nina Simone (1933)
Barbara Jordan (1936)
Gary Lockwood (1937)
Richard Beymer (1939)
Tyne Daly (1944)
Christopher Atkins (1961)

February 22
Fréderic Chopin (1810)
Edna St. Vincent Millay
   (1892)
Luis Buñuel (1900)
Seán O'Faoláin (1900)
Robert Young (1907)
John Mills (1908)
Sybil Leek (1917)
Edward Gorey (1925)
Guy Mitchell (1927)
Edward M. "Teddy" Kennedy
   (1932)
Julius Erving (1950)

February 23
W.E.B. Du Bois (1868)
Victor Fleming (1883)
Norman Taurog (1899)
William Shirer (1904)
Peter Fonda (1939)
Johnny Winter (1944)

February 24
Winslow Homer (1836)
Marjorie Main (1890)
Zachary Scott (1914)
Abe Vigoda (1921)
Michel Legrand (1932)
Renata Scotto (1934)
James Farentino (1938)
Barry Bostwick (1945)
Rupert Holmes (1947)

February 25
Auguste Renoir (1841)
Enrico Caruso (1873)
Zeppo Marx (1901)
Adelle Davis (1904)
Jim Backus (1913)
Anthony Burgess (1917)
Bobby Riggs (1918)
Lisa Kirk (1925)
Tom Courtenay (1937)
George Harrison (1943)

February 26
Victor Hugo (1802)
"Buffalo Bill" Cody (1846)
William Frawley (1893)
Robert Alda (1914)
Jackie Gleason (1916)
Betty Hutton (1921)
Margaret Leighton (1922)
Tony Randall (1924)
Fats Domino (1928)
Johnny Cash (1932)
Godfrey Cambridge (1933)
Brian Jones (1943)

February 27
David Sarnoff (1891)
William Demarest (1892)
John Steinbeck (1902)
James T. Farrell (1904)
Franchot Tone (1905)
Joan Bennett (1910)
Joanne Woodward (1930)
Elizabeth Taylor (1932)
Ralph Nader (1934)
Howard Hesseman (1940)

February 28
Vaslav Nijinsky (1890)
Molly Picon (1898)
Linus Pauling (1901)
Bugsy Siegel (1906)
Vincente Minnelli (1913)
Zero Mostel (1915)
Charles Durning (1923)
Gavin MacLeod (1930)
Tommy Tune (1939)
Bernadette Peters (1948)

February 29
William Wellman (1896)
Jean Negulesco (1900)
Jimmy Dorsey (1904)

March 1
Lionel Atwill (1885)
Glenn Miller (1904)
David Niven (1910)
Dinah Shore (1917)
Pete Rozelle (1926)
Harry Belafonte (1927)
Raymond Saint Jacques (1932)
Joan Hackett (1934)
Robert Conrad (1935)
Catherine Bach (1954)
Ron Howard (1954)

March 2
Kurt Weill (1900)
Dr. Seuss (1904)
Desi Arnaz (1917)
Jennifer Jones (1919)
John Cullum (1930)
Mikhail Gorbachev (1931)
Tom Wolfe (1931)
John Irving (1942)
Lou Reed (1944)

March 3
Alexander Graham Bell (1847)
Ring Lardner (1885)
Jean Harlow (1911)
Diana Barrymore (1921)
Gia Scala (1934)
Bobby Driscoll (1936)
Perry Ellis (1940)
Ed Marinaro (1950)

March 4
Knute Rockne (1888)
Charles Goren (1901)
John Garfield (1913)
Miriam Makeba (1932)
Barbara McNair (1937)
Paula Prentiss (1939)

March 5
Rex Harrison (1908)
Pier Paolo Pasolini (1922)
Jack Cassidy (1927)
Lorin Maazel (1930)
Dean Stockwell (1936)
Samantha Eggar (1940)
Eugene Fodor (1950)
Andy Gibb (1958)

March 6
Lou Costello (1908)
Ed McMahon (1923)
Gordon Cooper, Jr. (1927)
Gabriel García Márquez
(1928)
Rob Reiner (1947)
Kiri Te Kanawa (1947)

March 7
Marice Ravel (1875)
Anna Magnani (1909)
Anthony Armstrong-Jones
(1930)
Janet Guthrie (1938)
Daniel J. Travanti (1940)

March 8
Sam Jaffe (1893)
Claire Trevor (1909)
Cyd Charisse (1923)
Lynn Redgrave (1943)
Susan Clark (1944)
Mickey Dolenz (1945)
Carole Bayer Sager (1947)

March 9
Will Geer (1902)
Mickey Spillane (1918)
Keely Smith (1932)
Joyce Van Patten (1934)
Mickey Gilley (1936)
Marty Ingels (1936)
Raul Julia (1940)
Bobby Fischer (1943)
Trish Van Devere (1945)
Emmanuel Lewis (1971)

March 10
Barry Fitzgerald (1888)
Bix Beiderbecke (1903)
Warner Anderson (1911)
Heywood Hale Broun (1918)
Pamela Mason (1922)
David Rabe (1940)
Dean Torrence (1941)
Katharine Houghton (1945)

March 11
Raoul Walsh (1887)
Dorothy Gish (1898)
Lawrence Welk (1903)
Ralph Abernathy (1926)
Rupert Murdoch (1931)

Sam Donaldson (1934)
Antonin Scalia (1936)

March 12
Gordon MacRae (1921)
Jack Kerouac (1922)
Wally Schirra (1923)
Edward Albee (1928)
Andrew Young (1932)
Al Jarreau (1940)
Barbara Feldon (1941)
Liza Minnelli (1946)
James Taylor (1948)

March 13
Juan Gris (1887)
L. Ron Hubbard (1911)
Sammy Kaye (1913)
Neil Sedaka (1939)

March 14
Maxim Gorky (1868)
Albert Einstein (1879)
Hank Ketcham (1920)
Diane Arbus (1923)
Frank Borman (1928)
Michael Caine (1933)
Quincy Jones (1933)
Eugene Andrew Cernan
(1934)
Rita Tushingham (1942)
Billy Crystal (1947)

March 15
George Brent (1904)
John Osborne (1907)
Lightnin' Hopkins (1912)
MacDonald Carey (1914)
Harry James (1916)
Sabu (1924)
Alan Bean (1932)
Judd Hirsch (1935)
Mike Love (1941)
Sly Stone (1944)

March 16
Conrad Nagel (1897)
Robert Rossen (1908)
Josef Mengele (1911)
Patricia Nixon (1912)
William Westmoreland (1914)
Leo McKern (1920)
Jerry Lewis (1926)

Daniel Patrick Moynihan
(1927)
Bernardo Bertolucci (1940)
Erik Estrada (1949)
Kate Nelligan (1951)

March 17
Frank Buck (1884)
Shemp Howard (1900)
Bobby Jones (1902)
Mercedes McCambridge
(1918)
Nat King Cole (1919)
Monique Van Vooren (1933)
Rudolf Nureyev (1938)
Patrick Duffy (1949)
Kurt Russell (1951)
Lesley-Anne Down (1954)
Rob Lowe (1964)

March 18
Grover Cleveland (1837)
Nikolai A. Rimsky-Korsakov
(1844)
Neville Chamberlain (1869)
Edward Everett Horton
(1886)
Robert Donat (1905)
Mollie Parnis (1905)
Smiley Burnette (1911)
Peter Graves (1926)
George Plimpton (1927)
John Updike (1932)
Charley Pride (1938)
Wilson Pickett (1941)
Kevin Dobson (1944)
Brad Dourif (1950)
Irene Cara (1959)

March 19
Wyatt Earp (1848)
William Jennings Bryan
(1860)
Sergei Diaghilev (1872)
Earl Warren (1891)
Moms Mabley (1894)
Albert Speer (1905)
Adolf Eichmann (1906)
Kent Smith (1907)
Louis Hayward (1909)
Patrick McGoohan (1928)
Ornette Coleman (1930)

Philip Roth (1933)
Phyllis Newman (1935)
Ursula Andress (1936)
Sirhan Sirhan (1944)
Bruce Willis (1955)

March 20
Henrik Ibsen (1828)
Lauritz Melchior (1890)
Edgar Buchanan (1903)
B.F. Skinner (1904)
Ozzie Nelson (1906)
Michael Redgrave (1908)
Wendell Corey (1914)
Ray Goulding (1922)
Carl Reiner (1922)
Fred ("Mr.") Rogers (1928)
Hal Linden (1931)
Benno Schmidt, Jr. (1942)
Bobby Orr (1948)
William Hurt (1950)

Aries

March 21
Johann Sebastian Bach
(1685)
Benito Juarez (1806)
Nikolai Gogol (1809)
M.P. Mussorgsky (1839)
Florenz Ziegfeld (1867)
Peter Brook (1925)
James Coco (1929)
Al Freeman, Jr. (1934)
Kathleen Widdoes (1939)
Françoise Dorleac (1942)
Timothy Dalton (1946)

March 22
Richard Wagner (1813)
Chico Marx (1891)
Nicholas Monsarrat (1910)
Karl Malden (1913)
Werner Klemperer (1920)
Giulietta Masina (1921)
Marcel Marceau (1923)
Stephen Sondheim (1930)
William Shatner (1931)
May Britt (1933)
J.P. McCarthy (1934)
George Benson (1943)
Andrew Lloyd Webber (1948)
Stephanie Mills (1957)

March 23
Hazel Dawn (1898)
Erich Fromm (1900)
Joan Crawford (1908)
Akira Kurosawa (1910)
Wernher Von Braun (1912)
Roger Bannister (1929)
Chaka Khan (1953)
Amanda Plummer (1957)

March 24
Harry Houdini (1874)
Fatty Arbuckle (1887)
Wilhelm Reich (1897)
Malcolm Muggeridge (1903)
Clyde Barrow (1909)
Richard Conte (1914)
Lawrence Ferlinghetti (1919)
Gene Nelson (1920)
Norman Fell (1925)
Steve McQueen (1930)
Bob Mackie (1940)
Donna Pescow (1954)

March 25
Gutzon Borglum (1867)
Arturo Toscanini (1867)
Ed Begley (1901)
David Lean (1908)
Howard Cosell (1920)
Simone Signoret (1921)
Flannery O'Connor (1925)
Gloria Steinem (1935)
Hoyt Axton (1938)
Anita Bryant (1940)
Aretha Franklin (1942)
Paul Michael Glaser (1942)
Elton John (1947)
Bonnie Bedelia (1948)

March 26
Robert Frost (1874)
Condé Nast (1874)
Duncan Hines (1880)
Tennessee Williams (1911)
Sterling Hayden (1916)
Bob Elliot (1923)
Pierre Boulez (1925)
Sandra Day O'Connor (1930)
Leonard Nimoy (1931)
James Caan (1939)
Erica Jong (1942)

Bob Woodward (1943)
Diana Ross (1944)
Teddy Pendergrass (1950)
Martin Short (1950)
Curtis Sliwa (1954)

March 27
Edward Steichen (1879)
Mies van der Rohe (1886)
Gloria Swanson (1899)
Pee Wee Russell (1906)
Budd Schulberg (1914)
Snooky Lanson (1919)
Sarah Vaughan (1924)
David Janssen (1931)
Cale Yarborough (1940)
Michael York (1942)

March 28
Paul Whiteman (1891)
Rudolph Serkin (1903)
Pandro Berman (1905)
Nelson Algren (1909)
Dennis O'Keefe (1910)
Frank Lovejoy (1914)
Pearl Bailey (1918)
Freddie Bartholomew (1924)
Zbigniew Brzezinski (1928)
Ken Howard (1944)

March 29
Warner Baxter (1891)
Phil Foster (1914)
Sam Walton (1918)
Eileen Heckart (1919)
Dirk Bogarde (1921)

March 30
Vincent van Gogh (1853)
Sean O'Casey (1880)
Frankie Laine (1913)
John Astin (1930)
Peter Marshall (1930)
Warren Beatty (1937)
Eric Clapton (1945)

March 31
Jack Johnson (1878)
Henry Morgan (1915)
Richard Kiley (1922)
Leo Buscaglia (1925)
William Daniels (1927)
Liz Claiborne (1929)
John Jakes (1932)

Shirley Jones (1934)
Herb Alpert (1935)
Richard Chamberlain (1935)
Christopher Walken (1943)
Gabe Kaplan (1945)
Rhea Perlman (1946)

April 1
Edmond Rostand (1868)
Sergei Rachmaninoff (1873)
Lon Chaney (1883)
Wallace Beery (1886)
Laurette Taylor (1887)
Alberta Hunter (1897)
Nita Naldi (1899)
Abraham Maslow (1908)
Eddie Duchin (1909)
Hans Conreid (1915)
Toshiro Mifune (1920)
George Grizzard (1928)
Jane Powell (1928)
Debbie Reynolds (1932)
Ali McGraw (1938)

April 2
Hans Christian Andersen
  (1805)
Émile Zola (1840)
Buddy Ebsen (1908)
Alec Guinness (1914)
Jack Webb (1920)
Kenneth Tynan (1927)
Rita Gam (1928)
Marvin Gaye (1939)
Emmylou Harris (1948)

April 3
Boss Tweed (1823)
Allan Dwan (1885)
Dooley Wilson (1894)
George Jessel (1898)
Iron Eyes Cody (1915)
Marlon Brando (1924)
Doris Day (1924)
Virgil Grissom (1926)
Miyoshi Umeki (1929)
Jane Goodall (1934)
Marsha Mason (1942)
Wayne Newton (1942)
Tony Orlando (1944)
Eddie Murphy (1961)

April 4
Arthur Murray (1895)

John Cameron Swayze
  (1906)
Jerome Weidman (1913)
Muddy Waters (1915)
William Manchester (1922)
Maya Angelou (1928)
Christine Lahti (1950)
Nancy McKeon (1966)

April 5
Booker T. Washington (1856)
Spencer Tracy (1900)
Bette Davis (1908)
Gregory Peck (1916)
Arthur Hailey (1920)
Gale Storm (1922)
Rogert Corman (1926)
Frank Gorshin (1934)
Michael Moriarty (1942)

April 6
Butch Cassidy (1867)
Walter Huston (1884)
George Reeves (1914)
Gerry Mulligan (1927)
André Previn (1929)
Merle Haggard (1937)
Billy Dee Williams (1937)
Michelle Phillips (1944)
Marilu Henner (1953)

April 7
Bronislaw Malinowski (1884)
Irene Castle (1893)
Bert Wheeler (1895)
Walter Winchell (1897)
Percy Faith (1908)
Billie Holiday (1915)
James Garner (1928)
Alan Pakula (1928)
Donald Barthelme (1931)
Wayne Rogers (1933)
Francis Ford Coppola (1939)
David Frost (1939)
Tony Dorsett (1954)

April 8
Mary Pickford (1894)
Sonja Henie (1912)
Carmen McRae (1922)
Franco Corelli (1923)
Shecky Greene (1926)
Jacques Brel (1929)

John Gavin (1932)
Michael Bennett (1943)
John Schneider (1954)
Julian Lennon (1963)

April 9
Nikolai Lenin (1870)
Paul Robeson (1898)
Ward Bond (1904)
James W. Fulbright (1905)
Hugh Hefner (1926)
Michael Learned (1929)
Jean-Paul Belmondo (1933)
Dennis Quaid (1954)

April 10
Joseph Pulitzer (1847)
George Arliss (1868)
Kahlil Gibran (1883)
Tim McCoy (1891)
Clare Boothe Luce (1903)
Harry Morgan (1915)
Chuck Connors (1921)
Max von Sydow (1929)
David Halberstam (1934)
John Madden (1936)
Don Meredith (1938)
Paul Theroux (1941)

April 11
Charles Evans Hughes
 (1862)
Dean Acheson (1893)
Leo Rosten (1908)
Oleg Cassini (1913)
Ethel Kennedy (1928)
Joel Grey (1932)

April 12
Lily Pons (1904)
Tiny Tim (1922)
Ann Miller (1923)
Jane Withers (1926)
Montserrat Caballe (1933)
Alan Ayckbourn (1939)
Herbie Hancock (1940)
Charles Ludlam (1943)
David Letterman (1947)
David Cassidy (1950)
Elaine Zayak (1958)

April 13
Samuel Beckett (1906)
Eudora Welty (1909)

Howard Keel (1919)
Stanley Donen (1924)
Brad Dillman (1930)
Lyle Waggoner (1935)
Edward Fox (1937)
Garry Kasparov (1963)
Ricky Schroder (1970)

April 14
John Gielgud (1904)
Rod Steiger (1925)
Anthony Perkins (1932)
Loretta Lynn (1935)
Frank Serpico (1936)
Julie Christie (1940)
Pete Rose (1941)

April 15
Henry James (1843)
Thomas Hart Benton (1889)
Wallace Reid (1891)
Bessie Smith (1894)
Harvey Lembeck (1923)
Claudia Cardinale (1938)
Jeffrey Archer (1940)

April 16
Charlie Chaplin (1889)
Polly Adler (1900)
Fifi D'Orsay (1904)
John Hodiak (1914)
Spike Milligan (1918)
Merce Cunningham (1919)
Barry Nelson (1920)
Peter Ustinov (1921)
Kingsley Amis (1922)
Henry Mancini (1924)
Edie Adams (1929)
Bobby Vinton (1935)
Dusty Springfield (1939)
Kareem Abdul-Jabbar (1947)

April 17
Nikita Khrushchev (1894)
Thornton Wilder (1897)
Arthur Lake (1905)
William Holden (1918)
Lindsay Anderson (1923)
Harry Reasoner (1923)
Olivia Hussey (1951)

April 18
Clarence Darrow (1857)
Donald Crisp (1880)

Leopold Stokowski (1882)
Wendy Barrie (1910)
Clive Revill (1930)
Hayley Mills (1946)
James Woods (1947)

April 19
Constance Talmadge (1900)
Eliot Ness (1903)
Frank Fontaine (1920)
Don Adams (1927)
Hugh O'Brian (1930)
Fernando Botero (1932)
Jayne Mansfield (1932)
Dudley Moore (1935)
Paloma Picasso (1949)
Al Unser, Jr. (1962)

Taurus

April 20
Adolf Hitler (1889)
Harold Lloyd (1893)
Joan Miró (1893)
Gregory Ratoff (1893)
Bruce Cabot (1904)
Lionel Hampton (1914)
John Paul Stevens (1920)
Tito Puente (1923)
Nina Foch (1924)
Ryan O'Neal (1941)
Jessica Lange (1949)
Luther Vandross (1951)

April 21
Rollo May (1909)
Anthony Quinn (1916)
Don Cornell (1919)
Elizabeth II (1926)
Silvana Mangano (1930)
Elaine May (1932)
Charles Grodin (1935)
Patti LuPone (1949)
Tony Danza (1951)

April 22
Eddie Albert (1908)
Yehudi Menuhin (1916)
Charlie Mingus (1922)
Aaron Spelling (1925)
Charlotte Rae (1926)
Jack Nicholson (1937)
Peter Frampton (1950)

April 23
Vladimir Nabokov (1899)
Duncan Renaldo (1904)
Janet Blair (1921)
J.P. Donleavy (1926)
Shirley Temple Black (1928)
Halston (1932)
Rod McKuen (1933)
Shirley MacLaine (1934)
Roy Orbison (1936)
David Birney (1940)
Lee Majors (1940)
Sandra Dee (1942)
Hervé Villechaize (1943)
Joyce DeWitt (1949)
Valerie Bertinelli (1960)

April 24
Willem De Kooning (1904)
Jack E. Leonard (1911)
William Castle (1914)
Jill Ireland (1936)
Barbra Streisand (1942)

April 25
William Brennan (1906)
Fred Zinnemann (1907)
Ella Fitzgerald (1918)
Melissa Hayden (1928)
Paul Mazursky (1930)
Al Pacino (1940)
Talia Shire (1946)

April 26
Anita Loos (1893)
Bernard Malamud (1914)
I.M. Pei (1917)
Bambi Linn (1926)
Carol Burnett (1936)
Bobby Rydell (1942)

April 27
Ulysses S. Grant (1822)
Walter Lantz (1900)
Jack Klugman (1922)
Anouk Aimee (1934)
Sandy Dennis (1937)
Sheena Easton (1959)

April 28
Sidney Toler (1874)
Lionel Barrymore (1878)
Rowland Evans, Jr. (1921)
Blossom Dearie (1926)

Ann-Margret (1941)
Jay Leno (1950)

April 29
William Randolph Hearst
(1863)
Rafael Sabatini (1875)
Duke Ellington (1899)
Tom Ewell (1909)
Celeste Ewell (1919)
George J. Schulz (1925)
Keith Baxter (1935)
Zubin Mehta (1936)

April 30
Franz Lehar (1870)
Eve Arden (1912)
Robert Shaw (1916)
Sheldon Harnick (1924)
Corinne Calvet (1925)
Cloris Leachman (1925)
Johnny Horton (1927)
Willie Nelson (1933)
Burt Young (1940)
Jill Clayburgh (1944)
Perry King (1948)

May 1
General Mark W. Clark
(1896)
Kate Smith (1909)
Glenn Ford (1916)
Jack Paar (1918)
Joseph Heller (1923)
Terry Southern (1924)
Scott Carpenter (1925)
Judy Collins (1939)
Rita Coolidge (1945)
Steve Cauthen (1960)

May 2
Vernon Castle (1887)
Baron von Richthofen
(1892)
Lorenz Hart (1895)
Brian Aherne (1902)
Benjamin Spock (1903)
Bing Crosby (1904)
Philippe Halsman (1906)
Theodore Bikel (1924)
Saddam Hussein (1935)
Lesley Gore (1946)
Larry Gatlin (1949)

May 3
Beulah Bondi (1892)
Golda Meir (1898)
Jack LaRue (1902)
Walter Slezak (1902)
Mary Astor (1906)
William Inge (1913)
Betty Comden (1915)
Pete Seeger (1919)
James Brown (1934)
Engelbert Humperdinck
(1936)
Frankie Valli (1937)
Doug Henning (1947)

May 4
Howard DaSilva (1909)
Heloise (1919)
Hosni Mubarak (1928)
Audrey Hepburn (1929)
Roberta Peters (1930)
George F. Will (1941)
Tammy Wynette (1942)
Keith Haring (1958)

May 5
Søren Kierkegaard (1813)
Karl Marx (1818)
Henryk Sienkiewicz (1846)
Nellie Bly (1867)
Christopher Morley (1890)
Freeman Gosden (1899)
Tyrone Power (1914)
Alice Faye (1915)

May 6
Sigmund Freud (1856)
Robert E. Peary (1856)
Rudolph Valentino (1895)
Max Ophüls (1902)
Toots Shor (1905)
Carmen Cavallaro (1913)
Stewart Granger (1913)
Orson Welles (1915)
Theodore White (1915)
Willie Mays (1931)

May 7
Peter Ilyich
Tchaikovsky (1840)
Gabby Hayes (1885)
Archibald MacLeish (1892)
Gary Cooper (1901)

Eva Perón (1919)
Anne Baxter (1923)
Marvin Mitchelson (1928)
Totie Fields (1930)
Theresa Brewer (1931)
Johnny Unitas (1933)
Willard Scott (1934)
Janis Ian (1950)

May 8
Harry S. Truman (1884)
Bishop Fulton Sheen (1895)
Edmund Wilson (1895)
Fernandel (1903)
Roberto Rossellini (1906)
Lex Barker (1919)
David Attenborough (1926)
Don Rickles (1926)
Ted Sorensen (1928)
Arnold Scaasi (1931)
Thomas Pynchon (1937)
Peter Benchley (1940)
Toni Tennille (1943)
Beth Henley (1952)
Melissa Gilbert (1964)

May 9
José Ortega y Gasset (1883)
Richard Barthelmess (1895)
Pedro Armendariz (1912)
Mike Wallace (1918)
Pancho Gonzalez (1928)
Albert Finney (1936)
Glenda Jackson (1937)
James L. Brooks (1940)
Candice Bergen (1946)
Billy Joel (1949)

May 10
Fred Astaire (1899)
David O. Selznick (1902)
Nancy Walker (1921)
Ara Parseghian (1923)
Judith Jamison (1934)
Gary Owens (1935)
Arthur L. Kopit (1937)
Wayne Dyer (1940)
Mark David Chapman (1955)

May 11
Alma Gluck (1884)
Irving Berlin (1888)
Margaret Rutherford (1892)

Salvador Dali (1904)
Phil Silvers (1911)
Foster Brooks (1912)
Denver Pyle (1920)
Mort Sahl (1927)
Robert Jarvik (1946)
Randy Quaid (1950)

May 12
Wilfrid Hyde-White (1903)
Julius Rosenberg (1918)
Yogi Berra (1925)
Burt Bacharach (1929)
Tom Snyder (1936)
George Carlin (1937)
Millie Perkins (1940)
Lindsay Crouse (1948)
Bruce Boxleitner (1951)
Emilio Estevez (1962)

May 13
Daphne DuMaurier (1907)
Joe Louis (1914)
Beatrice Arthur (1926)
Clive Barnes (1927)
Herbert Ross (1927)
Richie Valens (1941)
Peter Gabriel (1940)

May 14
Otto Klemperer (1885)
Bobby Darin (1936)
George Lucas (1944)

May 15
Katherine Anne Porter (1894)
Joseph Cotton (1905)
James Mason (1909)
Constance Cummings (1910)
Paul Samuelson (1915)
Eddy Arnold (1918)
Richard Avedon (1923)
Jasper Johns (1930)
Anna Maria Alberghetti (1936)
Trini Lopez (1937)

May 16
Margaret Sullavan (1896)
Henry Fonda (1905)
Studs Terkel (1912)
Liberace (1919)
Billy Martin (1928)
Lainie Kazan (1940)
Pierce Brosnan (1953)

May 17
Ayatollah Khomeini (1900)
Jean Gabin (1904)
Maureen O'Sullivan (1911)
Birgit Nilsson (1918)
Dennis Hopper (1936)
Debra Winger (1955)
Sugar Ray Leonard (1956)

May 18
Ezio Pinza (1892)
Frank Capra (1897)
Perry Como (1912)
Margot Fonteyn (1919)
Pope John Paul II (1920)
Patrick Dennis (1921)
Robert Morse (1931)
Dwayne Hickman (1934)
Reggie Jackson (1946)

May 19
Nellie Melba (1859)
Ho Chi Minh (1890)
Malcolm X (1925)
Jim Lehrer (1934)
David Hartman (1935)
Pete Townshend (1945)
Glenn Close (1947)
Grace Jones (1952)

May 20
James Stewart (1908)
Moshe Dayan (1915)
George Gobel (1919)
Peggy Lee (1920)
Joe Cocker (1944)
Cher (1946)

Gemini

May 21
Horace Heidt (1901)
Robert Montgomery (1904)
Fats Waller (1904)
Harold Robbins (1916)
Raymond Burr (1917)
Dennis Day (1917)
Peggy Cass (1925)
Leo Sayer (1948)
Mr. T (1952)

May 22
Mary Cassatt (1844)
Arthur Conan Doyle (1859)

Laurence Olivier (1907)
Irene Pappas (1919)
Charles Aznavour (1924)
T. Boone Pickens (1928)
Richard Benjamin (1938)
Paul Winfield (1941)

May 23
Douglas Fairbanks (1883)
Scatman Crothers (1910)
Artie Shaw (1910)
John Payne (1912)
Helen O'Connell (1921)
Rosemary Clooney (1928)
Barbara Barrie (1931)
Anatoly Karpov (1951)

May 24
Lilli Palmer (1914)
Síobhán McKenna (1922)
Mai Zetterling (1925)
Bob Dylan (1941
Gary Burghoff (1943)
Patti LaBelle (1944)
Priscilla Presley (1946)

May 25
Béla Bartók (1881)
Marshal Tito (1892)
Gene Tunney (1898)
Claude Akins (1918)
John Weitz (1923)
Jeanne Crain (1925)
Miles Davis (1926)
Robert Ludlum (1927)
Beverly Sills (1929)
John Gregory Dunne (1932)
Ian McKellen (1939)
Leslie Uggams (1943)
Connie Selleca (1955)

May 26
Al Jolson (1886)
Paul Lukas (1894)
Norma Talmadge (1897)
John Wayne (1907)
Peter Cushing (1913)
Jay Silverheels (1922)
James Arness (1923)
Alex McCowen (1926)
Brent Musburger (1939)
Teresa Stratas (1939)
Pamela Grier (1949)

Philip Michael Thomas
(1949)
Sally Ride (1951)
Hank Williams, Jr. (1949)

May 27
Wild Bill Hickok (1837)
Isadora Duncan (1878)
Dashiell Hammett (1894)
Vincent Price (1911)
John Cheever (1912)
Sam Snead (1912)
Herman Wouk (1915)
Henry Kissinger (1923)
John Barth (1930)
Ramsey Lewis (1935)
Lee Meriwether (1935)
Lou Gossett, Jr. (1936)
Bruce Weitz (1943)

May 28
Jim Thorpe (1888)
Ian Fleming (1908)
Walker Percy (1916)
Dietrich Fischer-Dieskau
(1925)
Martha Vickers (1925)
Stephen Birmingham (1931)
Dionne Quintuplets (1934)
Carroll Baker (1935)
Gladys Knight (1944)
Sondra Locke (1947)

May 29
Josef von Sternberg (1894)
Beatrice Lillie (1898)
Bob Hope (1903)
John F. Kennedy (1917)
Herb Shriner (1918)
Felix Rohatyn (1928)
Paul Ehrlich (1932)
Al Unser (1939)
Helmut Berger (1944)
Anthony Geary (1948)
John W. Hinckley, Jr. (1955)
Lisa Whelchel (1963)

May 30
Howard Hawks (1898)
Irving Thalberg (1899)
Cornelia Otis Skinner (1901)
Stepin Fetchit (1902)
Mel Blanc (1908)

Benny Goodman (1909)
Christine Jorgensen (1926)
Clint Walker (1927)
Keir Dullea (1936)
Michael J. Pollard (1939)
Meredith MacRae (1944)

May 31
Fred Allen (1894)
Norman Vincent Peale (1898)
Don Ameche (1908)
Edward Bennett Williams
(1920)
Prince Rainier (1923)
Clint Eastwood (1930)
Shirley Verrett (1933)
Jim Hutton (1938)
Peter Yarrow (1938)
Johnny Paycheck (1941)
Sharon Gless (1943)
Tom Berenger (1950)
Brooke Shields (1965)

June 1
John Van Druten (1901)
Nelson Riddle (1921)
Joan Caulfield (1922)
Andy Griffith (1926)
Marilyn Monroe (1926)
Edward Woodward (1930)
Pat Boone (1934)
Reverend Ike (1935)
Cleavon Little (1939)
René Auberjonois (1940)
Frederica Von Stade (1945)
Lisa Hartman (1956)

June 2
Hedda Hopper (1890)
Johnny Weissmuller (1904)
Mike Todd (1907)
Milo O'Shea (1926)
Sally Kellerman (1937)
Stacy Keach (1941)
Marvin Hamlisch (1944)
Jerry Mathers (1948)

June 3
Maurice Evans (1901)
Jan Peerce (1904)
Josephine Baker (1906)
Paulette Goddard (1911)
Leo Gorcey (1915)

Tony Curtis (1925)
Colleen Dewhurst (1926)
Allen Ginsberg (1926)
Larry McMurtry (1936)

June 4
Robert Merrill (1919)
Gene Barry (1922)
Dennis Weaver (1925)
Bruce Dern (1936)
Freddy Fender (1937)
Parker Stevenson (1952)

June 5
John Maynard Keynes (1883)
Federico García Lorca (1899)
Cornelius Ryan (1920)
Tony Richardson (1929)
Jacques Demy (1931)
Bill Moyers (1934)
Ken Follett (1949)

June 6
William Inge (1860)
Thomas Mann (1875)
Kirk Kirkorian (1917)
Roy Innis (1934)
Harvey Fierstein (1954)
Dana Carvey (1955)
Bjorn Borg (1956)

June 7
Paul Gauguin (1848)
George Szell (1897)
Jessica Tandy (1909)
Rocky Graziano (1922)
Tom Jones (1940)
Nikki Giovanni (1943)
Prince (1958)

June 8
Robert Preston (1918)
Alexis Smith (1921)
George Kirby (1923)
Barbara Bush (1925)
LeRoy Neiman (1926)
Jerry Stiller (1926)
Dana Wynter (1932)
Joan Rivers (1933)
James Darren (1936)
William Rukeyser (1939)
Boz Scaggs (1944)
Bonnie Tyler (1953)

June 9
Cole Porter (1892)
Fred Waring (1900)
Bob Cummings (1910)
Robert McNamara (1916)
Les Paul (1916)
Marvin Kalb (1930)
Jackie Wilson (1932)
Michael J. Fox (1961)

June 10
Hattie McDaniel (1895)
Frederick Lowe (1904)
Terence Rattigan (1911)
Saul Bellow (1915)
Barry Morse (1918)
Prince Philip (1921)
Judy Garland (1922)
June Haver (1926)
Maurice Sendak (1928)
Jim McDivitt (1929)
F. Lee Bailey (1933)
Andrew Stevens (1955)

June 11
Risë Stevens (1913)
Richard Todd (1919)
Robert Hutton (1920)
Hazel Scott (1920)
William Styron (1925)
Charles Rangel (1930)
Athol Fugard (1932)
Gene Wilder (1934)
Chad Everett (1937)
Adrienne Barbeau (1945)
Joe Montana (1956)

June 12
Anthony Eden (1897)
William Lundigan (1914)
David Rockefeller (1915)
Uta Hagen (1919)
George Bush (1924)
Vic Damone (1928)
Anne Frank (1929)
Rona Jaffe (1932)
Jim Nabors (1932)
Chick Corea (1941)

June 13
William Butler Yeats (1865)
Joseph Stella (1880)

Basil Rathbone (1892)
Mark Van Doren (1894)
Red Grange (1903)
Ralph Edwards (1913)
Don Budge (1915)
Ben Johnson (1918)
Paul Lynde (1926)
Christo (1935)
Malcolm McDowell (1943)
Richard Thomas (1951)

June 14
Major Bowes (1874)
Margaret Bourke-White (1904)
Burl Ives (1909)
Dorothy McGuire (1918)
Pierre Salinger (1925)
Cy Coleman (1929)
Jerzy Kosinski (1933)
Christopher Lehmann-Haupt
    (1934)
Boy George (1961)

June 15
Harry Langdon (1884)
Erik Erikson (1902)
Yuri Andropov (1914)
Saul Steinberg (1914)
Erroll Garner (1921)
Mario Cuomo (1932)
Waylon Jennings (1937)
Jim Belushi (1954)
Terri Gibbs (1954)

June 16
Stan Laurel (1890)
Jack Albertson (1910)
Ilona Massey (1910)
Katharine Graham (1917)
John Howard Griffin (1920)
Erich Segal (1937)
Joyce Carol Oates (1938)
Joan Van Ark (1946)
Roberto Duran (1951)

June 17
Igor Stravinsky (1882)
Ralph Bellamy (1904)
Red Foley (1910)
John Hersey (1914)
Dean Martin (1917)
Barry Manilow (1946)
Joe Piscopo (1951)

June 18
Keye Luke (1904)
Jeanette MacDonald (1906)
Bud Collyer (1908)
E.G. Marshall (1910)
Sammy Cahn (1913)
Sylvia Porter (1913)
Richard Boone (1917)
Eva Bartok (1926)
Tom Wicker (1926)
Roger Ebert (1942)
Paul McCartney (1942)
Carol Kane (1952)
Isabella Rossellini (1952)

June 19
Dame May Whitty (1865)
Charles Coburn (1877)
Moe Howard (1897)
Laura Z. Hobson (1900)
Guy Lombardo (1902)
Lou Gehrig (1903)
Mildred Natwick (1908)
Louis Jourdan (1920)
Nancy Marchand (1928)
Gena Rowlands (1936)
Kathleen Turner (1954)

June 20
Helen Traubel (1899)
Lillian Hellman (1905)
Errol Flynn (1909)
Chet Atkins (1924)
Audie Murphy (1924)
Brian Wilson (1942)
Anne Murray (1945)
André Watts (1946)
Cyndi Lauper (1953)

June 21
Rockwell Kent (1882)
Reinhold Niebuhr (1892)
Al Hirschfeld (1903)
Jean-Paul Sartre (1905)
Mary McCarthy (1912)
Jane Russell (1921)
Judy Holliday (1922)
Maureen Stapleton (1925)
Françoise Sagan (1935)
Mariette Hartley (1940)
Meredith Baxter-Birney
    (1947)

Cancer

June 22
Erich Maria Remarque (1898)
Billy Wilder (1906)
Joseph Papp (1921)
Bill Blass (1922)
Kris Kristofferson (1937)
Ed Bradley (1941)
Meryl Streep (1949)
Lindsay Wagner (1949)
Freddie Prinze (1954)

June 23
Alfred Kinsey (1894)
Jean Anouilh (1910)
Irene Worth (1916)
Bob Fosse (1927)
June Carter (1929)
Ted Lapidus (1929)
James Levine (1943)
Ted Shackelford (1946)

June 24
Ambrose Bierce
Jack Dempsey (1895)
Chief Dan George (1899)
Claude Chabrol (1930)
Michele Lee (1942)

June 25
George Abbott (1887)
George Orwell (1903)
Sidney Lumet (1924)
June Lockhart (1925)
Carly Simon (1945)
Jimmie Walker (1948)
Phyllis George (1949)
George Michael (1963)

June 26
Pearl Buck (1892)
Peter Lorre (1904)
Babe Didrickson Zaharias (1912)
Eleanor Parker (1922)

June 27
Helen Keller (1880)
Bob Keeshan (1927)
H. Ross Perot (1930)
Anna Moffo (1934)
Isabelle Adjani (1955)

June 28
John Dillinger (1902)
Ashley Montagu (1905)
Eric Ambler (1909)
A.E. Hotchner (1920)
Mel Brooks (1928)
Pat Morita (1933)
Gilda Radner (1946)
John Elway (1960)
Danielle Brisebois (1969)

June 29
Antoine de Saint Exupéry (1900)
Nelson Eddy (1901)
Frank Loesser (1910)
John Toland (1912)
Bob Evans (1930)
Oriana Fallaci (1930)
Gary Busey (1944)
Fred Grandy (1948)

June 30
Czeslaw Milosz (1911)
Lena Horne (1917)
Susan Hayward (1919)
Martin Landau (1933)
Nancy Dussault (1936)

July 1
James M. Cain (1892)
Charles Laughton (1899)
William Wyler (1902)
Estée Lauder (1908)
Olivia DeHavilland (1916)
Jean-Pierre Rampal (1922)
Farley Granger (1925)
Leslie Caron (1931)
Jamie Farr (1934)
Jean Marsh (1934)
Sydney Pollack (1934)
Famous Amos (1936)
Twyla Tharp (1941)
Karen Black (1942)
Genevieve Bujold (1942)
Deborah Harry (1945)
Dan Aykroyd (1952)
Princess Diana (1961)

July 2
Hermann Hesse (1877)
Franz Kafka (1883)
Tyrone Guthrie (1900)
René Lacoste (1905)

Thurgood Marshall (1908)
Barry Gray (1916)
Cheryl Ladd (1952)

July 3
George M. Cohan (1878)
George Sanders (1906)
Dorothy Kilgallen (1913)
Ken Russell (1927)
Pete Fountain (1930)
David Shire (1937)
Tom Stoppard (1937)
Betty Buckley (1947)
Laura Branigan (1957)
Tom Cruise (1962)

July 4
Calvin Coolidge (1872)
Rube Goldberg (1883)
Louis B. Mayer (1885)
Louis Armstrong (1900)
Meyer Lansky (1902)
Tokyo Rose (1916)
Ann Landers (1918)
Abigail Van Buren (1918)
Eva Marie Saint (1924)
Neil Simon (1927)
Gina Lollobrigida (1928)
George Steinbrenner (1930)
Geraldo Rivera (1943)

July 5
P.T. Barnum (1810)
Cecil Rhodes (1853)
Jean Cocteau (1889)
Milburn Stone (1904)
Victor Navasky (1932)
Eliot Feld (1942)
Huey Lewis (1951)

July 6
Beatrix Potter (1866)
Nancy Reagan (1921)
Merv Griffin (1925)
Bill Haley (1925)
Janet Leigh (1927)
Della Reese (1932)
Dalai Lama (1935)
Ned Beatty (1937)
Sylvester Stallone (1946)
Shelley Hack (1949)

July 7
Marc Chagall (1887)

George Cukor (1899)
Gian Carlo Menotti (1911)
Pierre Cardin (1922)
Doc Severinsen (1927)
Ahmad Jamal (1930)
Ringo Starr (1940)
Shelley Duvall (1949)

July 8
John D. Rockefeller (1839)
Louis Jordan (1908)
Nelson A. Rockefeller (1908)
Billy Eckstine (1914)
Faye Emerson (1917)
Jerry Vale (1932)
Steve Lawrence (1935)
Kim Darby (1948)

July 9
Barbara Cartland (1901)
Ed Ames (1927)
Wally Post (1929)
David Hockney (1937)
Brian Dennehy (1940)
O.J. Simpson (1947)
Tom Hanks (1956)

July 10
Marcel Proust (1871)
Giorgio de Chirico (1888)
John Gilbert (1897)
David Brinkley (1920)
Jake La Motta (1921)
Fred Gwynne (1926)
Nick Adams (1931)
Jerry Herman (1933)
Arthur Ashe (1943)
Arlo Guthrie (1947)

July 11
Thomas Mitchell (1892)
Walter Wanger (1894)
E.B. White (1899)
Sally Blane (1910)
Yul Brynner (1920)
Nicolai Gedda (1925)
Brett Somers (1927)
Tab Hunter (1931)
Leon Spinks (1953)

July 12
Tod Browning (1884)
Amadeo Modigliani (1884)
Jean Hersholt (1886)

Kirsten Flagstad (1895)
Oscar Hammerstein (1895)
Pablo Neruda (1904)
Milton Berle (1908)
Andrew Wyeth (1917)
Vera Ralston (1919)
Donald Westlake (1933)
Van Cliburn (1934)
Bill Cosby (1937)
Richard Simmons (1948)

July 13
Father Flanagan (1886)
Sidney Blackmer (1896)
Bosley Crowther (1905)
Dave Garroway (1913)
Bob Crane (1928)
Harrison Ford (1942)

July 14
Irving Stone (1903)
Isaac Bashevis Singer (1904)
Terry-Thomas (1911)
Annabella (1912)
Woody Guthrie (1912)
Gerald R. Ford (1913)
Ingmar Bergman (1918)
Arthur Laurents (1918)
Dale Robertson (1923)
John Chancellor (1927)
Polly Bergen (1930)
Roosevelt Grier (1932)

July 15
Iris Murdoch (1919)
Julian Bream (1933)
Alex Karras (1935)
Jan-Michael Vincent (1944)
Linda Ronstadt (1946)

July 16
Mary Baker Eddy (1821)
Trygve Lie (1896)
Barbara Stanwyck (1907)
Ginger Rogers (1911)
Barnard Hughes (1915)
Bess Myerson (1924)
Rubén Blades (1948)
Pinchas Zukerman (1948)

July 17
Erle Stanley Gardner (1889)
James Cagney (1899)
William Gargan (1905)

Hardy Amies (1909)
Art Linkletter (1912)
Phyllis Diller (1917)
Donald Sutherland (1934)
Diahann Carroll (1935)
Gale Garnett (1942)
Lucie Arnaz (1951)
David Hasselhof (1952)
Nicolette Larson (1952)
Phoebe Snow (1952)

July 18
Gene Lockhart (1891)
Richard Dix (1894)
Jessamyn West (1902)
Chill Wills (1903)
S.I. Hayakawa (1906)
Clifford Odets (1906)
Lupe Velez (1908)
Hume Cronyn (1911)
Harriet Nelson (1912)
Red Skelton (1913)
Nelson Mandela (1918)
John Glenn (1921)
Dick Button (1929)
Hunter Thompson (1939)
James Brolin (1941)
Martha Reeves (1941)

July 19
Edgar Degas (1834)
Lizzie Borden (1860)
Lilly Damita (1901)
E.P. Snow (1905)
Pat Hingle (1924)
Helen Gallagher (1926)
Vikki Carr (1941)

July 20
Theda Bara (1890)
Lola Albright (1924)
Diana Rigg (1938)
Natalie Wood (1939)
Kim Carnes (1946)
Carlos Santana (1947)

July 21
C. Aubrey Smith (1863)
Ken Maynard (1895)
Hart Crane (1899)
Marshall McLuhan (1911)
Isaac Stern (1920)
Don Knotts (1924)

Norman Jewison (1926)
John Gardner (1933)
Jonathan Miller (1934)
Edward Herrmann (1943)
Cat Stevens (1948)
Robin Williams (1952)

July 22
Edward Hopper (1882)
Stephen Vincent Benét
 (1898)
Alexander Calder (1898)
Amy Vanderbilt (1908)
Jason Robards, Jr. (1922)
Margaret Whiting (1924)
Orson Bean (1928)
Vivien Merchant (1929)
Oscar De La Renta (1932)
Terence Stamp (1940)
Alex Trebek (1940)
Paul Schrader (1946)
Don Henley (1947)

Leo

July 23
Karl Menninger (1893)
Gloria De Haven (1925)
Bert Convy (1934)

July 24
Amelia Earhart (1898)
John MacDonald (1916)
Billy Taylor (1921)
Peter Yates (1929)
Patrick Oliphant (1935)
Ruth Buzzi (1936)
Lynda Carter (1951)

July 25
Walter Brennan (1894)
Eric Hoffer (1902)
Jack Gilford (1913)
Woody Strode (1914)
Estelle Getty (1924)
Ed Bullins (1935)
Adnan Khashoggi (1935)

July 26
Carl Jung (1875)
André Maurois (1885)
Emil Jannings (1886)
George Grosz (1893)
Paul Gallico (1897)

Gracie Allen (1906)
Vivian Vance (1912)
Virginia Gilmore (1919)
Blake Edwards (1922)
Stanley Kubrick (1928)
Jean Shepherd (1929)
Mary Jo Kopechne (1940)
Mick Jagger (1943)

July 27
Keenan Wynn (1916)
Norman Lear (1922)
Brock Peters (1927)
Bobbie Gentry (1944)
Peggy Fleming (1948)
Betty Thomas (1948)
Maureen McGovern (1949)

July 28
Marcel Duchamp (1887)
Barbara LaMarr (1896)
Rudy Vallee (1901)
Richard Rodgers (1902)
Malcolm Lowry (1909)
Jacqueline Onassis (1929)
Darryl Hickman (1931)
Jacques D'Amboise (1934)
Peter Duchin (1937)
Bill Bradley (1943)
Jim Davis (1945)
Sally Struthers (1948)

July 29
Booth Tarkington (1869)
Maria Ouspenskaya (1876)
Benito Mussolini (1883)
Sigmund Romberg (1887)
William Powell (1892)
Dag Hammarskjöld (1905)
Thelma Todd (1905)
Melvin Belli (1907)
Richard Egan (1923)
Peter Jennings (1938)

July 30
Casey Stengel (1891)
Thomas Sowell (1930)
Edd Byrnes (1933)
Peter Bogdanovich (1939)
Eleanor Smeal (1939)
Patricia Schroeder (1940)
Paul Anka (1941)
Arnold Schwarzenegger
 (1947)

July 31
Jean Dubuffet (1901)
Milton Friedman (1912)
Irv Kupcinet (1912)
Curt Gowdy (1919)
Geraldine Chaplin (1944)

August 1
Herman Melville (1819)
Arthur Hill (1922)
Meir Kahane (1932)
Dom DeLuise (1933)
Yves Saint Laurent (1936)
Giancarlo Giannini (1942)
Tempest Bledsoe (1973)

August 2
Helen Morgan (1900)
Myrna Loy (1905)
Ann Dvorak (1912)
James Baldwin (1924)
Carroll O'Connor (1924)
Peter O'Toole (1933)

August 3
Ernie Pyle (1900)
Dolores Del Rio (1905)
Leon Uris (1924)
Tony Bennett (1926)
Martin Sheen (1940)
Jay North (1952)

August 4
Raoul Wallenberg (1912)

August 5
Guy de Maupassant (1850)
Conrad Aiken (1889)
John Huston (1906)
Robert Taylor (1911)
Neil Armstrong (1930)
John Saxon (1935)
Loni Anderson (1946)

August 6
Leo Carrillo (1880)
Hoot Gibson (1892)
Guthrie McClintic (1893)
Dutch Schultz (1900)
Lucille Ball (1911)
Robert Mitchum (1917)
Andy Warhol (1927)

August 7
Grandma Moses (1860)

Mata Hari (1876)
Billie Burke (1886)
Ralph Bunche (1904)
Nicholas Ray (1911)
Garrison Keillor (1942)
B.J. Thomas (1942)

August 8
Marjorie Kinnan Rawlings
   (1896)
Sylvia Sidney (1910)
Dino De Laurentiis (1919)
Carl "Alfalfa" Switzer (1926)
Mel Tillis (1932)
Dustin Hoffman (1937)
Connie Stevens (1938)
Keith Carradine (1950)
Donny Most (1953)

August 9
Jean Piaget (1896)
Charles Farrell (1901)
Robert Shaw (1927)
David Steinberg (1942)
Melanie Griffith (1957)
Whitney Houston (1963)

August 10
Herbert C. Hoover (1874)
Jack Haley (1900)
Norma Shearer (1904)
Rhonda Fleming (1923)
Jimmy Dean (1928)
Eddie Fisher (1928)
Rosanna Arquette (1959)

August 11
Lloyd Nolan (1902)
Alex Haley (1921)
Mike Douglas (1925)
Carol Rowan (1925)
Arlene Dahl (1927)
Rev. Jerry Falwell (1933)

August 12
Cecil B. DeMille (1881)
Cantinflas (1911)
Michael Kidd (1919)
Ross and Norris McWhirter
   (1925)
John Derek (1926)
Buck Owens (1929)
William Goldman (1931)
George Hamilton (1939)

August 13
Annie Oakley (1860)
Bert Lahr (1895)
Alfred Hitchcock (1899)
Regis Toomey (1902)
Buddy Rogers (1904)
Ben Hogan (1912)
George Shearing (1919)
Pat Harrington (1929)
Robert Culp (1930)
Don Ho (1930)
Dan Fogelberg (1951)

August 14
John Galsworthy (1867)
Nehemiah Persoff (1920)
Russell Baker (1925)
Alice Ghostley (1926)
Lina Wertmuller (1928)
David Crosby (1941)
Susan St. James (1946)

August 15
Samuel Taylor Coleridge
   (1875)
Ethel Barrymore (1879)
Edna Ferber (1887)
Bill Baird (1904)
Julia Child (1912)
Wendy Hiller (1912)
Mike Connors (1921)
Phyllis Schlafly (1924)
Oscar Peterson (1925)
Jim Dale (1935)
Linda Ellerbee (1944)
Jim Webb (1946)

August 16
Menachem Begin (1913)
Shimon Peres (1923)
Fess Parker (1927)
Ann Blyth (1928)
Frank Gifford (1930)
Anita Gillette (1936)
Leslie Ann Warren (1946)
Madonna (1958)
Timothy Hutton (1960)

August 17
Marcus Garvey (1887)
Monty Woolley (1888)
Mae West (1892)
Ann Harding (1904)

Maureen O'Hara (1921)
Sean Penn (1960)

August 18
Jack Pickford (1896)
Caspar Weinberger (1917)
Shelley Winters (1922)
Roman Polanski (1933)
Rafer Johnson (1935)
Robert Redford (1937)
Martin Mull (1943)
Patrick Swayze (1952)
Malcolm-Jamal Warner (1970)

August 19
Bernard Baruch (1870)
Orville Wright (1871)
Coco Chanel (1882)
Colleen Moore (1902)
Ogden Nash (1902)
Malcolm Forbes (1919)
Willie Shoemaker (1931)
Johnny Nash (1940)

August 20
Paul Tillich (1886)
H.P. Lovecraft (1890)
Eero Saarinen (1910)
Jacqueline Susann (1921)
Regina Resnik (1922)
Isaac Hayes (1942)
Connie Chung (1946)

August 21
Aubrey Beardsley (1872)
Count Basie (1904)
Melvin Van Peebles (1932)
Kenny Rogers (1938)
Patty McCormick (1945)

August 22
Claude Debussy (1862)
Dorothy Parker (1893)
Denton Cooley (1920)
Ray Bradbury (1920)
James Kirkwood (1930)
Valerie Harper (1940)
Cindy Williams (1947)
Diana Nyad (1949)

Virgo

August 23
Edgar Lee Masters (1869)

Gene Kelly (1912)
Vera Miles (1929)
Barbara Eden (1934)
Shelley Long (1949)
Rick Springfield (1949)

August 24
Jorge Luis Borges (1899)
Durward Kirby (1912)
Gerry Cooney (1956)
Steve Guttenberg (1958)
Marlee Matlin (1965)

August 25
Clara Bow (1905)
Ruby Keeler (1909)
Mel Ferrer (1917)
Leonard Bernstein (1918)
Monty Hall (1923)
Sean Connery (1930)
Tom Skerrit (1933)
Frederick Forsyth (1938)
Gene Simmons (1949)
Elvis Costello (1955)

August 26
Earl Long (1895)
Christopher Isherwood
  (1904)
Albert Sabin (1906)
Lester Lanin (1911)
Ben Bradlee (1921)
Irving R. Levine (1922)
Ben Wattenberg (1933)

August 27
Theodore Dreiser (1871)
Samuel Goldwyn (1882)
Martha Raye (1916)
Ira Levin (1929)
Tommy Sands (1937)
Tuesday Weld (1943)
Barbara Bach (1947)

August 28
Charles Boyer (1899)
James Wong Howe (1899)
Bruno Bettelheim (1903)
Roger Tory Peterson (1908)
Van Johnson (1916)
Donald O'Connor (1925)
Ben Gazzara (1930)

Emma Samms (1961)
David Soul (1943)

August 29
Preston Sturges (1898)
Ingrid Bergman (1916)
George Montgomery (1916)
Charlie Parker (1920)
Richard Attenborough (1923)
Isabel Sanford (1933)
Elliott Gould (1938)
William Friedkin (1939)
Robin Leach (1941)
Richard Gere (1949)
Michael Jackson (1958)
Rebecca De Mornay (1962)

August 30
Raymond Massey (1896)
Shirley Booth (1907)
Fred MacMurray (1908)
Shirley Booth (1909)
Joan Blondell (1912)
Geoffrey Beene (1927)
Elizabeth Ashley (1939)
Peggy Lipton (1947)
Timothy Bottoms (1951)

August 31
Maria Montessori (1870)
Fredric March (1897)
Arthur Godfrey (1903)
Dore Schary (1905)
William Saroyan (1908)
Alan Jay Lerner (1918)
Richard Basehart (1919)
Buddy Hackett (1924)
James Coburn (1928)
Eldridge Cleaver (1935)
Warren Berlinger (1937)
Itzhak Perlman (1945)

September 1
Edgar Rice Burroughs (1875)
Richard Arlen (1899)
Yvonne De Carlo (1922)
Vittorio Gassman (1922)
George Maharis (1933)
Conway Twitty (1933)
Seiji Ozawa (1935)
Lily Tomlin (1939)

September 2
Cleveland Amory (1917)

Allen Drury (1918)
Marge Champion (1923)
Victor Spinetti (1933)
Mark Harmon (1951)

September 3
Alan Ladd (1913)
Kitty Carlisle (1915)
Anne Jackson (1926)
Alison Lurie (1926)
Eileen Brennan (1937)
Valerie Perrine (1943)
Judith Ivey (1951)
Charlie Sheen (1965)

September 4
Ida Kaminska (1899)
Edward Dmytryk (1908)
Richard Wright (1908)
Henry Ford II (1917)
Paul Harvey (1918)
Dick York (1928)
Mitzi Gaynor (1931)
Richard Castellano (1934)
Jennifer Salt (1944)

September 5
Florence Eldridge (1901)
Darryl F. Zanuck (1902)
Bob Newhart (1929)
Carol Lawrence (1932)
Werner Erhard (1935)
Raquel Welch (1940)
Cathy Guisewaite (1950)

September 6
Billy Rose (1899)
Jo Anne Worley (1937)
Swoosie Kurtz (1944)
Jane Curtin (1947)

September 7
Taylor Caldwell (1900)
Michael De Bakey (1908)
Elia Kazan (1909)
Anthony Quayle (1913)
Peter Lawford (1923)
Sonny Rollins (1930)
Buddy Holly (1936)
Richard Roundtree (1942)
Susan Blakely (1948)

Gloria Gaynor (1949)
Corbin Bernsen (1954)

September 8
Howard Dietz (1896)
Claude Pepper (1900)
Sid Caesar (1922)
Grace Metalious (1924)
Denise Darcel (1925)
Peter Sellers (1925)
Patsy Cline (1932)
Heather Thomas (1957)

September 9
Cliff Robertson (1925)
Cannonball Adderley (1928)
Sylvia Miles (1932)
Otis Redding (1941)
Michael Keaton (1951)
Tom Wopat (1952)
Kristy McNichol (1962)

September 10
Ian Fleming (1888)
Fay Wray (1907)
Edmund O'Brien (1915)
Yma Sumac (1927)
Arnold Palmer (1929)
Charles Kuralt (1934)
Stephen Jay Gould (1941)
Jose Feliciano (1945)
Amy Irving (1953)

September 11
O. Henry (1862)
Hedy Lamarr (1914)
Earl Holliman (1936)
Brian De Palma (1940)
Lola Falana (1943)

September 12
H.L. Mencken (1880)
Maurice Chevalier (1888)
Margaret Hamilton (1902)
Jesse Owens (1913)
Dickie Moore (1925)
George Jones (1931)
Linda Gray (1940)
Maria Muldaur (1943)

September 13
Jesse Lasky (1880)
Leland Hayward (1902)
Claudette Colbert (1905)

Roald Dahl (1916)
Dick Haymes (1917)
Scott Brady (1924)
Mel Tormé (1925)
Barbara Bain (1932)
Jacqueline Bisset (1944)
Nell Carter (1948)

September 14
Jack Hawkins (1910)
Zoe Caldwell (1933)
Nicol Williamson (1938)
Joey Heatherton (1944)

September 15
Robert Benchley (1889)
Agatha Christie (1890)
Jean Renoir (1894)
Margaret Lockwood (1916)
Jackie Cooper (1922)
Hank Williams (1923)
Bobby Short (1926)
Merlin Olsen (1940)
Tommy Lee Jones (1946)

September 16
Alexander Korda (1893)
Allen Funt (1914)
Janis Paige (1922)
Lauren Bacall (1924)
Charlie Byrd (1925)
B.B. King (1925)
Robert Schuller (1926)
Peter Falk (1927)
Anne Francis (1930)
Tony Trabert (1930)
Ed Begley, Jr. (1949)

September 17
Ben Turpin (1874)
Warren Burger (1907)
Roddy McDowall (1928)
Anne Bancroft (1931)
Dorothy Loudon (1933)
Ken Kesey (1935)
John Ritter (1948)

September 18
Agnes DeMille (1905)
Greta Garbo (1905)
Eddie Anderson (1905)
Rossano Brazzi (1916)
Jack Warden (1920)

Robert Blake (1933)
Frankie Avalon (1940)

September 19
Joseph Pasternak (1901)
Ricardo Cortez (1899)
Lewis F. Powell, Jr. (1907)
Rosemary Harris (1930)
Mike Royko (1932)
David McCallum (1933)
Freda Payne (1945)
Jeremy Irons (1948)
Twiggy (1949)
Joan Lunden (1951)

September 20
Jelly Roll Morton (1885)
Fernando Rey (1917)
Anne Meara (1924)
Sophia Loren (1934)
Pia Lindstrom (1938)

September 21
Ladislas Farago (1906)
Dawn Addams (1930)
Larry Hagman (1931)
Stephen King (1947)
Bill Murray (1950)

September 22
Erich Von Stroheim (1885)
Paul Muni (1895)
John Houseman (1902)
Tommy Lasorda (1927)
Shari Belafonte-Harper
    (1954)
Debby Boone (1956)
Scott Baio (1961)

September 23
Walter Pidgeon (1897)
Mickey Rooney (1920)
Gail Russell (1924)
Ray Charles (1930)
Romy Schneider (1938)
Julio Iglesias (1943)
Bruce Springsteen (1949)

Libra

September 24
Jim McKay (1921)
Sheila MacRae (1924)
Anthony Newley (1931)
Jim Henson (1936)

September 25
Mark Rothko (1903)
Red Smith (1905)
Dmitri Shostakovich (1906)
Phil Rizzuto (1918)
Aldo Ray (1926)
Barbara Walters (1931)
Glenn Gould (1932)
Juliet Prowse (1936)
Michael Douglas (1944)
Mark Hamill (1951)
Christopher Reeve (1952)
Heather Locklear (1961)

September 26
George Raft (1895)
George Gershwin (1898)
Jack LaLanne (1914)
Marty Robbins (1925)
Julie London (1926)
Patrick O'Neal (1927)
Olivia Newton-John (1948)

September 27
Louis Auchincloss (1917)
William Conrad (1920)
Arthur Penn (1922)
Jayne Meadows (1926)
Barbara Howar (1934)
Claude Jarman, Jr. (1934)
Meat Loaf (1947)
Mike Schmidt (1949)
Heather Watts (1943)
Shaun Cassidy (1958)

September 28
Elmer Rice (1892)
Al Capp (1909)
Peter Finch (1916)
Marcello Mastroianni (1924)
Brigitte Bardot (1934)

September 29
Gene Autry (1907)
Greer Garson (1908)
Virginia Bruce (1910)
Michelangelo Antonioni
   (1912)
Stanley Kramer (1913)
Trevor Howard (1916)
Lizabeth Scott (1922)
Anita Ekberg (1931)
Jerry Lee Lewis (1935)

Madeline Kahn (1942)
Lech Walesa (1943)
Bryant Gumbel (1948)

September 30
Renée Adorée (1898)
Kenny Baker (1912)
Deborah Kerr (1921)
Truman Capote (1924)
Angie Dickinson (1931)
Johnny Mathis (1935)
Len Cariou (1939)
Jody Powell (1943)
Deborah Allen (1953)

October 1
Stanley Holloway (1890)
George Coulouris (1903)
Vladimir Horowitz (1904)
Everett Sloane (1909)
James Whitmore (1921)
Tom Bosley (1927)
Laurence Harvey (1928)
George Peppard (1928)
Richard Harris (1930)
Edward Villella (1932)
Julie Andrews (1935)
Stella Stevens (1936)
Stephen Collins (1947)

October 2
Mahatma Gandhi (1869)
Wallace Stevens (1879)
Groucho Marx (1890)
Bud Abbott (1900)
Graham Greene (1904)
Jan Morris (1926)
Spanky MacFarland (1928)
Moses Gunn (1929)
Rex Reed (1940)
Don McLean (1945)
Persis Khambata (1950)
Sting (1951)

October 3
Warner Oland (1880)
Leo McCarey (1898)
Gertrude Berg (1899)
James Herriot (1916)
Charles Bronson (1922)
Gore Vidal (1925)
Chubby Checker (1941)

October 4
Frederic Remington (1861)
Damon Runyon (1884)
Buster Keaton (1896)
Brendan Gill (1914)
Jan Murray (1917)
Charlton Heston (1924)
Alvin Toffler (1928)
Clifton Davis (1945)
Susan Sarandon (1946)

October 5
Joshua Logan (1908)
Donald Pleasence (1919)
Glynis Johns (1923)
Diane Cilento (1933)
Vaclav Havel (1936)
Jeff Conaway (1950)
Karen Allen (1951)
Bob Geldof (1951)

October 6
Jerome Cowan (1897)
Janet Gaynor (1906)
Carole Lombard (1909)
Thor Heyerdahl (1914)
Anna Quayle (1936)
Britt Ekland (1942)

October 7
Niels Bohr (1895)
Andy Devine (1905)
Vaughn Monroe (1911)
Elizabeth Janeway (1913)
Alfred Drake (1914)
June Allyson (1917)
Diana Lynn (1926)
R.D. Laing (1927)
Gabe Dell (1923)
Bishop Tutu (1931)
John Cougar Mellencamp (1951)
Yo-Yo Ma (1955)

October 8
Eddie Rickenbacker (1890)
Juan Perón (1895)
Meyer Levin (1905)
Rona Barrett (1936)
Jesse Jackson (1941)
Chevy Chase (1943)
Stephanie Zimbalist (1956)

October 9
Aimee Semple McPherson (1890)
Bruce Catton (1899)
Jacques Tati (1908)
John Lennon (1940)
Jeffrey Osbourne (1948)
Jackson Browne (1950)

October 10
Helen Hayes (1900)
Vernon Duke (1903)
Thelonius Monk (1920)
James Clavell (1924)
Harold Pinter (1930)
Omar Sharif (1932)
Ben Vereen (1946)
David Lee Roth (1955)
Martina Navratilova (1956)
Tanya Tucker (1958)

October 11
Eleanor Roosevelt (1884)
Joseph Alsop (1910)
Jerome Robbins (1916)
Elmore Leonard (1925)
Roy Scheider (1935)
Ron Leibman (1937)
Peter Martins (1946)
Daryl Hall (1948)

October 12
Jean Nidetch (1923)
Dick Gregory (1932)
Luciano Pavarotti (1935)
Chris Wallace (1947)
Susan Anton (1950)
Kirk Cameron (1970)

October 13
Herblock (1909)
Burr Tillstrom (1917)
Cornel Wilde (1918)
Jack MacGowran (1918)
Laraine Day (1920)
Yves Montand (1921)
Nipsy Russell (1924)
Lenny Bruce (1925)
Margaret Thatcher (1925)
Art Garfunkel (1942)
Pamela Tiffin (1942)
Demond Wilson (1946)
Marie Osmond (1959)

October 14

Eamon DeValera (1882)
Dwight D. Eisenhower (1890)
E.E. Cummings (1894)
Lillian Gish (1896)
Allan Jones (1907)
Roger Moore (1927)
Ralph Lauren (1939)
Greg Evigan (1953)

October 15

Jane Darwell (1880)
Ina Claire (1895)
Mervyn LeRoy (1900)
John Kenneth Galbraith
   (1908)
Arthur Schlesinger, Jr. (1917)
Mario Puzo (1920)
Lee Iacocca (1924)
Evan Hunter (1926)
Jean Peters (1926)
Linda Lavin (1937)
Penny Marshall (1945)
Jim Palmer (1945)

October 16

Oscar Wilde (1856)
David Ben-Gurion (1886)
Eugene O'Neill (1888)
Linda Darnell (1921)
Angela Lansbury (1925)
Günter Grass (1927)
Suzanne Somers (1946)

October 17

Spring Byington (1893)
Nathanael West (1903)
Jean Arthur (1908)
Arthur Miller (1915)
Rita Hayworth (1918)
Montgomery Clift (1920)
Tom Poston (1927)
Jimmy Breslin (1930)
Margot Kidder (1948)
Howard Rollins (1950)

October 18

Leo G. Carroll (1892)
Lotte Lenya (1900)
Miriam Hopkins (1902)
Sidney Kingsley (1906)
Jesse Helms (1921)
Melina Mercouri (1925)

George C. Scott (1927)
Inger Stevens (1934)
Peter Boyle (1935)
Mike Ditka (1939)
Lee Harvey Oswald (1939)
Ntozake Shange (1948)
Pam Dawber (1951)
Wynton Marsalis (1961)

October 19

Jack Anderson (1922)
John LeCarré (1931)
Peter Max (1937)
John Lithgow (1945)
Jeannie C. Riley (1945)
Jennifer Holliday (1960)

October 20

Bela Lugosi (1882)
Margaret Dumont (1889)
Arlene Francis (1908)
Art Buchwald (1925)
Dr. Joyce Brothers (1928)
Mickey Mantle (1931)
Jerry Orbach (1935)

October 21

Peter Graves (1911)
George Solti (1912)
Dizzy Gillespie (1917)
Carrie Fisher (1956)

October 22

N.C. Wyeth (1882)
Constance Bennett (1905)
Joan Fontaine (1917)
Timothy Leary (1920)
Robert Rauschenberg (1925)
Derek Jacobi (1938)
Tony Roberts (1939)
Catherine Deneuve (1943)
Jeff Goldblum (1952)

October 23

James Daly (1918)
Ned Rorem (1923)
Johnny Carson (1925)
Bella Darvi (1929)
Diana Dors (1931)
Pelé (1940)
Michael Crichton (1942)
Weird Al Yankovic (1959)

Scorpio

October 24
Ted Lewis (1894)
Moss Hart (1904)
Tony Walton (1934)
F. Murray Abraham (1939)
Kevin Kline (1947)

October 25
Pablo Picasso (1881)
Henry Steele Commager
   (1902)
Minnie Pearl (1912)
John Berryman (1914)
Barbara Cook (1927)
Anthony Franciosa (1928)
Helen Reddy (1941)

October 26
Primo Carnera (1906)
Mahalia Jackson (1911)
Jackie Coogan (1914)
François Mitterrand (1916)
Bob Hoskins (1942)
Jaclyn Smith (1947)
Julian Schnabel (1951)

October 27
Theodore Roosevelt (1858)
Fred De Cordova (1910)
Leif Erickson (1911)
Dylan Thomas (1914)
Teresa Wright (1918)
Nanette Fabray (1922)
Roy Lichtenstein (1923)
Ruby Dee (1924)
Sylvia Plath (1932)
John Cleese (1939)
Pat Sajak (1946)
Simon LeBon (1958)

October 28
Elsa Lanchester (1902)
Evelyn Waugh (1903)
Edith Head (1907)
Jonas Salk (1914)
Joan Plowright (1929)
Suzy Parker (1933)
Jane Alexander (1939)
Bruce Jenner (1949)

October 29
Fanny Brice (1891)

Akim Tamiroff (1901)
Bill Mauldin (1921)
Melba Moore (1945)
Richard Dreyfuss (1947)
Kate Jackson (1948)

October 30
Emily Post (1873)
Ezra Pound (1885)
Charles Atlas (1894)
Ruth Gordon (1896)
Gordon Parks (1912)
Ruth Hussey (1914)
Herschel Bernardi (1923)
Louis Malle (1932)
Henry Winkler (1945)
Harry Hamlin (1951)

October 31
Chiang Kai-Shek (1886)
Ethel Waters (1900)
Dale Evans (1912)
Dick Francis (1920)
Barbara Bel Geddes (1922)
Lee Grant (1930)
Dan Rather (1931)
Michael Landon (1936)
John Candy (1950)
Jane Pauley (1950)

November 1
Stephen Crane (1871)
Sholem Asch (1880)
Walter Matthau (1920)
Victoria De Los Angeles
   (1924)
A.R. Gurney, Jr. (1930)
Larry Flynt (1942)

November 2
Paul Ford (1901)
Luchino Visconti (1906)
Burt Lancaster (1913)
Ann Rutherford (1917)
Patrick Buchanan (1938)

November 3
André Malraux (1901)
Yitzhak Shamir (1914)
Ken Berry (1933)
Terrence McNally (1939)

November 4
Isamu Noguchi (1904)

Pauline Trigère (1912)
Gig Young (1913)
Walter Cronkite (1916)
Art Carney (1918)
Martin Balsam (1919)
Loretta Swit (1937)

November 5
Eugene Debs (1855)
Ida Tarbell (1857)
Will Durant (1885)
Joel McCrea (1906)
Roy Rogers (1912)
Vivien Leigh (1913)
John McGiver (1913)
Ike Turner (1931)
Elke Sommer (1940)
Paul Simon (1942)
Sam Shepard (1943)
Tatum O'Neal (1963)

November 6
Juanita Hall (1901)
Mike Nichols (1931)
Jean Shrimpton (1942)
Sally Field (1946)
Maria Shriver (1955)

November 7
Madame Curie (1867)
Heinrich Himmler (1900)
Dean Jagger (1903)
Albert Camus (1913)
Rev. Billy Graham (1918)
Al Hirt (1922)
Joan Sutherland (1929)
Mary Travers (1937)
Barry Newman (1938)
Joni Mitchell (1943)

November 8
Leon Trotsky (1879)
Margaret Mitchell (1900)
Katharine Hepburn (1907)
June Havoc (1916)
Patti Page (1927)
Morley Safer (1931)
Esther Rolle (1933)
Alain Delon (1935)
Bonnie Raitt (1949)
Leif Garrett (1961)

November 9
Marie Dressler (1869)

Ed Wynn (1886)
Claude Rains (1889)
Peter Drucker (1909)
Spiro Agnew (1918)
Jerome Hines (1921)
Dorothy Dandridge (1922)
Carl Sagan (1934)
Lou Ferrigno (1952)

November 10
J.P. Marquand (1893)
Mabel Normand (1897)
Richard Burton (1925)
Ann Reinking (1949)
Mackenzie Phillips (1959)

November 11
George Patton (1885)
René Clair (1898)
Pat O'Brien (1899)
Sam Spiegel (1901)
Alger Hiss (1904)
Robert Ryan (1909)
Gene Tierney (1920)
Kurt Vonnegut, Jr. (1922)
Jonathan Winters (1925)
Carlos Fuentes (1928)
Charles Manson (1934)
Bibi Andersson (1935)

November 12
Jack Oakie (1903)
Kim Hunter (1922)
Grace Kelly (1929)
Stefanie Powers (1942)
Wallace Shawn (1943)
Neil Young (1945)

November 13
Louis Brandeis (1856)
Hermione Baddeley (1906)
Alexander Scourby (1913)
Nathaniel Benchley (1915)
Oskar Werner (1922)
Linda Christian (1923)
Richard Mulligan (1932)
Garry Marshall (1934)
Jean Seberg (1938)
George V. Higgins (1939)

November 14
Claude Monet (1840)
Jawaharlal Nehru (1889)

Aaron Copland (1900)
Louise Brooks (1906)
Barbara Hutton (1912)
Brian Keith (1921)
Johnny Desmond (1921)
McLean Stevenson (1929)
Prince Charles (1948)

November 15
Franklin P. Adams (1881)
Felix Frankfurter (1882)
Georgia O'Keeffe (1887)
Erwin Rommel (1891)
Veronica Lake (1919)
Edward Asner (1929)
Petula Clark (1932)
Sam Waterston (1940)
Beverly D'Angelo (1953)

November 16
W.C. Handy (1873)
George S. Kaufman (1889)
Burgess Meredith (1908)
Bo Derek (1956)
Lisa Bonet (1967)

November 17
Lee Strasberg (1901)
Mischa Auer (1905)
Rock Hudson (1925)
Peter Cook (1937)
Martin Scorsese (1942)
Lauren Hutton (1944)
Tom Seaver (1944)

November 18
Ignace Paderewski (1860)
Eugene Ormandy (1899)
Alan Shepard, Jr. (1923)
Dorothy Collins (1926)
Brenda Vaccaro (1939)
Linda Evans (1942)

November 19
Clifton Webb (1891)
Tommy Dorsey (1905)
Imogene Coca (1908)
Indira Gandhi (1917)
Alan Young (1919)
Jeane Kirkpatrick (1926)
Larry King (1933)
Dick Cavett (1936)
Ted Turner (1938)

Calvin Klein (1942)
Jodie Foster (1962)

November 20
Chester Gould (1900)
Alistair Cooke (1908)
Emilio Pucci (1914)
Judy Canova (1916)
Evelyn Keyes (1919)
Robert F. Kennedy (1925)
Maya Plisetskaya (1925)
Kaye Ballard (1926)
Estelle Parsons (1927)
Richard Dawson (1932)
Dick Smothers (1938)
Veronica Hamel (1945)

November 21
René Magritte (1898)
Eleanor Powell (1912)
Ralph Meeker (1920)
Vivian Blaine (1924)
Natalia Makarova (1940)
Marlo Thomas (1943)
Goldie Hawn (1945)
Mariel Hemingway (1961)

November 22
André Gide (1869)
Charles De Gaulle (1890)
Hoagy Carmichael (1899)
Wiley Post (1900)
Rodney Dangerfield (1921)
Geraldine Page (1924)
Robert Vaughn (1932)
Tom Conti (1941)
Jamie Lee Curtis (1958)

Sagittarius

November 23
Billy the Kid (1859)
Boris Karloff (1887)
Harpo Marx (1893)
Victor Jory (1903)
José Duarte (1926)

November 24
Bat Masterson (1853)
Henri de Toulouse-Lautrec
   (1864)
Scott Joplin (1868)
Dale Carnegie (1888)

Cathleen Nesbitt (1889)
Lucky Luciano (1897)
Dick Powell (1904)
Garson Kanin (1912)
Geraldine Fitzgerald (1914)
Howard Duff (1917)
William F. Buckley, Jr.
  (1925)

November 25
Carry Nation (1846)
Virgil Thomson (1896)
Helen Gahagan Douglas
  (1900)
Ricardo Montalban (1920)
John Larroquette (1947)

November 26
Charles Brackett (1892)
Emlyn Williams (1905)
Eugene Ionesco (1912)
Eric Severeid (1912)
Charles Schulz (1922)
Robert Goulet (1933)
Marian Mercer (1935)
Rich Little (1938)
Tina Turner (1938)

November 27
James Agee (1909)
David Merrick (1912)
William Simon (1927)
Bruce Lee (1940)
Eddie Rabbit (1941)
Jimi Hendrix (1942)
Danny De Vito (1944)
Caroline Kennedy (1951)

November 28
Brooks Atkinson (1894)
Jose Iturbi (1895)
Alberto Moravia (1907)
Gloria Grahame (1925)
Berry Gordy, Jr. (1929)
Hope Lange (1933)
Paul Warfield (1942)
Randy Newman (1943)
Alexander Godunov (1949)

November 29
Busby Berkeley (1895)
Adam Clayton Powell, Jr.
  (1908)

Merle Travis (1917)
Kahlil Gibran (1922)
Vin Scully (1927)
John Gary (1932)
Diane Ladd (1932)
Willie Morris (1934)
Chuck Mangione (1940)
Howie Mandel (1955)

November 30
Winston Churchill (1874)
Virginia Mayo (1920)
Efrem Zimbalist, Jr. (1923)
Richard Crenna (1927)
Dick Clark (1929)
G. Gordon Liddy (1930)
Robert Guillaume (1937)
Mandy Patinkin (1952)
Billy Idol (1955)
Bo Jackson (1962)

December 1
Cyril Ritchard (1897)
Mary Martin (1914)
Woody Allen (1935)
Lou Rawls (1936)
Lee Trevino (1939)
Richard Pryor (1940)
Dennis Wilson (1941)
Bette Midler (1945)
Charlene Tilton (1958)

December 2
George Seurat (1859)
Adolph Green (1915)
Ezra Stone (1917)
Alexander Haig (1924)
Julie Harris (1925)

December 3
Joseph Conrad (1857)
Larry Parks (1914)
Maria Callas (1923)
Jim Backus (1924)
Jean-Luc Godard (1930)
Andy Williams (1930)
Ozzy Osbourne (1948)

December 4
Wassily Kandinsky (1866)
Francisco Franco (1892)
Deanna Durbin (1921)
Horst Buchholz (1933)
Jeff Bridges (1949)

December 5
Fritz Lang (1890)
Walt Disney (1901)
Otto Preminger (1906)
Larry Kert (1930)
Joan Didion (1934)
Calvin Trillin (1935)
Morgan Brittany (1951)

December 6
William S. Hart (1872)
Lynn Fontanne (1887)
Ira Gershwin (1896)
Eve Curie (1904)
Agnes Moorehead (1906)
Dave Brubeck (1920)
Wally Cox (1924)
Bobby Van (1932)
Tom Hulce (1953)

December 7
Willa Cather (1873)
Rudolf Friml (1879)
Fay Bainter (1892)
Rod Cameron (1912)
Eli Wallach (1915)
Ted Knight (1923)
Ellen Burstyn (1932)

December 8
Diego Rivera (1886)
George Stevens (1904)
Sammy Davis, Jr. (1925)
Maximilian Schell (1930)
Flip Wilson (1933)
Jim Morrison (1943)
John Rubinstein (1946)
Kim Basinger (1953)

December 9
Hermione Gingold (1897)
Emmett Kelly (1898)
Dalton Trumbo (1905)
Douglas Fairbanks, Jr.
  (1909)
Broderick Crawford (1911)
Lee J. Cobb (1911)
Kirk Douglas (1916)
Redd Foxx (1922)
Dina Merrill (1925)
Dick Van Patten (1928)
John Cassavetes (1929)
Buck Henry (1930)

Beau Bridges (1941)
Donny Osmond (1957)

December 10
Una Merkel (1903)
Morton Gould (1913)
Dorothy Lamour (1914)
Dennis Morgan (1920)
Gloria Loring (1946)
Susan Dey (1952)

December 11
Fiorello La Guardia (1882)
Victor McLaglen (1886)
Gilbert Roland (1905)
Jean-Louis Trintignant (1930)
Rita Moreno (1931)
Donna Mills (1943)
Terri Garr (1945)
Jermaine Jackson (1954)

December 12
Edward G. Robinson (1893)
Jules Dassin (1911)
Curt Jurgens (1915)
Frank Sinatra (1915)
Joe Williams (1918)
Connie Francis (1938)
Dionne Warwick (1941)
Cathy Rigby (1952)

December 13
Marc Connelly (1890)
Drew Pearson (1897)
Carlos Montoya (1903)
Van Heflin (1910)
Lillian Roth (1910)
Dick Van Dyke (1925)
Christopher Plummer (1929)
Tim Conway (1933)
John Davidson (1941)

December 14
Morey Amsterdam (1914)
Dan Dailey (1915)
Abbe Lane (1932)
Charlie Rich (1932)
Lee Remick (1935)
Patty Duke (1946)

December 15
Maxwell Anderson (1888)
J. Paul Getty (1892)
Jeff Chandler (1918)

James E. Carter (1923)
Don Johnson (1949)

December 16
George Santayana (1863)
Noel Coward (1899)
Margaret Mead (1901)
Arthur C. Clarke (1917)
Liv Ullmann (1939)
Ben Cross (1947)

December 17
Arthur Fiedler (1894)
Erskine Caldwell (1903)
William Safire (1929)
Tommy Steele (1936)

December 18
Saki (H.H. Munro) (1870)
Paul Klee (1879)
Abe Burrows (1910)
Willy Brandt (1913)
Betty Grable (1916)
Ossie Davis (1917)
Steven Spielberg (1947)

December 19
Oliver La Farge (1901)
Ralph Richardson (1902)
Jean Genet (1910)
Gordon Jackson (1923)
Cicely Tyson (1939)
Robert Urich (1940)
Richard Leakey (1944)
Miguel Pinero (1946)
Jennifer Beals (1963)

December 20
Sidney Hook (1902)
Max Lerner (1902)
Irene Dunne (1904)
George Roy Hill (1922)

December 21
Joseph Stalin (1879)
Kurt Waldheim (1918)
Joe Paterno (1926)
Phil Donahue (1935)
Jane Fonda (1937)
Frank Zappa (1940)
Michael Tilson Thomas
  (1944)

Capricorn

December 22
Giacomo Puccini (1858)
Connie Mack (1862)
Andre Kostelanetz (1901)
Peggy Ashcroft (1907)
Gene Rayburn (1917)
Hector Elizondo (1936)
Diane Sawyer (1945)
Maurice and Robin Gibb
  (1949)

December 23
Yousef Karsh (1908)
José Greco (1918)
Ruth Roman (1924)
Harry Guardino (1925)
Elizabeth Hartman (1941)

December 24
Michael Curtiz (1898)
Howard Hughes (1905)
Ava Gardner (1922)
Robert Joffrey (1930)
Jill Bennett (1931)

December 25
Clara Barton (1821)
Maurice Utrillo (1883)
Conrad Hilton (1887)
Rebecca West (1892)
Robert Ripley (1893)
Humphrey Bogart (1899)
Moses and Raphael Soyer
  (1899)
Cab Calloway (1907)
Quentin Crisp (1908)
Tony Martin (1913)
Anwar el Sadat (1918)
Rod Serling (1924)
Jimmy Buffet (1946)
Larry Csonka (1946)
Barbara Mandrell (1948)
Sissy Spacek (1949)

December 26
Henry Miller (1891)
Mao Zedong (1893)
Elisha Cook, Jr. (1906)
Richard Widmark (1914)
Steve Allen (1921)
Alan King (1927)

December 27
Sydney Greenstreet (1879)
Marlene Dietrich (1901)
Oscar Levant (1906)
Moshe Arens (1925)
Gerard Depardieu (1948)

December 28
Woodrow Wilson (1856)
Earl Fatha Hines (1905)
Cliff Arquette (1905)
Lew Ayres (1908)
Sam Levenson (1911)
Lou Jacobi (1913)
Lee Bowman (1914)
Hildegarde Neff (1925)
Maggie Smith (1934)
Edgar Winter (1946)
Denzel Washington (1954)

December 29
Pablo Casals (1876)
Mary Tyler Moore (1937)
Jon Voight (1938)
Marianne Faithfull (1946)
Ted Danson (1947)

December 30
Rudyard Kipling (1865)
Carol Reed (1906)
Bert Parks (1914)
Bo Diddley (1928)
Jack Lord (1930)
Russ Tamblyn (1935)
Tracey Ullman (1959)

December 31
Henri Matisse (1869)
George C. Marshall (1880)
Elizabeth Arden (1884)
Pola Negri (1894)
Jule Styne (1905)
Odetta (1930)
Anthony Hopkins (1937)
John Denver (1943)
Ben Kingsley (1943)
Sarah Miles (1943)
Patti Smith (1946)
Tim Matheson (1948)
Donna Summer (1948)

★ # Famous Adopted/Foster Children ★

Edward Albee
Art Buchwald
Deborah Harry

Steven Jobs
Art Linkletter
Greg Louganis

James MacArthur
James Michener
Jim Palmer

★ # Famous People Born in Canada ★

Canada has a serious "brain drain," to say the least. The only people who seem to stay are the politicians (and, sometimes, their wives) and the fishermen. Here are over two hundred people who increased their incomes tenfold just by crossing the border:

	Place of Birth
Paul Anka	Ottawa
Elizabeth Arden	Woodbridge, Ontario
Margaret Atwood	Ottawa
Dan Aykroyd	Ottawa

Conrad Bain	Lethbridge, Alberta
Saul Bellow	Lachine, Quebec
Richard Bennett	Hopewell, N.B.
Billy Bishop	Owen Sound, Ontario
Ben Blue	Montreal
Oscar Brand	Winnipeg
Bobby Breen	Toronto
Genevieve Bujold	Montreal
Raymond Burr	New Westminster, B.C.
Sebastian Cabot	Victoria
Rod Cameron	Calgary
Len Cariou	Saint Boniface, Manitoba
Jack Carson	Carman, Manitoba
Susan Clark	Sarnia, Ontario
Dorothy Collins	Windsor, Ontario
Thomas Costain	Brantford, Ontario
James J. Couzens	Chatham, Ontario
Hume Cronyn	London, Ontario
Yvonne De Carlo	Vancouver
Katharine DeMille	Vancouver
Colleen Dewhurst	Montreal
Selma Diamond	London, Ontario
Dionne Sisters	Callander, Ontario
Edward Dmytryk	Grand Forks, B.C.
Denny Doherty	Halifax, N.S.
Fifi D'Orsay	Montreal
Marie Dressler	Cobourg, Ontario
Deanna Durbin	Winnipeg
Allan Dwan	Toronto
Richard Eagan	Windsor, Ontario
Paul Erdman	Stratford, Ontario
Percy Faith	Toronto
Maynard Ferguson	Verdun, Quebec
Glenn Ford	Quebec
Michael J. Fox	Edmonton, Alberta
John Kenneth Galbraith	Iona Station, Ontario
Chief Dan George	North Vancouver
Glenn Gould	Toronto
Lorne Greene	Ottawa
Monty Hall	Winnipeg
S.I. Hayakawa	Vancouver
Doug Henning	Fort Gary, Manitoba
Arthur Hill	Melfort, Saskatchewan
Arthur Hiller	Edmonton
Walter Huston	Toronto
John Ireland	Victoria
Lou Jacobi	Toronto
Peter Jennings	Toronto
Norman Jewison	Toronto

Ruby Keeler	Halifax, N.S.
Margot Kidder	Yellowknife, N.W.
Alexander Knox	Strathroy, Ontario
Gordon Lightfoot	Orillia, Ontario
Beatrice Lillie	Toronto
Art Linkletter	Saskatchewan
Rich Little	Ottawa
Gene Lockhart	London, Ontario
Guy Lombardo	London, Ontario
Gisele MacKenzie	Winnipeg
Raymond Massie	Toronto
Marshall McLuhan	Edmonton
Robert McNeil	Montreal
Aimee Semple McPherson	Ingersoll, Ontario
Lorne Michaels	Toronto
Joni Mitchell	McLeod, Alberta
Farley Mowat	Belleville, Ontario
Anne Murray	Springhill, N.S.
Bronko Nagurski	Rainy River, Ontario
Kate Nelligan	London, Ontario
Barbara Parkins	Vancouver
Oscar Peterson	Montreal
Jack Pickford	Toronto
Mary Pickford	Toronto
Walter Pidgeon	E. Saint John, N.B.
Christopher Plummer	Toronto
John Qualen	Vancouver
The Amazing Randi	Toronto
Mordecai Richler	Montreal
Franklin D. Roosevelt, Jr.	Campobello, N.B.
Morley Safer	Toronto
Mort Sahl	Montreal
Buffy Sainte-Marie	Craven, Saskatchewan
Michael Sarrazin	Quebec
Arnold Scaasi	Montreal
Mack Sennett	Quebec
William Shatner	Montreal
Norman Shearer	Montreal
Martin Short	Hamilton, Ontario
Jay Silverheels	Ontario
Alexis Smith	Penticton, B.C.
Hank Snow	Liverpool, N.S.
David Steinberg	Winnipeg
Teresa Stratas	Toronto
Dorothy Stratten	Vancouver
Donald Sutherland	Saint John, N.B.
Alan Thicke	Kirkland Lake, Ontario
Cecil Thompson	Sandon, B.C.
Alex Trebek	Sudbury, Ontario

Robert Urich	Toronto
Jon Vickers	Prince Albert, Saskatchewan
Lila Acheson Wallace	Virden, Manitoba
Jack Warner	London, Ontario
Joseph Wiseman	Montreal
Fay Wray	Alberta
Neil Young	Toronto

Also many hockey greats (Orr, Gilbert, Howe, Hull, et al.).

★ Famous People Born in Russia ★

Place of Birth

Sholem Aleichem	Pereyaslavl
Boris Aronson	Kiev
Isaac Asimov	Petrovichi
Mischa Auer	St. Petersburg
George Balanchine	St. Petersburg
Mikhail Baryshnikov	Riga
Irving Berlin	Tenum
Yul Brynner	Sakhalin
Marc Chagall	Vitebsk
Fyodor Chaliapin	Kazan
Tom Conway	St. Petersburg
Alexandra Danilova	Peterhof
Vernon Duke	Pskov
Ariel Durant	Proskurov
Sergei Eisenstein	Riga
Alexander Godunov	Sakhalin
Sir Lew Grade	Tokmak
Philippe Halsman	Riga
Jascha Heifetz	Vilna
Vladimir Horowitz	Kiev
Sol Hurok	Pogar
Al Jolson	St. Petersburg
Ida Kaminska	Odessa
Andre Kostelanetz	St. Petersburg
Meyer Lansky	Grodno
Max Lerner	Minsk
Alexis Lichine	Moscow
Anatole Litvak	Kiev
Natalia Makarova	Leningrad
Golda Meir	Kiev
Lewis Milestone	Chisinau
Nathan Milstein	Odessa
M.P. Mussorgsky	Karevo
Vladimir Nabokov	St. Petersburg

	Place of Birth
Louise Nevelson	unspecified
Vaslav Nijinsky	Kiev
Rudolf Nureyev	Irkutsk
Serge Obolensky	Tsarskoe Selo
Maria Ouspenskaya	Tula
Ayn Rand	St. Petersburg
Gregory Ratoff	Petrograd
Mark Rothko	unspecified
Albert Sabin	Bialystok
George Sanders	St. Petersburg
David Sarnoff	Minsk
Joseph Schenk	Rybinsk
Alan Schneider	Kharkov
Moses Soyer	Tambov
Raphael Soyer	Tambov
Isaac Stern	Kreminiecz
Jo Swerling	unspecified
Akim Tamiroff	Baku
Jacobo Timerman	Bar
Leon Trotsky	Elisavetgrad
Sophie Tucker	unspecified
Efrem Zimbalist	Rostov

★ Famous People Born in Poland ★

	Place of Birth
Polly Adler	Yanow
Jerzy Andrzejewski	Warsaw
Sholem Asch	Kutno
Menachem Begin	Brest-Litovsk
David Ben-Gurion	Plonsk
Jacob Bronowski	unspecified
Zbigniew Brzezinski	Warsaw
Frederic Chopin	Zelazowa
Myron Cohen	Grodno
Joseph Conrad	Berdichev
Copernicus	Torun
Marie Curie	Warsaw
Bella Darvi	Sosnowiec
David Dubinsky	Brest-Litovsk
Max Factor	Lodz
Casimir Funk	Warsaw
Samuel Goldwyn	Warsaw
Wojciech Jaruzelski	Kurow
Thaddeus Kosciuszko	Belorussia
Jerzy Kosinski	Lodz
Bronislaw Malinowski	Cracow

Ross Martin	Gradek
Helena Modjeska	Cracow
Pola Negri	Janowa
Olga	Cracow
Ignace Paderewski	Kurilovka
Shimon Peres	Wolozyn
Pope John Paul II	Wadowice
Kazimierz Pulaski	Winiary
Wladyslaw Stanislaw Reymont	Kobiele Wielkie
Admiral Hyman G. Rickover	Makow
Leo Rosten	Lodz
Arthur Rubinstein	Lodz
Helena Rubinstein	Cracow
Haym Salomon	Leszno
Elisabeth Schwarzkopf	Jarotschin
Yitzhak Shamir	Kuzinoy
Henryk Sienkiewicz	Okrzejska
Isaac Bashevis Singer	Radzymin
Menasha Skulnik	Warsaw
Sam Spiegel	Jaroslaw
Andrzej Wajda	Suwalki
Lech Walesa	Popow
Harry Warner	Kraznashiltz
Simon Wiesenthal	Buczacz

400 Famous People Born or
★ Raised in Brooklyn ★

Eddie Murphy, Eddie Rabbit, and Eddie Money have more than first names and fame in common—all three were born in Brooklyn, New York, the most fabled and infamous of New York's five boroughs and a spawning ground for the rich and famous. Brooklyn has such a mystique that author Norman Mailer (born in Long Branch, New Jersey) still insists on living in the borough, unlike those Brooklynites who now live in Scarsdale, Beverly Hills, and on Fifth Avenue. Brooklyn is the city's largest borough and boasts a population that would make it the fourth-largest city in the United States. Brooklyn is not just a part of New York—it is a state of mind. Reaching the age of eighteen in Brooklyn is the equivalent of getting a college degree in Survival, Self-Defense, Salesmanship, Chutzpah, and Making Big Bucks.

Joey Adams
Woody Allen
Lyle Alzado
Warner Anderson
Red Auerbach
Scott Baio
Ina Balin
Pat Benatar
William Bennett
Alan Bergman
Marilyn Bergman
Warren Berlinger
Clarence F.
  Birdseye
Mr. Blackwell
Kermit
  Bloomgarten
Helen Boehm
Neil Bogart
Joseph Bologna
James Brady
Scott Brady
Danielle Brisebois
Jane Brody
Mel Brooks
Heywood Broun
Susan Brownmiller
Julie Budd
Mary Bunting
Louis Calhern
Joseph Califano
Charlie Callas
Al Capone
Hugh Carey
Jeff Chandler
Saul Chaplin
Shirley Chisholm
Andrew Dice Clay
Herb Cohen
Mickey Cohen
Betty Comden
Barry Commoner
Chuck Connors
Gerry Cooney
Aaron Copland
Peter Criss
Alan Dale
Alfonse D'Amato
Vic Damone
William Daniels
Frederic Dannay

Tony Danza
Clive Davis
Jerry Della Femina
Dom De Luise
Alan Dershowitz
William De Vries
Neil Diamond
J.P. Donleavy
Dan Dorfman
Frank N.
  Doubleday
Richard Dreyfuss
Chris Economaki
Herb Edelman
Vince Edwards
Florence Eldridge
Stanley Ellin
Clifton Fadiman
James Farentino
Richard Farina
Eliot Feld
Lou Ferrigno
Harvey Fierstein
Bobby Fisher
Phil Foster
Sonny Fox
Milton Friedman
David Frye
Wilfred Funk
Allen Funt
Helen Gallagher
William Gargan
Leonard Garment
David Geffen
George Gershwin
Vitas Gerulaitis
Ralph Ginzburg
Jackie Gleason
G.W. Goethals
Sid Gordon
Lou Gosset
Elliott Gould
Hank Greenspun
Harry Guardino
Bob Guccione
Arlo Guthrie
Steve Guttenburg
Philip Habib
Buddy Hackett
Briton Haddon
Pete Hamill

Richie Havens
Susan Hayward
Joseph Heller
Joel Hirschorn
Tommy Holmes
Elizabeth Holtzman
Lena Horne
Edward Everett
  Horton
Curly Howard
Moe Howard
Waite Hoyt
Robert M. Hutchins
Elizabeth Janeway
Meir Kahane
Roger Kahn
Gabe Kaplan
Lainie Kazan
Alfred Kazin
Danny Kaye
Wee Willie Keeler
Harvey Keitel
Patsy Kelly
Michael Kidd
Alan King
Carole King
Larry King
Anne Klein
C. Everett Koop
Bernie Kopell
Sandy Koufax
Paul Krassner
Veronica Lake
Martin Landau
Abbe Lane
Cindy Lauper
Steve Lawrence
Manfred Lee
Mitch Leigh
David Levine
Emmanuel Lewis
Bambi Linn
Vincent Lopez
Sid Luckman
Bernard Malamud
Albert Maltz
Barry Manilow
Abraham Maslow
Paul Mazursky
Lee Mazzilli
Robert Merrill

Stephanie Mills
Eddie Money
Mary Tyler Moore
Cousin Brucie
   Morrow
Jerry Moss
Donny Most
Zero Mostel
Eddie Murphy
Jean Nidetch
Joseph Papp
Joe Paterno
Joe Pepitone
S.J. Perelman
Rhea Perlman
Rico Petrocelli
Norman Podhoretz
Priscilla Presley
Gilbert Price
Eddie Rabbitt
Buddy Rich
Joan Rivers
Mickey Rooney
Herbert Ross
Eugene Rostow
Raymond Rubicam
Theodore Rubin
Albert Salmi

Olga San Juan
Andrew Sarris
John Saxon
Dick Schaap
Joe Schenck
Murray Schisgal
Julian Schnabel
Arthur Schwartz
Delmore Schwartz
Alexander Scourby
Neil Sedaka
Erich Segal
Jerry Seinfeld
Maurice Sendak
Rogers Sessions
Irwin Shaw
Irving Shulman
Bugsy Siegel
Beverly Sills
Phil Silvers
Jo Sinclair
Curtis Sliwa
Mickey Spillane
Lawrence Spivak
Barbara Stanwyck
Connie Stevens
Barbra Streisand
Lyle Stuart

Constance
   Talmadge
Vic Tayback
Irving Thalberg
Gene Tierney
Joe Torre
Richard Tucker
Helen Twelvetrees
Earl Ubell
Brenda Vaccaro
Vince Van Patten
Jerry Wald
Eli Wallach
Fred Waller
Jessica Walter
Harry Warren
Wendy
   Wasserstein
Charlie Watters
Jerry Weintraub
Sonny Werblin
Mae West
Cara Williams
Manny Wolf
Wolfman Jack
Peggy Wood

★ Famous People Born in Texas ★

Until recent decades, Texas had a relatively small population, yet it has produced many famous people in diverse careers. Here are a few hundred of the state's finest offspring.

Alvin Ailey
Debbie Allen
Jay Presson Allen
Lance Alworthy
Donny Anderson
Stephen Austin
Gene Autry
Tex Avery
Bonnie Baker
James Baker
Ernie Banks
Clyde Barrow
Florence Bates

Les Baxter
Don Baylor
Alan Bean
Tex Benecke
Robby Benson
Robert Benton
Lloyd Bentsen
Dan Blocker
Larry Blyden
E. Powers Boothe
The Big Bopper
Bill Bradley
Tom Bradley

Edmund Lee
   Browning
Frank Buck
Betty Buckley
Don Buford
Carol Burnett
Gary Busey
Kate Capshaw
Liz Carpenter
Vicki Carr
Mark David
   Chapman
Cyd Charisse

Claire Chennault
George Church
Ramsey Clark
Tom Clark
Dabney Coleman
Ornette Coleman
John Connally
Tom Connally
Maureen Connelly
Denton Cooley
Cecil Cooper
Ben Crenshaw
Kathryn Crosby
Bebe Daniels
Linda Darnell
Cullen Davis
Mac Davis
Jimmy Dean
Jimmy Demaret
Martin Dies, Jr.
J. Frank Dobie
Sam Donaldson
Allen Drury
Sandy Duncan
Shelley Duvall
David Eichelberger
Dwight D.
  Eisenhower
Lee Elder
Linda Ellerbee
Ron Ely
Doug English
Dale Evans
Ferris Fain
Morgan Fairchild
John Henry Falk
"Cissy" Farenthold
James Farmer
Farrah Fawcett
Freddie Fender
Curt Flood
George Foreman
Percy Foreman
Robert Foxworth
A.J. Foyt
Al Freeman, Jr.
Lee Gaines
John Nance Garner
Larry Gatlin
Lynda Day George
Phyllis George

Euell Gibbons
Andie Granatelli
Joe Greene
Nan Grey
John Howard
  Griffin
Steve Grogan
Texas Guinan
Reed Hadley
Larry Hagman
Najib Halaby
Jerry Hall
Ann Harding
Billy Joe Hargis
Lisa Hartman
Ted Healy
Heloise
Hollywood
  Henderson
Don Henley
John Hillerman
Oveta Culp Hobby
Roy Hofheinz
Ben Hogan
Buddy Holly
Sam "Lightnin' "
  Hopkins
Rogers Hornsby
Johnny Horton
Susan Howard
Howard Hughes
Sarah Tilghman
  Hughes
Gayle Hunnicutt
Bunker Hunt
Nelson Hunt
Ivory Hunter
Martha Hyer
Maynard Jackson
Leon Jaworski
Jack Johnson
Lady Bird Johnson
Lyndon B. Johnson
Rafer Johnson
Carolyn Jones
Dickie Jones
George Jones
Tommy Lee Jones
Janis Joplin
Scott Joplin
Barbara Jordan

Mary Kay
Steven Kemp
Evelyn Keyes
Suzy
  Knickerbocker
Kris Kristofferson
Tom Landry
Esther Little
Daniel Logan
Josh Logan
Alan Lomax
Trini Lopez
Bessie Love
Barbara Mandrell
Stanley Marcus
Steve Martin
Eddie Matthews
Tex McCrary
Spanky McFarland
Ray McKinley
Larry McMurtry
Meredith McRae
Meat Loaf
John Mecom
Don Meredith
Ann Miller
Nolan Miller
Roger Miller
Steve Miller
Joe Morgan
Mark Moseley
Clint Murchison
Audie Murphy
Johnny Nash
Byron Nelson
Willie Nelson
Chester Nimitz
Phil Ochs
Sanda Day
  O'Connor
Roy Orbison
Buck Owens
Bonnie Parker
Buddy Parker
Fess Parker
Suzy Parker
Wright Patman
Van Patrick
H. Ross Perot
Valerie Perrine
Esther Phillips

Katherine Anne Porter	Bob Schieffer	Y.A. Tittle
Wiley Post	Zachary Scott	Rip Torn
Paula Prentiss	Bobby Seale	John Tower
Billy Preston	Jim Seals	Lee Trevino
Greg Pruitt	Ann Sheridan	Ernest Tubb
Dennis Quaid	Willie Shoemaker	Tanya Tucker
Dan Rather	Stephen Sills	Tommy Tune
Robert Rauschenberg	Bubba Smith	Jack Valenti
Rex Reed	Jaclyn Smith	King Vidor
Mel Renfro	Liz Smith	Richard Viguerie
Debbie Reynolds	Tommy Smith	Doak Walker
Paul Richards	Terry Southern	Stanley Walker
Sid Richardson	Sissy Spacek	T. Bone Walker
Jeannie C. Riley	Tris Speaker	Lisa Whelchel
Tex Ritter	Aaron Spelling	Barry White
Frank Robinson	David Stockman	Ed White
Johnny Rodriguez	Sly Stone	Kathy Whitworth
Bill Rogers	Gale Storm	Delvin Williams
Kenny Rogers	Patrick Swayze	Bob Wills
Kyle Rote	Sharon Tate	Chill Wills
Schoolboy Rowe	Garry Templeton	Dooley Wilson
Nolan Ryan	B.J. Thomas	Teddy Wilson
Boz Scaggs	Hank Thompson	Edgar Winter
	Tommy Thompson	Johnny Winter
	Charles Thornton	James Wright, Jr.

Born in Babylon: Famous People Born in ★ Hollywood, Beverly Hills, and Malibu ★

Once a vast terrain of orange groves, the area now cynically referred to as "Tinseltown" quickly became a mecca for waitresses and gas station attendants with stars and stardom in their eyes. The place has been around long enough that people—usually second-generation show business folk—are actually born there. Here is a list of luminaries who were born in the area.

	Place
Lucie Arnaz	Hollywood
Diane Baker	Hollywood
Candice Bergen	Beverly Hills
Belinda Carlisle	Hollywood
Kim Carnes	Hollywood
David Carradine	Hollywood
Richard Chamberlain	Beverly Hills
Tina Cole	Hollywood
Christina Crawford	Hollywood

	Place
Kim Darby	Hollywood
John Derek	Hollywood
Tony Dow	Hollywood
Carrie Fisher	Beverly Hills
Terri Garr	Hollywood
Leif Garrett	Hollywood
Dan Haggerty	Hollywood
Barbara Hershey	Hollywood
Jerome Hines	Hollywood
Tim Holt	Beverly Hills
Timothy Hutton	Malibu
Jack Jones	Beverly Hills
John Philip Law	Hollywood
Elizabeth Montgomery	Hollywood
Don Murray	Hollywood
Jay North	North Hollywood
Bud Palmer	Hollywood
Stefanie Powers	Hollywood
Katharine Ross	Hollywood
John Rubinstein	Beverly Hills
Jan Smithers	North Hollywood
K.T. Stevens	Hollywood
Dean Stockwell	Hollywood
Michael Tilson Thomas	Hollywood

NAMES

Famous People Not Known by Their First Names

★ ★

George Edward (Eddie) Arcaro
Yitzak Eddie Asner
Orvon Gene Autry
Francis Lee Bailey
Henry Warren Beaty (Beatty)
Ernest Ingmar Bergman
George Richard Beymer
James Hubert (Eubie) Blake
Charles Eugene (Pat) Boone
Edmund Gerald (Jerry) Brown, Jr.
William Nigel Bruce
Charles Victor Buono
Edward MacDonald Carey
Mary Margaret (Peggy) Cass
Beatrice Joan Caulfield
George Richard Chamberlain
Leroy Eldridge Cleaver
Edward Montgomery Clift
Pierino (Perry) Como
Alfred Alistair Cooke
John Michael Crichton
Ellen Tyne Daly
Morris Mac Davis
Ruth Elizabeth (Bette) Davis
Dorothy Faye Dunaway
Henry Havelock Ellis
Mary Farrah Fawcett
Arthur John Gielgud
Herbert John (Jackie) Gleason
Hugh Marjoe Ross Gortner
Samuel Dashiell Hammett
Emmet Evan (Van) Heflin, Jr.
James Langston Hughes
Charles Van Johnson

Frederick Lawrence (Larry) Kert
John Charles Julian Lennon
Alice (Ali) McGraw
Terrence Stephen (Steve) McQueen
Keith Rupert Murdoch
George Robert (Bob) Newhart
James David Niven
Patrick Ryan O'Neal
Olive Marie Osmond
Margaret Jane Pauley
Eldred Gregory Peck
David Samuel (Sam) Peckinpah
Charles Robert Redford, Jr.
Ernestine Jane Russell
Christa Brooke Camille Shields
Robert Sargent Shriver
Marvin Neil Simon
Michael Sylvester Stallone
Mary Louise (Meryl) Streep
Margaret (Marlo) Thomas
Mary Jean (Lily) Tomlin
Eugene (Gore) Vidal
Stanley Robert (Bobby) Vinton
Myron (Mike) Wallace
Peter John (Johnny) Weissmuller
George Orson Welles
Howard Andrew (Andy) Williams
Walter Bruce Willis
Clerow (Flip) Wilson
Mary Debra Winger

★ Odd Names of Celebrity Children ★

Parent(s)' Names	Children's Names
Don Adams	Beige Dawn
Woody Allen and Mia Farrow	Satchel
Cher and Greg Allman	Elijah Blue
Robby Benson	Lyric
Marisa Berenson	Starlite Melody
Cher and Sonny Bono	Chastity
David Bowie	Zowie
David Carradine and Barbara Hershey	Free
Aretha Franklin	Kecalf (acronym of Ken E. Cunningham and Aretha L. Franklin)
Bob Geldof	Fifi Trixibelle, Pixie
J.P. Getty II	Tara Gabriel, Galaxy Gramaphone
Melissa Gilbert	Dakota Paul
Elliot Gould	Sam Bazooka
Mick and Bianca Jagger	Jade
Casey Kasem	Liberty
Norman Mailer	John Buffalo
Peter Max	Adam Cosmo, Libra Astro
Dorothy McGuire	Topo
Bill Murray	Homer Banks
Tony Perkins	Elvis, Osgood
Mia Farrow and André Previn	Lark Song, Summer Song
Richard Pryor	Rain
Keith Richard	Dandelion
Kurt Russell	Boston
Susan St. James	Harmony, Sunshine
Sam Shepard	Jesse Mojo
Sylvester Stallone	Sage Moonblood
Ringo Starr	Zak
Frank Zappa	Moon Unit, Dweezil, Diva, and Ahmet Emuukha Rodan

★ Real Names of Famous People ★

	Real Name
Kareem Abdul-Jabbar	Ferdinand Lewis Alcindor, Jr.
Edie Adams	Elizabeth Edith Enke
Joey Adams	Joseph Abramowitz
Maud Adams	Maud Solveig Christina Wikstrom

Nick Adams	Nicholas Adamshock
Anouk Aimee	Françoise Sorya
Edward Albee	Edward Franklin Albee III
Eddie Albert	Edward Albert Heimberger
Alan Alda	Alphonso d'Abruzzo
Robert Alda	Alphonso Roberto d'Abruzzo
Sholem Aleichem	Solomon J. Rabinowitz
Jane Alexander	Jane Quigley
Shana Alexander	Shana Ager
Nelson Algren	Nelson Algren Abraham
Muhammad Ali	Cassius Marcellus Clay, Jr.
Fred Allen	John Florence Sullivan
Mel Allen	Melvin Allen Israel
Woody Allen	Allen Stewart Konigsberg
June Allyson	Ella Geisman
Don Ameche	Dominic Felix Amici
Julie Andrews	Julia Elizabeth Wells
Victoria de los Angeles	Victoria Gamez Cima
Pier Angeli	Anna Maria Pierangeli
Annabella	Suzanne Georgette Charpentier
Ann-Margret	Ann Margret Olsson
Ray Anthony	Raymond Antonini
Guillaume Apollinaire	Guillaume Kostrowitsky
Fatty Arbuckle	Roscoe Conkling Arbuckle
Elizabeth Arden	Florence Nightingale Graham
Eve Arden	Eunice Quedens
Harold Arlen	Hyman Arluck
Richard Arlen	Richard Cornelius Van Mattemore
George Arliss	George Augustus Andrews
Henry Armstrong	Henry Jackson
Desi Arnaz	Desiderio Albert Arnaz de Acha III
James Arness	James Aurness
Peter Arno	Curtis Arnoux Peters, Jr.
Sig Arno	Siegfried Aron
Danny Arnold	Arnold Rothman
Edward Arnold	Guenther Edward Arnold Schneider
Bea Arthur	Bernice Frankel
Jean Arthur	Gladys Georgianna Greene
Elizabeth Ashley	Elizabeth Ann Cole
Merrill Ashley	Linda Merrill
Fred Astaire	Frederick Austerlitz
Mary Astor	Lucille Vasconcells Langhanke
William Atherton	William Atherton Knight II
Charles Atlas	Angelo Siciliano

W.H. Auden	Wystan Hugh Auden
Mischa Auer	Mischa Ounskowski
Jean-Pierre Aumont	Jean-Pierre Salomons
Frankie Avalon	Francis Thomas Avalonne
Axis Sally (Berlin)	Mildred Gillars Sisk
Axis Sally (Rome)	Rita Louise Zucca
Lew Ayres	Lewis Frederick Ayres III
Charles Aznavour	Shahnour Varenaugh Aznavourian
Lauren Bacall	Betty Joan Perske
Barbara Bach	Barbara Goldbach
Catherine Bach	Catherine Bachman
Wee Bonnie Baker	Evelyn Nelson
George Balanchine	Georgi Melitonovitch Balanchivadze
Ina Balin	Ina Rosenberg
Kaye Ballard	Catherine Gloria Balotta
Anne Bancroft	Anna Maria Louisa Italiano
Vilma Banky	Vilma Lonchit
Theda Bara	Theodosia Goodman
Imamu Amiri Baraka	Leroi Jones
Red Barber	Walter Lanier Barber
Lynn Bari	Majorie Schuyler Fisher
Lex Barker	Alexander Crichlow Barker, Jr.
P.T. Barnum	Phineas Taylor Barnum
Candy Barr	Juanita Slusher
Richard Barr	Richard Baer
Rona Barrett	Rona Burstein
Wendy Barrie	Margaret Wendy Jenkins
Don Barry	Donald Barry de Acosta
Gene Barry	Eugene Klass
Jack Barry	Jack Barasch
Diana Barrymore	Diana Blanche Blythe
Ethel Barrymore	Ethel Mae Blythe
John Barrymore	John Blythe
Lionel Barrymore	Lionel Blythe
Lionel Bart	Lionel Begleiter
Eva Bartok	Eva Martha Szoke
Florence Bates	Florence Rabe
Nora Bayes	Dora Goldberg
Orson Bean	Dallas Frederick Burrows
Warren Beatty	Henry Warren Beaty
Bonnie Bedelia	Bonnie Culkin
Harry Belafonte	Harold George Belanfonte, Jr.
Barbara Bel Geddes	Barbara Geddes Lewis
August Belmont	August Shoenberg
Pat Benatar	Patricia Andrzejewski
David Ben-Gurion	David Green

Bruce Bennett	Herman Brix
Michael Bennett	Michael Bennett DiFiglia
Tony Bennett	Antonio Dominic Benedetto
Jack Benny	Benjamin Kubelsky
Barbi Benton	Barbara Klein
Gertrude Berg	Gertrude Edelstein
Edgar Bergen	Edgar John Bergren
Polly Bergen	Nellie Paulina Burgin
Helmut Berger	Helmut Steinberger
Busby Berkeley	William Berkeley Enos
Milton Berle	Milton Berlinger
Irving Berlin	Israel Baline
Paul Bern	Paul Levy
Sarah Bernhardt	Rosine Bernard
Turhan Bey	Turhan Gilbert Selahettin Saultavey
Billy the Kid	William H. Bonney
Joey Bishop	Joseph Abraham Gottlieb
Karen Black	Karen Blanchie Ziegler
Vivian Blaine	Vivian S. Stapleton
Betsy Blair	Betsy Boger
Janet Blair	Martha Lafferty
Amanda Blake	Beverly Louise Neill
Robert Blake	Michael Gubitosi
Sally Blane	Elizabeth Jane Young
Ben Blue	Benjamin Bernstein
Nellie Bly	Elizabeth Cochrane Seaman
Larry Blyden	Ivan Lawrence Blieden
Betty Blythe	Elizabeth Blythe Slaughter
Helen Boehm	Helen Francesca Stefanie Franzolin
Dirk Bogarde	Derek Van Den Bogaerde
Gary U.S. Bonds	Gary Anderson
Sonny Bono	Salvatore Phillip Bono
Shirley Booth	Thelma Booth Ford
Big Bopper	Jiles Perry Richardson
Victor Borge	Borge Rosenbaum
Ernest Borgnine	Ermes Effron Borgnino
David Bowie	David Robert Hayward-Jones
Stephen Boyd	William Millar
Scott Brady	Gerald Kenneth Tierney
Max Brand	Frederick Faust
Willy Brandt	Herbert Ernst Karl Frahm
Keefe Brasselle	John J. Brasselli
Evelyn Brent	Mary Elizabeth Riggs
George Brent	George Brent Nolan
Fanny Brice	Fanny Borach
Beau Bridges	Lloyd Vernet Bridges III
Lloyd Bridges	Lloyd Vernet Bridges II

	Real Name
May Britt	Maybritt Wilkens
Morgan Brittany	Suzanne Cupito
Barbara Britton	Barbara Brantingham
Bronco Billy	Max Aaronson
Steve Brodie	John Stevens
Charles Bronson	Charles Bunchinsky (later, Buchinsky)
Geraldine Brooks	Geraldine Stroock
Mel Brooks	Melvin Kaminsky
Dr. Joyce Brothers	Joyce Diane Bauer
Vanessa Brown	Smylla Brind
Lenny Bruce	Leonard Alfred Schneider
Virginia Bruce	Helen Virginia Briggs
Yul Brynner	Youl Bryner
John Bubbles	John William Sublett
Pearl Buck	Pearl Comfort Sydenstricker
Anthony Burgess	John Anthony Burgess Wilson
Billie Burke	Mary William Ethelbert Appleton Burke
George Burns	Nathan Birnbaum
Raymond Burr	William Stacey Burr
Ellen Burstyn	Edna Rae Gillooly
Richard Burton	Richard Jenkins
Red Buttons	Aaron Chwatt
Edd "Kookie" Byrnes	Edward Breitenberger
Bruce Cabot	Jacques Etienne de Bujac
Nicholas Cage	Nicholas Coppola
Sammy Cahn	Sam Cohen
Michael Caine	Maurice J. Micklewhite
Calamity Jane	Martha Jane Canary Burke
Louis Calhern	Carl Henry Vogt
Rory Calhoun	Francis Timony Durgin
Michael Callan	Martin Caliniff
Maria Callas	Maria Calogeropoulos
Corinne Calvet	Corinne Dibos
Rod Cameron	Rod Cox
Dyan Cannon	Samile Diane Friesen
Cantinflas	Mario Moreno August
Eddie Cantor	Isidore Itzkowitz
Truman Capote	Truman Streckfus Persons
Al Capp	Alfred Gerald Caplin
Kate Capshaw	Kathy Sue Nail
Capucine	Germaine Lefebvre
Harry Carey	Henry De Witt Carey II
Kitty Carlisle	Catherine Conn
Judy Carne	Judy Botterill
Allan Carr	Allan Solomon
Vicki Carr	Florencia Bisenta de Casillas Martinez Cardona

John Carradine	Richmond Reed Carradine
Diahann Carroll	Carol Diahann Johnson
Lewis Carroll	Charles Lutwidge Dodgson
Madeline Carroll	Marie-Madeline Bernadette O'Carroll
Jack Carter	Jack Chakrin
Nell Carter	Nell Hardy
Butch Cassidy	George Leroy Parker
Hopalong Cassidy	William Lawrence Boyd
Joanna Cassidy	Joanna Virginia Caskey
Oleg Cassini	Oleg Loiewski-Cassini
Irene Castle	Irene Foote
William Castle	William Schloss
Phoebe Cates	Phoebe Katz
Whittaker Chambers	J. Vivian Chambers
Marge Champion	Marjorie Celeste Belcher
Jeff Chandler	Ira Grossel
Lon Chaney, Jr.	Creighton Chaney
Lita Crey Chaplin	Lillita Louis McMurray
Cyd Charisse	Tula Elice Finklea
Ray Charles	Ray Charles Robinson
Charo	Maria Rosario Pilar Martinez Melina Baeza
Charlie Chase	Charles Parrott
Chevy Chase	Cornelius Crane Chase
Chubby Checker	Ernest Evans
Cher	Cher Sarkesian (later, Cher La Piere)
G.K. Chesterton	Gilbert Keith Chesterton
Judy Chicago	Judy Cohen
Linda Christian	Blanca Rosa Welter
Agatha Christie	Agatha Mary Clarissa Miller
Christo	Christo Javacheff
Ina Claire	Ina Fagan
Eric Clapton	Eric Clapp
Dane Clark	Bernard Zanville
Mae Clarke	Mary Klotz
Andrew Dice Clay	Andrew Silverstein
Van Cliburn	Harvey Lavan Cliburn, Jr.
Colin Clive	Clive Greig
Lee J. Cobb	Lee Jacob
Claudette Colbert	Lily Chauchoin
Nat King Cole	Nathaniel Adams Coles
Cy Coleman	Seymour Kaufman
Dorothy Collins	Marjorie Chandler
Bud Collyer	Clayton Collyer
Betty Comden	Betty Cohen
Perry Como	Pierino Roland Como
Chuck Connors	Kevin Joseph Connors

Mike Connors	Krekor "Kirk" Ohanian
Joseph Conrad	Teodor Konrad Korzeniowski
Robert Conrad	Conrad Robert Falk
Hans Conreid	Frank Foster Conreid
Tom Conway	Thomas Sanders
Alice Cooper	Vincent Damon Furnier
Gary Cooper	Frank James Cooper
Pat Cooper	Pasquale Caputo
David Copperfield	David Kotkin
Ellen Corby	Ellen Hansen
Alex Cord	Alexander Viespi
El Cordobes	Manuel Benetez Perez
Jill Corey	Norma Jean Spearanza
Don Cornell	Louis F. Varlaro
Ray "Crash" Corrigan	Ray Benard
Ricardo Cortez	Jacob Krantz
Stanley Cortez	Stanislaus Krantz
Howard Cosell	Howard Kosell (later, Cohen)
Elvis Costello	Declan Patrick McManus
Frank Costello	Francesco Castiglia
Lou Costello	Louis Francis Cristillo
Wally Cox	Wallace Maynard Cox
Buster Crabbe	Clarence Linden Crabbe
Joan Crawford	Lucille LeSueur
Quentin Crisp	Denis Pratt
Judith Crist	Judith Klein
Linda Cristal	Victoria Maya
Michael Cristofer	Michael Procaccino
Bing Crosby	Harry Lillis Crosby
Christopher Cross	Christoper Geppert
Scatman Crothers	Benjamin Sherman Crothers
Tom Cruise	Thomas Cruise Mapother IV
Constance Cummings	Constance Halverstadt
E.E. Cummings	Edward Estlin Cummings
Ken Curtis	Curtis Gates
Tony Curtis	Bernard Schwartz
Michael Curtiz	Mihaly Kertesz
Dagmar	Virginia Ruth Egnor
Dalai Lama	Gejong Tenzin Gyatsho
Jim Dale	Jim Smith
John Dall	John Jenner Thompson
Jacques D'Amboise	Jacques Joseph D'Amboise Ahearn
Lily Damita	Liliane-Marie-Madeleine Carre
Vic Damone	Vito Farinola
Rodney Dangerfield	Jacob Cohen (later, Jack Roy)
Ted Danson	Edward Bridge Danson III
Tony Danza	Anthony Iadanza

Kim Darby	Deborah Zerby
Denise Darcel	Denise Billecard
Bobby Darin	Walden Robert Cassotto
Linda Darnell	Monetta Eloyse Darnell
James Darren	James Ercolani
Frankie Darro	Frank Johnson
Henry Darrow	Henry Thomas Delgado
Bella Darvi	Bayla Wegier
Jane Darwell	Patti Woodward
Howard Da Silva	Howard Silverblatt
Marion Davies	Marion Douras
Hazel Dawn	Hazel Letout
Dennis Day	Eugene Denis McNulty
Doris Day	Doris Kappelhof
Laraine Day	Laraine Johnson
Dizzy Dean	Jan Hanna Dean
Jimmy Dean	Seth Ward
Yvonne De Carlo	Peggy Yvonne Middleton
Ruby Dee	Ruby Ann Wallace
Sandra Dee	Alexandra Zuck
Gabe Dell	Gabriel Del Vecchio
Dolores Del Rio	Lolita Dolores Asunsolo Martinez
Catherine Deneuve	Catherine Dorleac
Patrick Dennis	Edward Everett Tanner III
Reginald Denny	Reginald Leigh Daymore
John Denver	Henry John Deutschendorf, Jr.
Bo Derek	Mary Cathleen Collins
John Derek	Derek Harris
Rick Derringer	Rick Zehringer
Johnny Desmond	Giovanni Alfredo DeSimone
Andy Devine	Jeremiah Schwartz
Billy De Wolfe	William Andrew Jones
Legs Diamond	John T. Nolan
Angie Dickinson	Angeline Brown
Bo Diddley	Elias McDaniels
Marlene Dietrich	Maria Magdalene Dietrich (later, von Losch)
Phyllis Diller	Phyllis Driver
Richard Dix	Ernest Carlton Brimmer
Jean Dixon	Jeane Pinckert
E.L. Doctorow	Edgar Laurence Doctorow
Luis Miguel Dominguin	Luis Miguel Gonzalez Lucas
Troy Donahue	Merle Johnson, Jr.
Donovan	Donald P. Leitch
Philip Dorn	Hein Van Der Niet (later, Fritz Van Dongen)
Diana Dors	Diana "Daisy" Fluck

Fifi D'Orsay	Yvonne Lussier
Kirk Douglas	Issur Danielovitch Demsky
Melvyn Douglas	Melvin Hesselberg
Mike Douglas	Michael Delaney Dowd, Jr.
Billy Dove	Lillian Bohny
Eddie Dowling	Joseph Nelson Goucher
Alfred Drake	Alfred Capurro
Tom Drake	Alfred Alderdice
Louise Dresser	Louise Kerlin
Marie Dressler	Leila Marie Koerber
Joanne Dru	Joanne la Cock
W.E.B. DuBois	William Edward Burghardt DuBois
Patty Duke	Anna Marie Duke
Vernon Duke	Vladimir Dukelsky
Margaret Dumont	Margaret Baker
Michael Dunn	Gary Neil Miller
Ann Dvorak	Ann McKim
Bob Dylan	Robert Zimmerman
Sheena Easton	Sheena Shirley Orr
Abba Eban	Aubrey Solomon
Buddy Ebsen	Christian Rudolph Ebsen, Jr.
Barbara Eden	Barbara Huffman
Blake Edwards	William Blake McEdwards
Vince Edwards	Vincent Edward Zoino
Elaine	Elaine Kaufman
Florence Eldridge	Florence McKechnie
George Eliot	Mary Ann Evans
T.S. Eliot	Thomas Stearns Eliot
Linda Ellerbee	Linda Jane Smith
Duke Ellington	Edward Kennedy Ellington
Cass Elliott	Ellen Naomi Cohen
Ziggy Elman	Harry Finkelman
Ron Ely	Ronald Pierce
Werner Erhard	John Paul "Jack" Rosenberg
David Essex	David Cook
Dale Evans	Frances Octavia Smith
Linda Evans	Linda Evenstad
Chad Everett	Raymond Lee Cramton
Tom Ewell	S. Yewell Tompkins
Fabian	Fabian Anthony Forte
Nanette Fabray	Ruby Bernadette Nanette Fabares
Douglas Fairbanks	Douglas Elton Ulman
Douglas Fairbanks, Jr.	Douglas Elton Ulman, Jr.
Morgan Fairchild	Patsy Ann McClenny
Donna Fargo	Yvonne Vaughan
Jamie Farr	Jameel Farah
Mia Farrow	Maria de Lourdes Villiers Farrow

	Real Name
Alice Faye	Alice Leppert
Joey Faye	Joseph Anthony Palladino
Michael Feinstein	Michael Cohen
Freddie Fender	Baldemar G. Huerta
Fernandel	Fernand Joseph Desire Contandin
José Ferrer	Jose Vicente Ferrer Otero y Cintron
Stepin Fetchit	Lincoln Theodore Perry
Gracie Fields	Grace Stansfield
Totie Fields	Sophie Feldman
W.C. Fields	William Claude Dukenfield
Peter Finch	William Mitchell
Barry Fitzgerald	William Joseph Shields
Bud Flanagan	Robert Winthrop
Rhonda Fleming	Marilyn Louis
Nina Foch	Nina Consuelo Maud Fock
Joan Fontaine	Joan De Havilland
Margot Fonteyn	Margaret Hookham
Ford Madox Ford	Ford Madox Hueffer
Gerald R. Ford	Leslie Lynch King, Jr.
Glenn Ford	Gwyllyn Ford
John Ford	Sean O'Fearna
Paul Ford	Paul Ford Weaver
Wallace Ford	Samuel Jones Grundy
Steve Forrest	William Forrest Andrews
E.M. Forster	Edward Morgan Forster
John Forsythe	John Lincoln Freund
Jodie Foster	Alicia Christian Foster
Phil Foster	Philip Feldman
Redd Foxx	John Elroy Sanford
Eddie Foy	Edward Fitzgerald
Anthony Franciosa	Anthony Papaleo
Connie Francis	Concetta Maria Franconero
Kay Francis	Katherine Gibbs
Betty Friedan	Betty Naomi Goldstein
Fred Friendly	Ferdinand Wachenheimer
David Frye	David Shapiro
Diane von Fürstenberg	Diane Halfin
Jean Gabin	Jean-Alexis Moncourge
Greta Garbo	Greta Louisa Gustaffson
Vincent Gardenia	Vincent Scognamiglio
John Garfield	Julius Garfinkle
Beverly Garland	Beverly Lucy Fessenden
Judy Garland	Frances Gumm
James Garner	James Scott Baumgarner
Cyndy Garvey	Cynthia Thuhan
Romain Gary	Romain Kacew
Crystal Gayle	Brenda Webb

Janet Gaynor	Laura Gainor
Mitzi Gaynor	Francesca Mitzi Marlene de Czanyi von Gerber
John Gavin	John Anthony Golenor
Genevieve	Ginette Marguerite Auger
Bobbie Gentry	Roberta Streeter
Boy George	George Alan O'Dowd
Gladys George	Gladys Clare
Estelle Getty	Estelle Scher
Georgia Gibbs	Fredda Lipson
Hoot Gibson	Edmund Richard Gibson
John Gilbert	John Pringle
Lou Gilbert	Lou Gitlitz
Jack Gilford	Jacob Gellman
Dizzy Gillespie	John Birks Gillespie
Virginia Gilmore	Sherman Virginia Poole
Gloria Jean	Gloria Jean Schoonover
Alma Gluck	Reba Fiersohn
Paulette Goddard	Pauline Levy
Whoopi Goldberg	Caryn Johnson
Harry Golden	Harry Goldenhurst
Samuel Goldwyn	Samuel Gelbfisch (later, Goldfish)
Bert Gordon	Barney Gorodetsky
Gale Gordon	Charles Aldrich, Jr.
Max Gordon	Michael Salpeter
Ruth Gordon	Ruth Gordon Jones
Elliott Gould	Elliott Goldstein
Bill Graham	Wolfgang Grajonca
Sheilah Graham	Lily Shiel
Virginia Graham	Virginia Komiss
Gloria Grahame	Gloria Grahame Hallward
Stewart Granger	James Lablache Stewart
Cary Grant	Archibald Alexander Leach
Gogi Grant	Myrtle Audrey Arinsberg
Kathryn Grant	Olive Kathryn Grandstaff
Kirby Grant	Kirby Grant Hoon, Jr.
Lee Grant	Lyova Haskell Rosenthal
Peter Graves	Peter Aurness
Barry Gray	Bernard Yaroslaw
Kathryn Grayson	Zelma Hedrick
Rocky Graziano	Rocco Barbella
Lorne Greene	Lorne Green
Shecky Greene	Fred Sheldon Greenfield
Joel Grey	Joel Katz
Zane Grey	Pearl Zane Grey
D.W. Griffith	David Wark Griffith
C.Z. Guest	Lucy Douglas Cochrane
Robert Guillaume	Robert Peter Williams

Buddy Hackett	Leonard Hacker
Reed Hadley	Reed Herring
Jean Hagen	Jean Shirley Verhagen
Connie Haines	Yvonne Marie Jamais
H.R. Haldeman	Harry Robert Haldeman
Alan Hale	Rufus Alan McKahan
Gus Hall	Arvo Kusta Halberg
Huntz Hall	Henry Hall
Jon Hall	Charles Hall Locher
Monty Hall	Monte Halparin
Halston	Roy Halston Frowick
Walter Hampden	Walter Hampden Dougherty
W.C. Handy	William Christopher Handy
Ty Hardin	Orson Whipple Hungerford II
Ann Harding	Dorothy Walton Gatley
Jean Harlow	Harlean Carpentier
Barbara Harris	Sandra Markowitz
Rex Harrison	Reginald Carey Harrison
Dolores Hart	Dolores Hicks
Gary Hart	Gary Warren Hartpence
Moss Hart	Robert Arnold Conrad
Laurence Harvey	Larushka Mischa Skikne
Paul Harvey	Paul Harvey Aurandt
June Haver	June Stovenour
June Havoc	Ellen Evangeline Hovick
S.I. Hayakawa	Samuel Ichiye Hayakawa
Melissa Hayden	Mildred Herman
Sterling Hayden	John Hamilton
Gabby Hayes	George Francis Hayes
Helen Hayes	Helen Hayes Brown
Peter Lind Hayes	Joseph Conrad Lind, Jr.
Louis Hayward	Seafield Grant
Susan Hayward	Edithe Marrener
Rita Hayworth	Margarita Cansino
Tippi Hedren	Natalie Kay Hedren
Van Heflin	Emmett Evan Heflin, Jr.
Heloise	Heloise Bowles Reese
Skitch Henderson	Lyle Russell Cedric Henderson
Paul Henreid	Paul Julius von Hernreid
Buck Henry	Buck Henry Zuckerman
O. Henry	William Sidney Porter
Pat Henry	Patrick Henry Scarnato
Audrey Hepburn	Audrey Hepburn-Ruston
Herblock	Herbert Lawrence Block
Pee Wee Herman	Paul Rubenfeld (later, Paul Reubens)
Hildegarde	Hildegarde Loretta Sell
Laura Z. Hobson	Laura Zametkin

	Real Name
Dennis Hoey	Samuel David Hyams
Hulk Hogan	Terry Jean Bollette
Hal Holbrook	Harold Rowe Holbrook, Jr.
William Holden	William Franklin Beedle, Jr.
Billie Holiday	Eleanora Fagan
Judy Holliday	Judith Tuvim
Earl Holliman	Anthony Numkena
Buddy Holly	Charles Hardin Holley
Tim Holt	John Charles Holt, Jr.
Bob Hope	Leslie Townes Hope
Hedda Hopper	Elda Furry
A.E. Hotchner	Aaron Edward Hotchner
Harry Houdini	Ehrich Weiss
John Houseman	Jacques Haussmann
Leslie Howard	Leslie Howard Stainer
Moe, Curly, and Shemp Howard	Moses, Jerome, and Samuel Horowitz
Susan Howard	Jeri Lynn Mooney
James Wong Howe	Wong Tung Jim
L. Ron Hubbard	Lafayette Ronald Hubbard
Rock Hudson	Roy Scherer, Jr. (later, Roy Fitzgerald)
Josephine Hull	Josephine Sherwood
Engelbert Humperdinck	Arnold Gerry Dorsey
Jeffrey Hunter	Henry Herman McKinnies
Kim Hunter	Janet Cole
Ross Hunter	Martin Fuss
Tab Hunter	Arthur Andrew Gelien
Ruth Hussey	Ruth Carol O'Rourke
Walter Huston	Walter Houghston
Will Hutchins	Marshall Lowell Hutchason
Betty Hutton	Betty June Thornberg
Robert Hutton	Robert Bruce Winne
Diana Hyland	Joan Diana Genter
Janis Ian	Janis Fink
Billy Idol	William Board
Robert Indiana	Robert Clarke
Frieda Inescort	Frieda Wightman
Marty Ingels	Martin Ingerman
Rex Ingram	Reginald Ingram Montgomery Hitchcock
George Irving	George Irving Shelasky
Burl Ives	Burle Icle Ivanhoe
Dean Jagger	Dean Jeffries
Joni James	Joan Carmella Babbo
Rick James	James Johnson
Elsie Janis	Elsie Bierbower
Emil Jannings	Theodor Friedrich Emil Janenz

David Janssen	David Harold Meyer
Allen Jenkins	Allen McGonegal
Jimmy the Greek	Demetrios George Synodinos (later, James G. Snyder)
Robert Joffrey	Abdullah Jaffa Bey Khan
Elton John	Reginald Kenneth Dwight
Chic Johnson	Harold Ogden Johnson
Don Johnson	Don Wayne
Al Jolson	Asa Hesselson (later, Asa Yoelson)
Buck Jones	Charles Frederick Gebhart
Candy Jones	Jessica Wilcox
Jennifer Jones	Phyllis Isley (later, Walker)
Spike Jones	Lindley Armstrong Jones
Tom Jones	Thomas Jones Woodward
Christine Jorgensen	George Jorgensen, Jr.
Louis Jourdan	Louis Gendre
Letrice Joy	Leatrice Joy Zeidler
Peggy Hopkins Joyce	Margaret Upton
Raul Julia	Raul Rafael Carlos Julia y Arcelos
Katy Jurado	Maria Christina Jurado Garcia
Ish Kabibble	Merwin A. Bogue
Helen Kane	Helen Schroder
Boris Karloff	William Henry Pratt
Casey Kasem	Kemal Amin Kasem
Danny Kaye	David Daniel Kominski
Nora Kaye	Nora Koreff
Elia Kazan	Elia Kazanjoglous
Lainie Kazan	Lainie Levine
Kurt Kaznar	Kurt Serwischer
Buster Keaton	Joseph Frank Keaton
Diane Keaton	Diane Hall
Michael Keaton	Michael Douglas
Howard Keel	Harold Clifford Leek
Ruby Keeler	Ethel Hilda Keeler
Brian Keith	Robert Keith, Jr.
Ricky Keith	Ricky Thibodeaux
Kay Kendall	Justine McCarthy
Suzy Kendall	Frieda Harrison
Jack Kerouac	Jean Louis Lebris de Kerouac
Deborah Kerr	Deborah Kerr-Trimmer
Jean Kerr	Bridget Jean Collins
Chaka Khan	Yvette Marie Stevens
Michael Kidd	Milton Greenwald
Alan King	Irwin Alan Kniberg
Alexander King	Alexander Koenig
B.B. King	Riley B. King

Carole King	Carole Klein
Larry King	Larry Zieger
Martin Luther King, Jr.	Michael Luther King, Jr.
Ben Kingsley	Krishna Bhanji
Sidney Kingsley	Sidney Kirschner
Nastassia Kinski	Nastassja Nakszybski
Phyllis Kirk	Phyllis Kirkegaard
Cholly Knickerbocker	Igor Loiewski-Cassini
Ted Knight	Tadewurz Wladziu Konopka
Judith Krantz	Judith Tarcher
Kreskin, The Amazing	George Joseph Kresge, Jr.
Kay Kyser	James Kern Kyser
Patti LaBelle	Patricia Louise Holte
Cheryl Ladd	Cheryl Stoppelmoor
Diane Ladd	Rose Diane Ladner
Bert Lahr	Irving Lahrheim
Frankie Laine	Frank Paul Lo Vecchio
R.D. Laing	Ronald David Laing
Arthur Lake	Arthur Silverlake
Veronica Lake	Constance Frances Marie Ockleman
Barbara La Marr	Rheatha Watson
Hedy Lamarr	Hedwig Eva Marie Kiesler
Dorothy Lamour	Dorothy Kaumeyer
Elsa Lanchester	Elsa Sullivan
Ann Landers	Esther Pauline Friedman
Carole Landis	Frances Lillian Mary Ridste
Michael Landon	Eugene Michael Orowitz
Abbe Lane	Francine Lassman
Burton Lane	Burton Levy
Lola Lane	Dorothy Mullican
Priscilla Lane	Priscilla Mullican
Rosemary Lane	Rosemary Mullican
Frances Langford	Frances Newbern
Lillie Langtry	Emilie Charlotte LeBreton
Meyer Lansky	Maier Suchowljansky
Snooky Lanson	Roy Landman
Mario Lanza	Alfred Arnold Cocozza
Jack La Rue	Gaspare Biondolillo
Lassie	Pal
Stan Laurel	Arthur Stanley Jefferson
Ralph Lauren	Ralph Lifshitz
Piper Laurie	Rosetta Jacobs
Carol Lawrence	Carol Maria Laraia
D.H. Lawrence	David Herbert Lawrence
Gertrude Lawrence	Gertrud Alexandra Dagmar Lawrence-Klasen
Lawrence of Arabia	Thomas Edward Lawrence
Steve Lawrence	Sidney Liebowitz

	Real Name
John Le Carré	David John Moore Cornwell
Brenda Lee	Brenda Mae Tarpley
Bruce Lee	Lee Siu Loong
Canada Lee	Leonard Lionell Cornelius Canegata
Christopher Lee	Christoper Frank Carandini Lee
Dixie Lee	Wilma Winifred Wyatt
Gypsy Rose Lee	Rose Louise Hovick
Lila Lee	Augusta Appel
Michele Lee	Michele Lee Dusiak
Peggy Lee	Norma Engstrom
Pinky Lee	Pincus Leff
Spike Lee	Shelton Lee
Sybil Leek	Sybil Falk
Janet Leigh	Jeanette Helen Morrison
Mitch Leigh	Irwin Michnick
Vivien Leigh	Vivian Mary Hartley
Jack Lemmon	John Uhler Lemmon III
Nikolai Lenin	Vladimir Ilyich Ulyanov
Lotte Lenya	Karoline Blamauer
Benny Leonard	Benjamin Leiner
Jack E. Leonard	Leonard Lebitsky
Sheldon Leonard	Sheldon Leonard Bershad
Sugar Ray Leonard	Ray Charles Leonard
Baby Le Roy	Le Roy Winnebrenner
Huey Lewis	Hugh Anthony Cregg III
Jerry Lewis	Joseph Levitch
Joe E. Lewis	Joe Klewan
Shari Lewis	Shari Hurwitz
Ted Lewis	Theodore Leopold Friedman
Liberace	Wladziu Valentino Liberace
Beatrice Lillie	Constance Sylvia Munston
Elmo Lincoln	Otto Elmo Linkenhelter
Hal Linden	Harold Lipschitz
Viveca Lindfors	Elsa Viveca Torstendsotter
Virna Lisi	Virna Peralisi
Little Richard	Richard Penniman
Mary Livingstone	Sadye Marks
Gary Lockwood	John Gary Yusolfsky
Margaret Lockwood	Margaret Day
John Loder	John Lowe
Herbert Lom	Herbert C. Angelo Kuchacevich
Carole Lombard	Carol Jane Peters
Julie London	Julie Peck
Jack Lord	John Joseph Ryan
Sophia Loren	Sofia Scicolone
Peter Lorre	Lazlo Lowenstein

	Real Name
Joe Louis	Joe Louis Barrow
Anita Louise	Anita Louise Fremault
Tina Louise	Tina Blacker
Bessie Love	Juanita Horton
Myrna Loy	Myrna Williams
Emil Ludwig	Emil Ludwig Cohn
Bela Lugosi	Bela Blasko
Paul Lukas	Paul Lucacs
Lulu	Marie McDonald McLaughlin
Magda Lupescu	Elena Wolff
Carol Lynley	Carol Lee
Diana Lynn	Dolly Loehr
Jeffrey Lynn	Ragnar Godfrey Lind
Loretta Lynn	Loretta Webb
Leonard Lyons	Leonard Sucher
Moms Mabley	Loretta Mary Aiken
Ross MacDonald	Kenneth Millar
Connie Mack	Cornelius Alexander McGillicuddy
Ted Mack	William Edward Maguiness
Gisele MacKenzie	Marie Marguerite Louise Gisele La Fleche
Shirley MacLaine	Shirley MacLean Beaty
Guy Madison	Robert Moseley
Madonna	Madonna Louise Ciccone
Marjorie Main	Mary Tomlinson Krebs
Lee Majors	Harvey Lee Yeary
Malcolm X	Malcolm Little
Karl Malden	Mladen Sekulovich
Dorothy Malone	Dorothy Eloise Maloney
Herbie Mann	Herbert Jay Solomon
David Manners	Rauff de Ryther Acklom
Manolete	Manuel Rodriguez y Sanchez
Jayne Mansfield	Jayne Palmer
Fredric March	Frederick McIntyre Bickel
Rocky Marciano	Rocco Francis Marchegiano
Marisol	Marisol Escobar
Hugh Marlowe	Hugh Hipple
Julia Marlowe	Sarah Frances Frost
Jean Marsh	Jean Lyndsey Torren Marsh
Brenda Marshall	Ardis Anderson Gaines
E.G. Marshall	Edda Gunnar Marshall
Peter Marshall	Pierre la Cock
Dean Martin	Dino Crocetti
Ross Martin	Martin Rosenblatt
Tony Martin	Alvin Morris
Wink Martindale	Winston Conrad Martindale
Al Martino	Alfred Cini
Chico Marx	Leonard Marx

Groucho Marx	Julius Marx
Gummo Marx	Milton Marx
Harpo Marx	Adolph Marx
Zeppo Marx	Herbert Marx
Jackie Mason	Jacob Masler
Ilona Massey	Ilona Hajmassy
André Maurois	Emile Salomon Herzog
Lois Maxwell	Lois Hooker
Elaine May	Elaine Berlin
Virginia Mayo	Virginia Jones
Mike Mazurki	Mikhail Mazurwski
Spanky McFarland	George Emmett McFarland
Jim McKay	James Kenneth McManus
Scott McKay	Carl Chester Gose
Butterfly McQueen	Thelma McQueen
Audrey Meadows	Audrey Cotter
Jayne Meadows	Jayne Cotter
Meat Loaf	Marvin Lee Adair
Ralph Meeker	Ralph Rathgeber
Golda Meir	Golda Mabovitz (later, Meyerson)
Melanie	Melanie Safka
Nellie Melba	Helen Porter Mitchell
H.L. Mencken	Henry Louis Mencken
Vivien Merchant	Ada Thompson
Ethel Merman	Ethel Zimmermann
David Merrick	David Margulois
Dina Merrill	Nedenia Hutton
Robert Merrill	Moishe Miller
Vera Miles	Vera Ralston
Ray Milland	Reginald Truscott-Jones
Ann Miller	Lucy Ann Collier
Spike Milligan	Terence Alan Milligan
Donna Mills	Donna Jean Miller
Minnesota Fats	R. Wanderone
Carmen Miranda	Maria da Carmo Miranda de Cunha
Cameron Mitchell	Cameron Mizell
Guy Mitchell	Al Cernick
Joni Mitchell	Roberta Joan Anderson
Eddie Money	Edward Mahoney
Marilyn Monroe	Norma Jean Mortensen (later, Baker)
Bull Montana	Luigi Montagna
Yves Montand	Ivo Montand Livi
Lola Montez	Marie Dolores Eliza Rosanna Gilbert
George Montgomery	George Montgomery Letz
Ron Moody	Ronald Moodnick

Archie Moore	Archibald Lee Wright
Colleen Moore	Kathleen Morrison
Demi Moore	Demi Gynes
Garry Moore	Thomas Garrison Morfit
Melba Moore	Beatrice Moore
Terry Moore	Helen Koford
Alberto Moravia	Alberto Pincherie
Rita Moreno	Rosita Dolores Alverio
Dennis Morgan	Stanley Morner
Frank Morgan	Francis Wupperman
Harry Morgan	Harry Bratsburg
Henry Morgan	Henry Lerner Von Ost, Jr.
J.P. Morgan	John Pierpont Morgan
Ralph Morgan	Ralph Wupperman
Wayne Morris	Bert De Wayne Morris
Toni Morrison	Chloe Wofford
Grandma Moses	Anna Mary Robertson
Zero Mostel	Samuel Joel Mostel
Paul Muni	Muni Weisenfreund
Patrice Munsel	Patrice Munsil
F.W. Murnau	Friedrich W. Plumpe
Arthur Murray	Arthur Murray Teichman
Jan Murray	Murray Janofsky
Kathryn Murray	Kathryn Kohnfelder
Ken Murray	Don Court
Mae Murray	Marie Adrienne Koenig
Edward R. Murrow	Egbert Roscoe Murrow
Nita Naldi	Anita Anne Dooley
Anna Neagle	Marjorie Robertson
Pola Negri	Apolonia Mathias-Chalupec
Kate Nelligan	Patricia Colleen Nelligan
Barry Nelson	Robert Haakon Nielson
Gene Nelson	Gene Berg
Peter Nero	Bernie Nierow
Pablo Neruda	Neftali Richardo Reyes y Basoalto
Louise Nevelson	Louise Berliawsky
Julie Newmar	Julia Charlene Newmeyer
Juice Newton	Judy Cohen
Mike Nichols	Michael Igor Peschkowsky
Jean Nidetch	Jean Slutsky
Mabel Normand	Mabel Fortescue
Chuck Norris	Carlos Ray Norris
Sheree North	Dawn Bethel
Kim Novak	Marilyn Novak
Ramon Novarro	Ramon Samaniegoes
France Nuyen	France Nguyen Vannga
Louis Nye	Louis Nyestadt
Jack Oakie	Lewis Delaney Offield

Annie Oakley	Phoebe Annie Oakley Mozee
Merle Oberon	Estelle Merle O'Brien Thompson
Hugh O'Brian	Hugh J. Krampe
Margaret O'Brien	Angela Maxine O'Brien
Pat O'Brien	William Joseph O'Brien, Jr.
Odetta	Odetta Holmes Felious Gordon
Maureen O'Hara	Maureen Fitzsimmons
Dennis O'Keefe	Edward "Bud" Vance Flanagan
Olga	Olga Erteszek
Tony Orlando	Michael Anthony Orlando Cassavitis
Eugene Ormandy	Jeno Blau
Max Ophüls	Max Oppenheimer
George Orwell	Eric Arthur Blair
Gilbert O'Sullivan	Raymond Edward O'Sullivan
Jesse Owens	James Cleveland "J.C." Owens
Amos Oz	Amos Klausner
Frank Oz	Frank Richard Oznowicz
Patti Page	Clara Ann Fowler
Debra Paget	Debralee Griffin
Janis Paige	Donna Mae Jaden
Jack Palance	Walter Jack Palahnuik
Lilli Palmer	Lilli Peiser
Joseph Papp	Joseph Papirofsky
Dorothy Parker	Dorothy Rothschild
Jean Parker	Luise Stephanie Zelinska
Suzy Parker	Cecilia Parker
Bert Parks	Bert Jacobson
Larry Parks	Samuel Klausman
Louella Parsons	Louella Oettinger
Mandy Patinkin	Mandel Patinkin
Les Paul	Lester William Polfus
Marisa Pavan	Marisa Pierangeli
Johnny Paycheck	Don Lytle
Minnie Pearl	Sarah Ophelia Colley Cannon
Jan Peerce	Jacob Pincus Perelmuth
Pelé	Edson Arantes do Nascimento
J.C. Penney	James Cash Penney
Gigi Perreau	Ghislaine Perreau-Saussine
Bernadette Peters	Bernadette Lazzara
Brock Peters	Brock Fisher
Roberta Peters	Roberta Peterman
Suzanne Peters	Suzanne Carnahan

Esther Phillips	Esther Mae Jones
Michelle Phillips	Holly Michelle Gilliam
Edith Piaf	Edith Giovanna Gassion
Slim Pickens	Louis Bert Lindley, Jr.
Jack Pickford	Jack Smith
Mary Pickford	Glady Mary Smith
Molly Pitcher	Mary Ludwig Hays McCauley
ZaSu Pitts	Eliza Susan Pitts
Christopher Plummer	Arthur Christopher Ormf
Pocahontas	Mataoka
Michael J. Pollard	Michael J. Pollack
Snub Pollard	Harold Fraser
Rosa Ponselle	Rose Ponzillo
Iggy Pop	James Jewel Osterburg
Sylvia Porter	Sylvia Feldman
Jane Powell	Suzanne Burce
Jody Powell	Joseph Lester Powell
Stefanie Powers	Stefanie Zofia Federkiewicz
Paula Prentiss	Paula Ragusa
Priscilla Presley	Priscilla Wagner (later, Beaulieu)
Robert Preston	Robert Preston Meservey
Prince	Prince Rogers Nelson
Emilio Pucci	Marchese di Barsento
Lily Pulitzer	Lillian McKim Rousseau
Sarah Purcell	Sarah Pentecost
John Qualen	John Oleson
Charlotte Rae	Charlotte Lubotsky
George Raft	George Ranft
Ella Raines	Ella Wallace Raubes
Ma Rainey	Gertrude Malissa Nix Pridgett
Prince Rainier III	Louis Henri Maxence Bertrand
Sally Rand	Helen Gould Beck
Phylicia Rashad	Phylicia Ayers-Allen
Aldo Ray	Aldo de Re
Nicholas Ray	Raymond N. Kienzle
Gene Rayburn	Eugene Rubessa
Martha Raye	Margaret Theresa Yvonne Reed
Nancy Reagan	Anne Frances Robbins
Robert Redford	Charles Robert Redford, Jr.
Donna Reed	Donna Belle Mullenger
Jerry Reed	Jerry Hubbard
Harry Reems	Herbert Streicher
Della Reese	Deloreese Patrica Early
George Reeves	George Basselo
Regine	Regina Zylberberg
Max Reinhardt	Maximilian Goldman

	Real Name
Duncan Renaldo	Renaldo Duncan
Fernando Rey	Fernando Arambillet
Debbie Reynolds	Mary Frances Reynolds
Marjorie Reynolds	Marjorie Moore
R.J. Reynolds	Richard Joshua Reynolds
Elmer Rice	Elmer Leopold Reizenstein
Cliff Richard	Harold Roger Webb
Jeannie C. Riley	Jeannie C. Stephenson
Tex Ritter	Woodward Maurice Ritter
Joan Rivers	Joan Sandra Molinsky
Larry Rivers	Yitzroch Loiza Grossberg
Al Ritz	Al Joachim
Cliff Robertson	Clifford Parker Robertson III
Harold Robbins	Francis Kane
Jerome Robbins	Jerome Rabinowitz
Marty Robbins	Martin David Robinson
Edward G. Robinson	Emanuel Goldenberg
Sugar Ray Robinson	Walker Smith, Jr.
Ginger Rogers	Virginia Katherine McMath
Roy Rogers	Leonard Slye
Eric Rohmer	Jean-Marie Maurice Scherer
Gilbert Roland	Luis Antonio Damaso de Alonso
Mike Romanoff	Harry F. Gerguson
Mickey Rooney	Joe Yule, Jr.
Billy Rose	William Samuel Rosenberg
Barney Ross	Barnet David Rasofsky
Lillian Roth	Lillian Rutstein
Mark Rothko	Marcus Rothkovich
Alma Rubens	Alma Smith
Jack Ruby	Jacob Rubenstein
Lillian Russell	Helen Louise Leonard
Mark Russell	Mark Ruslander
Bobby Rydell	Robert Riderelli
Alfred Ryder	Alfred Jacob Corn
Mitch Ryder	Williams S. Levise, Jr.
Winona Ryder	Winona Horowitz
Sabu	Sabu Dastagir
Sade	Helen Folasade Adu
Françoise Sagan	Françoise Quoirez
Lili St. Cyr	Marie Van Schaak
Raymond St. Jacques	James Arthur Johnson
Susan St. James	Susan Miller
Jill St. John	Jill Oppenheim
Yves St. Laurent	Henri Donat Mathieu
Pat Sajak	Pat Sadjak
S.Z. Sakall	Eugene Gero Szakall
Saki	Hector Hugh Munro
Soupy Sales	Milton Supman

J.D. Salinger	Jerome David Salinger
George Sand	Amandine Lucille Aurore Dupin Dudevant
Paul Sand	Paul Sanchez
Dominique Sanda	Dominique Varaigne
Susan Sarandon	Susan Abigail Tomalin
Michael Sarrazin	Jacques Michel Andre Sarazin
John Saxon	Carmen Orrico
Arnold Scaasi	Arnold Isaacs
Boz Scaggs	William Royce Scaggs
Gia Scala	Giovanna Scoglio
Romy Schneider	Rosemarie Albach-Retty
Dutch Schultz	Arthur Flegenheimer
Gordon Scott	Gordon M. Werschkul
Elizabeth Scott	Emma Matzo
Randolph Scott	Randolph Crane
Mack Sennett	Michael Sinnott
Dr. Seuss	Theodor Seuss Geisel
Jane Seymour	Joyce Penelope Frankenberg
Yitzhak Shamir	Yitzhak Yezernitsky
Ntozake Shange	Paulette L. Williams
Del Shannon	Charles Westover
Omar Sharif	Michael Shalhoub
Jack Sharkey	Joseph Paul Zukauskas
Artie Shaw	Arthur Isaac Arshawsky
Dick Shawn	Richard Schulefand
Al Shean	Alfred Shoenberg
Moira Shearer	Moira Shearer King
Charlie Sheen	Carlos Irwin Estevez
Martin Sheen	Ramon Estevez
Sam Shepard	Sam Shepard Rogers
Ann Sheridan	Clara Lou Sheridan
Brooke Shields	Christa Brooke Camille Shields
Talia Shire	Talia Coppola
Anne Shirley	Dawn Evelyn Paris (later, Dawn O'Day)
Dinah Shore	Frances "Fanny" Rose Shore
Nevil Shute	Nevil Shute Norway
Sylvia Sidney	Sophie Kosow
Simone Signoret	Simone Kaminker
Beverly Sills	Belle "Bubbles" Miriam Silverman
Jay Silverheels	Harold J. Smith
Phil Silvers	Phil Silversmith
Nina Simone	Eunice Kathleen Waymon
Adele Simpson	Adele Smithline
O.J. Simpson	Orenthal James Simpson

Penny Singleton	Mariana Dorothy McNulty
Red Skelton	Richard Bernard Skelton
B.F. Skinner	Burrhus Frederic Skinner
Grace Slick	Grace Wing
Adam Smith	George J. Goodman
Betty Smith	Betty Wehner
Red Smith	Walter Wellesley Smith
Smith and Dale	Joseph Seltzer and Charles Marks
Tommy Smothers	Thomas Bolyn Smothers III
Phoebe Snow	Phoebe Laub
Suzanne Somers	Suzanne Mahoney
Elke Sommer	Elke Schletz
Jack Soo	Goro Suzuki
Ann Sothern	Harriet Lake
Georgia Sothern	Hazel Anderson
Ned Sparks	Edward A. Sparkman
Dusty Springfield	Mary Isobel Catherine O'Brien
Joseph Stalin	Josif V. Dzhugashvili
Stanislavsky	Konstantin Sergeyevitch Alekseyev
Kim Stanley	Patricia Kimberly Reid
Barbara Stanwyck	Ruby Stevens
Jean Stapleton	Jeanne Murray
Ringo Starr	Richard Starkey
Bob Steele	Robert North Bradbury, Jr.
Tommy Steele	Tommy Hicks
Anna Sten	Anjuchka Stenska
Stendhal	Marie Henri Beyle
Princess Stephanie	Stephanie Marie Elisabeth Grimaldi
Jan Sterling	Jane Sterling Adriance
Cat Stevens	Stephen Dmitri Georgiou (later, Yosef Islam)
Connie Stevens	Concetta Ingolia
Craig Stevens	Gail Shekles, Jr.
Inger Stevens	Inger Stensland
K.T. Stevens	Gloria Wood
Ray Stevens	Harold Ray Ragsdale
Shadoe Stevens	Terry Ingstad
Risë Stevens	Risë Steenberg
Stella Stevens	Estelle Egglestone
Michael Stewart	Michael Rubin
Sting	Gordon Matthew Sumner
I.F. Stone	Isidor Feinstein Stone
Irving Stone	Irving Tennebaum
Tom Stoppard	Thomas Straussler

Gale Storm	Josephine Cottle
Dorothy Stratten	Dorothy Hoogstratten
Lyle Stuart	Lionel Simon
Preston Sturges	Edmund P. Biden
Jule Styne	Julius Kerwin Stein
Yma Sumac	Emperatriz Chavarri Yma Sumac
Donna Summer	La Donna Andrea Gaines
Sundance Kid	Harry Longabaugh
Suzy	Aileen Elder Mehle
Vic Tanny	Victor A. Iannidinardo
Jacques Tati	Jacques Tatischeff
Estelle Taylor	Estelle Boylan
Kent Taylor	Louis Weiss
Laurette Taylor	Laurette Cooney
Robert Taylor	Spangler Arlington Brugh
Alan Thicke	Alan Jeffery
Betty Thomas	Betty Thomas Nienhauser
Danny Thomas	Muzyad Yakhoob (later, Amos Jacobs)
Marlo Thomas	Margaret Julia Thomas
Terry-Thomas	Thomas Terry Hoar-Stevens
Tom Thumb	Charles Sherwood Stratton
Tiny Tim	Herbert Khaury
Titian	Tiziano Vecelli
Tito	Josip Broz
Y.A. Tittle	Yelberton Abraham Tittle
Mike Todd	Avrom Hirsch Goldborgen
Tokyo Rose	Iva Ikiko Toguri D'Aquino
J.R.R. Tolkien	John Ronald Reuel Tolkien
Rip Torn	Elmore Torn
Raquel Torres	Paula Marie Osterman
B. Traven	Berick Traven Torsvan
Robert Traver	John Donaldson Voelker
Randy Travis	Randy Traywick
Arthur Treacher	Arthur T. Veary
Leon Trotsky	Lev Davidovich Bronstein
Garry Trudeau	Garretson Beckman Trudeau
Richard Tucker	Reuben Ticker
Sophie Tucker	Sophie Kalish (later, Abuza)
Sonny Tufts	Bowen Charleston Tufts III
Lana Turner	Julia Jean Turner
Tina Turner	Annie Mae Bullock
Madame Tussaud	Marie Gresholtz
Mark Twain	Samuel Langhorne Clemens
Boss Tweed	William Marcy Tweed
Helen Twelvetrees	Helen Jurgens
Twiggy	Leslie Hornby
Conway Twitty	Harold Jenkins

Bonnie Tyler	Gaynor Hopkins
Tom Tyler	Vincent Markowsky
Kenneth Tynan	Kenneth Peacock
Ukelele Ike	Cliff Edwards
Roger Vadim	Roger Vadim Plemiannikov
Jerry Vale	Gerano Louis Vitaliamo
Ritchie Valens	Richard Valenzuela
Valentino	Valentino Garavani
Rudolph Valentino	Rodolpho Gugielmi di Valentino d'Antonguolla
Rudy Vallee	Hubert Prior Vallee
Alida Valli	Alida Maria Altenburger
Frankie Valli	Francis Castelluccio
Bobby Van	Robert Van Stein
Abigail Van Buren	Pauline Esther Friedman
Mamie Van Doren	Joan Lucille Olander
Jimmy Van Heusen	Edward Chester Babcock
Melvin Van Peebles	Melvin Peebles
Lupe Velez	Maria Guadeloupe Velez de Villalobos
Benay Venuta	Venuta Rose Crooke
Vera-Ellen	Vera Ellen Westmeyr Rohe
John Vernon	Adolphus Vernon Agopsowicz
Veruschka	Countess Vera Von Lehndorff
Sid Vicious	John Simon Ritchie
Martha Vickers	Martha MacVicar
Gore Vidal	Eugene Luther Vidal
Florence Vidor	Florence Cobb
Pancho Villa	Doroteo Arango
Luchino Visconti	Count Don Luchino Visconti di Modrone
Monica Vitti	Monica Luisa Ceciarelli
Josef Von Sternberg	Josef Stern
Erich Von Stroheim	Hans Erich Maria Stroheim
Lindsay Wagner	Lindsay Jean Ball
Jersey Joe Walcott	Arnold Raymond Cream
Christopher Walken	Ronald Walken
Mort Walker	Mort Walker Addison
Nancy Walker	Anne Myrtle Swoyer
Irving Wallace	Irving Wallechinsky
Mike Wallace	Myron Leon Wallace
Bruno Walter	Bruno Walter Schlesinger
Walter Wanger	Walter Feuchtwanger
Burt Ward	Bert John Gervais, Jr.
Andy Warhol	Andrew Warhola
Harry Warren	Salvatore Guaragna
Dionne Warwick	Marie Dionne Warrick
Dinah Washington	Ruth Jones
Muddy Waters	McKinley Morganfield

	Real Name
David Wayne	David McMeekan
John Wayne	Marion Michael Morrison
Charlie Weaver	Cliff Arquette
Doodles Weaver	Winstead Sheffield Glendening Dixon
Sigourney Weaver	Susan Weaver
Clifton Webb	Webb Parmelee Hollenbeck
Raquel Welch	Raquel Tejada
Tuesday Weld	Susan Kerr Weld
H.G. Wells	Herbert George Wells
Kitty Wells	Muriel Deason
Oskar Werner	Oskar Josef Bschliessmayer
Lina Wertmuller	Arcangela Felice Assunta Wertmuller von Elgg
Rebecca West	Cecily Isabel Fairfield
Nathanael West	Nathan Wallenstein Weinstein
Jack Weston	Morris Weinstein
Jesse White	Jesse Marc Wiedenfeld
Gene Wilder	Jerome Silberman
Anson Williams	Anson Williams Heimlick
Tennessee Williams	Thomas Lanier Williams
Flip Wilson	Clerow Wilson
Walter Winchell	Walter Winechel
Claire Windsor	Claire Viola Cronk
Marie Windsor	Emily Marie Bertelson
George "Foghorn" Winslow	George Wenzlaff
Johnny Winter	John Dawson Winter III
Shelley Winters	Shirley Schrift
Estelle Winwood	Estelle Goodwin
Googie Withers	Georgina McCallum
Wolfman Jack	Robert Smith
Stevie Wonder	Steveland Judkins (later, Steveland Morris)
Anna May Wong	Liu Tsong Wong
Natalie Wood	Natasha Gurdin
Holly Woodlawn	Harold Danhaki
Monty Woolley	Edgar Montillion Woolley
Jane Wyman	Sarah Jane Fulks
Tammy Wynette	Wynette Pugh
Ed Wynn	Isaiah Edwin Leopold
Dana Wynter	Dagmar Spencer-Marcus
Diana Wynyard	Dorothy Isobel Cox
Susannah York	Susannah Yolande Fletcher
Chic Young	Murat Bernard Young
Gig Young	Byron Ellsworth Barr
Loretta Young	Gretchen Young
Tony Zale	Anthony Florian Zaleski
Frank Zappa	Francis Vincent Zappa, Jr.
Vera Zorina	Eva Brigitta Hartwig

★ FAMILY ★

★   ★

Ethnic Origins of Famous People

Jack Albertson	German-Jewish, Russian-Jewish
Jane Alexander	Irish
Muhammad Ali	African, Irish
Woody Allen	Orthodox Jewish
Herb Alpert	Russian-Jewish, Hungarian-Jewish
Don Ameche	Italian, German, Irish, Scottish
Ann-Margret	Swedish
Edward Asner	Orthodox Jewish
Lauren Bacall	German-Jewish, Romanian-Jewish
Joan Baez	Mexican, English, Irish, Scottish
Lucille Ball	Irish, Scottish, English, French
Anne Bancroft	Italian
John Belushi	Albanian
Jacqueline Bisset	English, Scottish, French
Judy Blume	Orthodox Jewish
David Bowie	Anglo-Catholic, Jewish
Benjamin Bradlee	English, German, Polish
Marlon Brando	French, English, Irish, Dutch
Charles Bronson	Lithuanian, Russian
Mel Brooks	Russian-Jewish, Polish-Jewish
Anita Bryant	French, Dutch, English, Scottish, Irish, Cherokee
Yul Brynner	Swiss-French, Gypsy
Ellen Burstyn	Irish
James Caan	Dutch-Jewish, German-Jewish
Sammy Cahn	Polish-Jewish
Roy Campanella	African, Italian
Leslie Caron	French, American
Cher	Armenian, Turkish, French, Cherokee
Walter Cronkite	Dutch
Blythe Danner	German
Dr. Michael De Bakey	Lebanese
Robert De Niro	Italian, Jewish
Colleen Dewhurst	Irish, Scottish, English
Neil Diamond	Polish-Jewish, Russian-Jewish
Joan Didion	English, Alsatian
Phil Donahue	Irish
Sandy Duncan	Irish, Cherokee
Werner Erhard	Russian-Jewish, English, Swedish
Farrah Fawcett	French, English, Choctaw
Dianne Feinstein	Jewish, Russian-Catholic
Jane Fonda	Italian, Dutch, English
Arlene Francis	Armenian, English
John Frankenheimer	Jewish, Irish

Sir John Gielgud	Lithuanian, Polish, English
Barry Goldwater	Polish-Jewish, English
Sir Lew Grade	Russian-Jewish
Alex Haley	African, Irish
Valerie Harper	Spanish, English, Scottish, Irish, Welsh, French
Goldie Hawn	Jewish, English
George Roy Hill	Irish
John Irving	Scottish
Anne Jackson	Irish, Croatian
Billy Joel	Alsatian-Jewish, Russian-Jewish, English
Elia Kazan	Greek
Harvey Korman	Russian-Jewish
Liberace	Italian, Polish
G. Gordon Liddy	German, Italian, Scottish
Rich Little	English, Irish
Moms Mabley	African, Irish, Cherokee
Penny Marshall	Italian
Billy Martin	Portuguese, Italian
Marsha Mason	Irish, English, Russian, German
Ann Miller	Irish, French, Cherokee
Vincente Minnelli	Italian, French
Robert Mitchum	Irish, Norwegian, Native American
Olivia Newton-John	Welsh, German-Jewish
Jerry Orbach	Irish, Jewish
Dolly Parton	Dutch, Irish, Cherokee
Harold Pinter	Sephardic Jewish
Sylvia Porter	Russian-Jewish
Freddie Prinze	Hungarian-Jewish, Puerto Rican
Anthony Quinn	Mexican (Aztec), Irish
Regine	Polish-Jewish
Geraldo Rivera	Jewish, Puerto Rican
Linda Ronstadt	German, Mexican
Morley Safer	Austrian-Jewish
Neil Sedaka	Sephardic Jewish
Martin Sheen	Spanish, Irish
Carly Simon	German-Jewish, Spanish
Curtis Sliwa	Italian, Polish
Sissy Spacek	Czechoslovakian
Dr. Benjamin Spock	Dutch, English
Bruce Springsteen	Dutch, Italian
Sylvester Stallone	Italian, French
Willie Stargell	African, Seminole
George Steinbrenner	German, Irish
Meryl Streep	Dutch
Sally Struthers	Norwegian, Scottish
Kiri Te Kanawa	Maori, Irish, English
Paul Theroux	French-Canadian, Italian
Mel Tormé	Russian-Jewish

John Travolta	Italian, Irish
Tommy Tune	English, Shawnee
Leon Uris	Russian-Jewish, Polish-Jewish
Bobby Vinton	Polish, Lithuanian
Jon Voight	Czechoslovakian
Mike Wallace	Russian-Jewish
Joseph Wambaugh	German, Irish
Dennis Weaver	Irish, Scottish, English, Cherokee, and Osage
Raquel Welch	Bolivian, Spanish
Lawrence Welk	Alsatian-German
Henry Winkler	German-Jewish
Darryl F. Zanuck	Swiss

Famous People of Native American Descent
★   ★

Pearl Bailey (part Creek)
Kim Basinger (part Cherokee)
Anita Bryant (part Cherokee)
Johnny Cash (one-fourth Cherokee)
Cher (part Cherokee)
Kevin Costner (one-eighth Cherokee)
Johnny Depp (part Cherokee)
Sandy Duncan (part Cherokee)
Farrah Fawcett (part Choctaw)
Redd Foxx (one-fourth Seminole)
James Garner (part Cherokee)
Alex Haley*
Jimi Hendrix (part Cherokee)
Lena Horne (one-eighth Blackfoot)
Jesse Jackson*
Waylon Jennings (part Cherokee and part Comanche)
Eartha Kitt (half Cherokee)
Moms Mabley (part Cherokee)
Rue McClanahan*
Robert Mitchum*
Joe Montana (one-sixty-fourth Sioux)
Wayne Newton (one-fourth Powhatan and one-fourth Cherokee)
Chuck Norris (part Cherokee)
Lou Diamond Philips (part Cherokee)
Jon Peters (half Cherokee)
John Phillips (half Cherokee)
Robert Rauschenberg (one-fourth Cherokee)
Johnnie Ray (part Blackfoot)
Burt Reynolds (one-fourth Cherokee)

*Claims Native American heritage but tribe not specified.

Oral Roberts (part Cherokee)
Roy Rogers (part Choctaw)
Will Rogers (part Cherokee)
Jay Silverheels (full-blooded Canadian Red)
Glenn Strange (part Cherokee)
Willie Stargell (part Seminole)
Ernest Tubb (one-eighth Cherokee)
Tommy Tune (part Shawnee)
Fernando Valenzuela (part Mayo)
Alice Walker*
Dennis Weaver (part Cherokee and part Osage)

★ Famous Ancestors and Relatives ★

Actress **Lauren Bacall** (née Perske)	First cousin of Israel's Prime Minister **Shimon Peres** (né Perske)
Raconteur-actor **Orson Bean**	Third cousin of **Calvin Coolidge**, 30th U.S. President. His maternal great-grandmother and Coolidge's mother were sisters.
Singer **Pat Boone** and oil magnate **T. Boone Pickens**	Descendants of pioneer **Daniel Boone.**
Actor **Bruce Dern**	Grandfather **George H. Dern** was Secretary of War during one of Franklin D. Roosevelt's administrations and was governor of Utah. Dern is also a great-nephew of poet **Archibald MacLeish**.
Actor **Glenn Ford** and singer **Nelson Eddy**	Descendants of **Martin Van Buren**, 8th U.S. President.
The late choreographer **Martha Graham**	Descendant of Captain **Miles Standish**, early American settler and *Mayflower* passenger.
Actress **Mariette Hartley**	Maternal grandfather was behavioral psychologist **John B. Watson**.
The late NBC newscaster **Chet Huntley**	Descendant of **John Adams**, 2nd U.S. President, and **John Quincy Adams**, 6th U.S. President.
Former baseball commissioner **Bowie Kuhn**	Received his unusual first name because he is a descendant of Alamo defender **Jim Bowie**, after whom the Bowie knife was named.
Actor **Burt Lancaster**	Has claimed that his ancestry can be traced to England's royal House of Lancaster.

Actress **Sophia Loren**	Her sister, Maria, married Romano Mussolini, a son of Italian premier **Benito Mussolini**.
TV commentator **Roger Mudd**	Descendant of Dr. **Samuel Mudd**, the Maryland doctor who gave medical assistance to John Wilkes Booth, Lincoln's wounded assassin. Also, playwright **William Inge** was a distant relative of Booth and of actor **Edwin Booth**.
Singer **Olivia Newton-John**	Her maternal grandfather was Nobel Prize-winning German-Jewish physicist **Max Born**.
Former U.S. President **Richard M. Nixon**	Descendant of **King Edward III** of England.
Comedic actor **Maclean Stevenson**	Paternal great-uncle **Adlai E. Stevenson** was Grover Cleveland's Vice President (second administration).

★ Famous Twins ★

Mario Andretti
José Canseco
Montgomery Clift
Laraine Day
John Elway
Jerry Falwell
Jerry Hall

William Randolph
    Hearst*
Laura Z. Hobson
Liberace*
Laraine Newman
Elvis Presley*
Lori Singer

Ed Sullivan*
Kiefer Sutherland
Jim Thorpe
Paul Tsongas
Clint Walker
Billy Dee Williams
Derek Wolcott

*Twin died at birth or in infancy.

★ Twins Who Both Achieved Fame ★

Pier Angeli and
    Marisa Pavan
John and Roy
    Boulting
Julius and Philip
    Epstein
Maurice and Robin
    Gibb

Tim and Tom
    Gullikson
Ann Landers and
    Abigail Van
    Buren
Norris and Ross
    McWhirter

Charles and John
    Panozzo (Styx)
Anthony and Peter
    Shaffer
Moses and
    Raphael Soyer
Dick and Tom
    Van Arsdale

Famous Parents of Twins

Ed Asner
Alan Bates
Meredith Baxter
and David Birney
Ingrid Bergman
Debby Boone
Jimmy Breslin
Jim Brown
Anita Bryant
Bing Crosby
Jacques D'Amboise

Donald Dell
Mike Douglas
Mia Farrow and
André Previn
Milos Forman
Andy Gibb
Mel Gibson
Günter Grass
Susan Hayward
Ron Howard
Loretta Lynn

Henry Mancini
Rick Nelson
Jane Pauley and
Garry Trudeau
Otto Preminger
Nelson Rockefeller
Eric Severeid
Cybill Shepherd
James Stewart
Donald Sutherland
Margaret Thatcher

Famous Siblings

Pier Angeli and Marisa Pavan*
James Arness and Peter
Graves
Ethel, John, and Lionel
Barrymore
Warren Beatty and Shirley
MacLaine
John and Jim Belushi
Marlon and Jocelyn Brando
Beau and Jeff Bridges
James and Jeanne Cagney
Francis Ford Coppola and Talia
Shire
Ricardo and Stanley Cortez
Olivia De Havilland and Joan
Fontaine
Catherine Deneuve and
Françoise Dorleac
Joanne Dru and Peter
Marshall
Emilio Estevez and Charlie
Sheen

Jane and Peter Fonda
Lillian and Dorothy Gish
Darryl and Dwayne Hickman
Betty and Marion Hutton
Anna Landers and Abigail Van
Buren*
Gypsy Rose Lee and June
Havoc
Audrey and Jane Meadows
Hayley and Juliet Mills
Frank and Ralph Morgan
Gigi Perreau and Peter Miles
Mary and Jack Pickford
Vanessa and Lynn Redgrave
Eric and Julia Roberts
George Sanders and Tom
Conway
Maximilian and Maria Schell
Natalie and Lana Wood
And, of course, the Marx
Brothers, the Ritz Brothers,
et al.

*See also *Famous Twins.*

★ Celebrities with Five or More Children ★

	No. of Children		No. of Children
Sun Myung Moon	13	Sidney Poitier	6
Mickey Rooney	11	Jason Robards, Jr.	6
Dennis Day	10	Roy Rogers	6
Dick Gregory	10	Andy Rooney	6
Marlon Brando	9	George C. Scott	6
Glen Campbell	9	Gene Shalit	6
Michael Landon	9	Paul Anka	5
Danielle Steele	9	Johnny Cash	5
Frankie Avalon	8	Bill Cosby	5
Mia Farrow	8	Phil Donahue	5
Al Hirt	8	Bob Dylan	5
Norman Mailer	8	Jim Henson	5
Werner Erhard	7	Jesse Jackson	5
Dean Martin	7	Burt Lancaster	5
Mario Puzo	7	Cloris Leachman	5
Harry Reasoner	7	Patricia Neal	5
Muhammad Ali	6	Jack Nicklaus	5
Charles Bronson	6	Gregory Peck	5
Jerry Lewis	6	Charles Schulz	5
Loretta Lynn	6	Mel Tillis	5
Paul Newman	6	Ben Vereen	5

★ Famous Only Children ★

Ann-Margret	Stan Freberg	Hal Prince
Lauren Bacall	William Friedkin	Nancy Reagan
Frank Borman	Elliot Gould	Cliff Robertson
Lenny Bruce	Cary Grant	Jean-Paul Sartre
Billie Burke	Arsenio Hall	Charles Schulz
Carol Burnett	Carl Icahn	Frank Sinatra
Dick Cavett	Derek Jacobi	Oliver Stone
John Cleese	Swoosie Kurtz	William Styron
Tom Conti	Mervyn LeRoy	Gloria Swanson
Bert Convy	Fred MacMurray	François Truffaut
Tim Conway	Ann Miller	Sarah Vaughan
Walter Cronkite	Farley Mowat	John Weitz
Alain Delon	Patrice Munsel	Oskar Werner
Robert De Niro	Anthony Newley	Betty White
Keir Dullea	Jerry Orbach	Robin Williams
Linda Ellerbee	George Peppard	David Wolper
Perry Ellis	Lou Diamond Phillips	

Famous In-Laws

★   ★

	Parent(s)-in-Law
W.H. Auden	Thomas Mann
Debby Boone	Rosemary Clooney and José Ferrer
Pat Boone	Red Foley
Robert Clary	Eddie Cantor
Phil Donahue	Danny Thomas
Tom Ewell	George Abbott
Dorothy Hamill	Dean Martin
Tom Hayden	Henry Fonda
Jacob Javits	Alfred T. Ringling
Sandy Koufax	Richard Widmark
Burt Lancaster	Ernie Kovacs
Peter Lawford	Dan Rowan
Laurence Luckinbill	Lucille Ball and Desi Arnaz
Sydney Lumet	Lena Horne
Denny McLain	Lou Boudreau
Jason Miller	Jackie Gleason
Rick Nelson	Tom Harmon
Anthony Quinn	Cecil B. De Mille
Geraldo Rivera	Kurt Vonnegut, Jr.
David O. Selznick	Louis B. Mayer
Artie Shaw	Jerome Kern
Frank Sinatra	Maureen O'Sullivan and John Farrow
Robert Walker	John Ford (first marriage)
Robert Walker	Ward Bond (second marriage)
Oskar Werner	Tyrone Power

Famous Military Brats

★   ★

	Father
Pat Conroy	Marine colonel
John Denver	Air Force lieutenant colonel
Faye Dunaway	Army sergeant
Nancy Dussault	Navy captain
Robert Duvall	Navy rear admiral
Samantha Eggar	British Army brigadier general
Michael J. Fox	Canadian Army Signal Corps officer
Cyndy Garvey	Air Force lieutenant colonel, pilot
Newt Gingrich	Army officer
Mark Hamill	Navy officer
Ann Harding	Army officer

	Father
Emmylou Harris	Marine officer
Robert Hays	Marine pilot
Engelbert Humperdinck	British Army captain
Christopher Isherwood	British Army officer
Elton John	British RAF squadron leader
Kris Kristofferson	Air Force general (pilot)
Swoosie Kurtz	Air Force B-17 pilot
Timothy Leary	Army captain
Christopher Lee	British colonel
Heather Locklear	Marine colonel
John Loder	British general
Steve McQueen	Navy pilot
Jim Morrison	Navy rear admiral
John Phillips	Marine major
Priscilla Presley	Navy pilot (father)
	Air Force major (stepfather)
Victoria Principal	Air Force master sergeant
Sally Quinn	Army lieutenant general
Charlotte Rampling	British Army colonel
Lionel Richie	Army captain
Sharon Tate	Army colonel
James Woods	Army officer

★ Occupations of Celebrities' Fathers ★

	Father's Occupation
Kareem Abdul-Jabbar	Transit policeman
Muhammad Ali	Sign painter
Horatio Alger	Unitarian minister
Woody Allen	Jewelry engraver
Herb Alpert	Clothing designer
Don Ameche	Bar owner
Dana Andrews	Baptist minister
Alan Arkin	Industrial draftsman
Louis Armstrong	Turpentine-factory worker
Chester Arthur	Baptist minister
Eddie Arnold	Farmer
Arthur Ashe	Playground caretaker
Fred Astaire	Salesman
W.H. Auden	Doctor
Joan Baez	Physicist
F. Lee Bailey	Newspaper-ad salesman
Pearl Bailey	Minister
James Baldwin	Minister
Kaye Ballard	Construction worker
Alan Bates	Insurance worker

Orson Bean	Campus policeman
Warren Beatty	Realtor; school superintendent
Jean-Paul Belmondo	Sculptor
Barbi Benton	Gynecologist
Ingmar Bergman	Lutheran minister
Joey Bishop	Machinist; bicycle-shop owner
Jacqueline Bisset	Doctor
Shirley Temple Black	Banker
Bill Blass	Wholesale hardware dealer
Dirk Bogarde	Art editor
Richard Boone	Corporate lawyer
William F. Buckley, Jr.	Oil-company owner
Smiley Burnette	Minister
John Byner	Truck mechanic
Michael Caine	Fish-market porter
Erskine Caldwell	Presbyterian minister
Glen Campbell	Minister
Diahann Carroll	Subway conductor
Johnny Carson	Utility-company lineman and manager
Johnny Cash	Farmer
John Cassavetes	Businessman
Dick Cavett	English teacher
Richard Chamberlain	Manufacturing-plant owner
Maurice Chevalier	House painter
Julia Child	Farm consultant
Julie Christie	Tea-plantation manager
Dick Clark	Cosmetics salesman
Petula Clark	Hospital orderly
Grover Cleveland	Congregational minister
Sean Connery	Truck driver
Alistair Cooke	Methodist minister
Sam Cooke	Minister
Rita Coolidge	Baptist minister
Alice Cooper	Minister
Wendell Corey	Congregational minister
Bill Cosby	Navy mess steward
Kevin Costner	Utility-company executive
Walter Cronkite	Dentist
Tom Cruise	Electrical engineer
Dorothy Dandridge	Minister
Ted Danson	Archeologist and museum director
Tony Danza	Garbage man
John Davidson	Baptist minister
Miles Davis	Dentist
Ruby Dee	Railroad porter and waiter
Olivia De Havilland	Patent attorney
Cecil B. De Mille	Episcopal minister
Sandy Dennis	Mail clerk

Gerard Depardieu	Sheet-metal worker
Johnny Depp	City engineer
William Devane	Chauffeur
Danny De Vito	Pool-hall owner
James Dickey	Lawyer
William O. Douglas	Presbyterian minister
Robert Evans	Dentist
Louise Fletcher	Episcopal minister
Steve Forrest	Baptist minister
Aretha Franklin	Baptist minister
Stan Freberg	Baptist minister
David Frost	Methodist minister
James Garner	Upholsterer; carpet layer; carpenter
Steve Garvey	Bus driver
Marvin Gaye	Minister
Ben Gazzara	Carpenter
Jean-Luc Godard	Doctor
Jeff Goldblum	Doctor
Eydie Gormé	Tailor
Lou Gosset, Jr.	Porter
Cary Grant	Clothing-firm presser
Lorne Greene	Shoemaker
Joel Grey	Clarinet player; Yiddish comic
Merv Griffin	Stockbroker
Melanie Griffith	Advertising executive
Tammy Grimes	Hotel and club owner
Charles Grodin	Supply salesman
Bryant Gumbel	Probate judge
Jasmine Guy	Minister
Buddy Hackett	Upholsterer
Arsenio Hall	Baptist minister
Halston	Accountant
Tess Harper	Hardware-store owner
George Harrison	School-bus driver
Paul Harvey	Policeman
Eric Heiden	Doctor
Joseph Heller	Truck driver for a bakery
Katharine Hepburn	Urologist
Benny Hill	Pharmacist
Dustin Hoffman	Furniture designer
Bob Hope	Stonemason
Trevor Howard	Insurance underwriter
John Hurt	Anglican minister
Julio Iglesias	Gynecologist
Glenda Jackson	Bricklayer; construction jobber
Leon Jaworski	Evangelical minister
Van Johnson	Plumbing contractor
Grace Jones	Pentecostal minister

James Earl Jones	Actor
Louis Jourdan	Hotel owner
Danny Kaye	Tailor
Elia Kazan	Rug merchant
Stacy Keach	Dialogue coach
Garrison Keillor	Railway mail clerk and carpenter
Arthur Kennedy	Dentist
Dorothy Kenyon	Minister
Alan King	Handbag cutter
Ben Kingsley	Doctor
Sam Kinison	Pentecostal minister
Kevin Kline	Record store owner
Christine Lahti	Surgeon
Melvin Laird	Presbyterian minister
Burt Lancaster	Postal worker
Jessica Lange	Traveling salesman
Angela Lansbury	Lumber merchant
Steve Lawrence	Cantor; part-time house painter
Michele Lee	Hollywood make-up man
Peggy Lee	Railwood-station agent
John Lennon	Merchant marine
Jay Leno	Insurance salesman
Alan Jay Lerner	Founder of Lerner apparel stores
Mervyn LeRoy	Department-store owner
Jerry Lewis	Nightclub singer
Henry Luce	Presbyterian minister and missionary
Susan Lucci	Building contractor
Paul Lynde	Butcher
Fred MacMurray	Violinist
Norman Mailer	Accountant
Marjorie Main	Minister
Marcel Marceau	Kosher butcher
Lee Marvin	Advertising executive
Marcello Mastroianni	Carpenter
Johnny Mathis	Chauffeur; painter; handyman
Paul Mazursky	Laborer
Paul McCartney	Cotton salesman
Marilyn McCoo	Doctor
Hattie McDaniel	Baptist minister
Kelly McGillis	Doctor
George McGovern	Methodist minister
Clyde McPhatter	Minister
Sal Mineo	Coffin maker
Robert Mitchum	Railroad worker
Walter Mondale	Methodist minister
Dudley Moore	Railroad electrician
Agnes Moorehead	Presbyterian minister
Jeanne Moreau	Restaurant owner

Robert Morse	Theater-chain owner; record-store owner
Zero Mostel	Rabbi
Patrice Munsel	Doctor
Eddie Murphy	NY City transit policeman
George Murphy	Track coach
Anne Murray	Doctor
Jim Nabors	Policeman
Joe Namath	Steel-mill worker
Patricia Neal	Transportation manager
Bob Newhart	Heating engineer
Anthony Newley	Shipping clerk
Randy Newman	Doctor
Huey P. Newton	Baptist minister
Jack Nicklaus	Drugstore owner
Ramon Novarro	Dentist
Laurence Olivier	Anglican minister
Geraldine Page	Doctor
Patti Page	Railroad foreman
Minnie Pearl	Owner of lumber business
Gregory Peck	Pharmacist
George Peppard	Building contractor
Walker Percy	Lawyer
Sylvia Porter	Doctor
Pointer Sisters	Minister
John Qualen	Minister
Lou Rawls	Minister
Harry Reasoner	School superintendent
Nancy Reagan	Car salesman; surgeon (stepfather)
Ronald Reagan	Shoe salesman
Otis Redding	Minister
Robert Redford	Accountant; milkman
Della Reese	Factory worker
Judge Reiner	Lawyer
Lee Remick	Department store owner
Renee Richards	Doctor
Bobby Riggs	Church of Christ minister
Molly Ringwald	Musician
Joan Rivers	Doctor
Cliff Robertson	Rancher
Ginger Rogers	Electrical engineer
Linda Ronstadt	Inventor of grease gun and electric stove
David Lee Roth	Ophthalmologist
Dean Rusk	Presbyterian minister
Morley Safer	Upholsterer
William Saroyan	Presbyterian mnister
Jessica Savitch	Clothing merchant

Diane Sawyer	Judge
Maximilian Schell	Poet; playwright
Romy Schneider	Actor
Arnold Schwarzenegger	Police chief
Albert Schweitzer	Lutheran minister
George C. Scott	Mine surveyor; executive
Jean Seberg	Pharmacist
Erich Segal	Rabbi
Doc Severinsen	Dentist
Jane Seymour	Doctor
Gene Shalit	Pharmacist
Omar Sharif	Timber merchant
Robert Shaw	Doctor
Dinah Shore	Department-store owner
Nina Simone	Methodist minister
Jaclyn Smith	Dentist
Maggie Smith	Public-health doctor
Suzanne Somers	High school coach
Elke Sommer	Lutheran minister
Bruce Springsteen	Bus driver
Ringo Starr	House painter
Mary Steenburgen	Freight-train conductor
Shadoe Stevens	Clothing-store owner
James Stewart	Hardware-store owner
Sting	Milkman
Barbra Streisand	Teacher
Sally Struthers	Doctor
Fran Tarkenton	Methodist minister
Lester Thurow	Methodist minister
Cheryl Tiegs	Mortician
Lily Tomlin	Factory worker
Sen. John Tower	Methodist minister
Tina Turner	Cotton sharecropper
Twiggy	TV-studio carpenter
John Updike	Teacher
Rudy Vallee	Drugstore owner
Dick Van Dyke	Trucking agent
Vincent van Gogh	Pastor
Robert Vaughn	Radio actor
Virginia Wade	Anglican minister
DeWitt Wallace	Presbyterian minister
Barbara Walters	Nightclub owner
Fritz Weaver	Economist
Raquel Welch	Engineer
Richard Widmark	Salesman
Paul Williams	Architectural engineer
Bruce Willis	Mechanic
Woodrow Wilson	Presbyterian minister

	Father's Occupation
Jonathan Winters	Bank officer
Tom Wolfe	College professor
Natalie Wood	Movie-set designer
Andrew Young	Dentist

EDUCATION

Famous High School Dropouts

★   ★

Danny Aiello
Richard Avedon
Brigitte Bardot
Harry Belafonte
Robert Blake
Sonny Bono
Bjorn Borg
David Bowie
Ellen Burstyn
Michael Caine
Glen Campbell
George Carlin
John Chancellor
Cher
Jackie Collins
Sean Connery
Roger Daltry
Gerard Depardieu*
Bo Derek
Lola Falana
Carrie Fisher
Michael J. Fox
Redd Foxx

Jerry Garcia
James Garner
Boy George
Andy Gibb*
Marjoe Gortner
Cary Grant
Gene Hackman
Merle Haggard
George Harrison
Lena Horne
Peter Jennings
Waylon Jennings
Tom Jones
Eartha Kitt
Evel Knievel
Jerry Lewis
Sophia Loren*
Loretta Lynn
Charles Manson
Rod McKuen*
Steve McQueen
Dean Martin
Lee Marvin

Elaine May
Melina Mercouri
Robert Mitchum
Roger Moore
Olivia Newton-John
Peter O'Toole
Al Pacino
Sidney Poitier*
Prince
Richard Pryor
Harold Robbins
Anthony Quinn
Vidal Sassoon
Frank Sinatra
Ringo Starr
Rod Steiger
Danny Thomas
Randy Travis
John Travolta
Peter Ustinov
Robert Wagner
Flip Wilson

*Grammar school dropout—never made it to high school.

High School and College Cheerleaders of Note

★   ★

Kirstie Alley
Ann-Margret
Kim Basinger
Ellen Burstyn
Dyan Cannon
Dick Cavett
Marilyn Chambers
Rita Coolidge
Jamie Lee Curtis
Eydie Gormé

Mariette Hartley
Patty Hearst
Cheryl Ladd
Vicky Lawrence
Brenda Lee
Jerry Lewis
Shirley MacLaine
Steve Martin
Bill Moyers
Gilda Radner

Susan Sarandon
Cybill Shepherd
Dinah Shore
Carly Simon
Dick Smothers
Meryl Streep
Cheryl Tiegs
Lily Tomlin
Raquel Welch

★ The Preppy Guide: Who Went Where ★

James Agee	St. Andrew's Sewanee
Edward Albee	Rye Country Day, Lawrenceville, Valley Forge Military Academy, Choate
Robert Aldrich	Moses Brown School
Jane Alexander	Beaver Country Day
Gregg Allman	Castle Heights Military Academy
Kingsley Amis	City of London School
Cleveland Amory	Milton Academy
Prince Andrew	Gordonstoun
Walter Annenberg	Peddie
Diane Arbus	Fieldston
Jeffrey Archer	Wellington School
Brooke Astor	Madeira
Chris Atkins	Rye Country Day
Louis Auchincloss	Groton
John Badham	Indian Springs School
F. Lee Bailey	Kimball Union Academy
Letitia Baldrige	Miss Porter's
Anne Baxter	Brearley
Barbara Bel Geddes	Putney
Peter Benchley	Exeter
Candice Bergen	Westlake, Montesano
Busby Berkeley	Mohegan Lake Military Academy
Stephen Birmingham	Hotchkiss
Shirley Temple Black	Westlake
Humphrey Bogart	Trinity, Andover
Peter Bogdanovich	Collegiate
Derek Bok	Harvard School
Debby Boone	Westlake
Bill Bradley	St. Mark's
Marlon Brando	Shattuck Military Academy
Kingman Brewster	Belmont Hill School
Matthew Broderick	Walden School
James Conant Bryan	Roxbury Latin
William F. Buckley, Jr.	Beaumont, Millbrook
McGeorge Bundy	Groton
Barbara Bush	Rye Country Day
George Bush	Andover
James Caan	Rhodes School
Truman Capote	Trinity, St. John's Military Academy
John Carradine	Episcopal Academy
John Chancellor	DePaul Academy
Stockard Channing	Chapin, Madeira
Prince Charles	Gordonstoun
Chevy Chase	Dalton
John Cheever	Thayer Academy

Julia Child	Katherine Branson School
Jill Clayburgh	Brearley
Glenn Close	Rosemary Hall
Natalie Cole	Northfield–Mount Hermon
Christina Crawford	Chadwick
Jamie Lee Curtis	Choate–Rosemary Hall
Ted Danson	Kent
Bette Davis	Northfield
Pete Dawkins	Cranbrook
John Dean	Staunton Military Academy
Frank Deford	Gilman School
Dana Delany	Andover
Cecil B. DeMille	Pennsylvania Military Academy
Brian DePalma	Friends Central
Bruce Dern	Choate
Danny De Vito	Oratory School
Princess Diana	West Heath
Sam Donaldson	New Mexico Military Academy
John Dos Passos	Choate
Michael Douglas	Choate
Keir Dullea	George School
Michael Eisner	Lawrenceville
T.S. Eliot	Milton Academy
Daniel Ellsberg	Cranbrook School
Douglas Fairbanks, Jr.	Collegiate, Harvard Military Academy
King Farouk	Le Rosey
Mia Farrow	Marymount, Cygnet House
Lawrence Ferlinghetti	Mount Hermon
Mark Fidrych	Worcester Academy
Frances Fitzgerald	Dalton School, Foxcroft
F. Scott Fitzgerald	St. Paul Academy
Jane Fonda	Emma Willard
Peter Fonda	Westminster
Malcolm Forbes	Lawrenceville
Malcolm Forbes, Jr.	Brooks School
Jodie Foster	Lycée Français
Arlene Francis	Convent of Mount St. Vincent Academy
John Frankenheimer	LaSalle Military Academy
Helen Frankenthaler	Brearley
John A. Gambling	Horace Mann
John Gavin	St. John's Military Academy, Villanova Prep
Barry Goldwater	Staunton Military Academy
Albert Gore, Jr.	St. Alban's
Fred Grandy	Phillips Exeter
Tammy Grimes	Beaver Country Day
Learned Hand	Albany Academy
Mark Harmon	Harvard School
Averill Harriman	Groton

Julie Harris	Grosse Pointe Country Day
David Hartman	Mount Hermon
Helen Hayes	Sacred Heart Convent
Richard Helms	Le Rosey
Florence Henderson	St. Francis Academy
Katharine Hepburn	Hartford School for Girls
John Hersey	Hotchkiss
Abbie Hoffman	Worcester Academy
Hal Holbrook	Suffield Academy, Culver Military Academy
Oliver Wendell Holmes	Phillips Andover
John Irving	Phillips Exeter
Rona Jaffe	Dalton
Tommy Lee Jones	St. Mark's–Texas
Raul Julia	Colegio San Ignacio
Thomas Kean	St. Mark's
Caroline Kennedy	Brearley, Concord Academy
Edward M. Kennedy	Milton Academy
John F. Kennedy	Choate
Robert Kennedy	Milton Academy
Ana Khan	Le Rosey
Michael Kinsley	Cranbrook
Lewis Lapham	Hotchkiss
Jack Lemmon	Phillips Andover
Alan Jay Lerner	Choate
Huey Lewis	Lawrenceville
G. Gordon Liddy	St. Benedict's Prep
Anne Morrow Lindbergh	Chapin
Charles Lindbergh	Sidwell Friends
June Lockhart	Westlake
Vince Lombardi	St. Francis Prep
Walter Lord	Gilman School
Allard Lowenstein	Horace Mann
Clare Booth Luce	St. Mary's
J. Anthony Lukas	Putney
Stuart Margolin	St. Andrew's Sewanee
Lee Marvin	St. Leo's Prep
John McEnroe	Trinity
Ali McGraw	Rosemary Hall
John McLaughlin	LaSalle Military Academy
Herman Melville	Albany Academy
Johnny Mercer	Woodberry Forest
Steve Miller	St. Mark's–Texas
Liza Minnelli	Chadwick School
Elizabeth Montgomery	Spence
Samuel Eliot Morrison	Noble and Greenough
Samuel F.B. Morse	Phillips Andover
George Murphy	Pawling
Brent Musberger	Shattuck Academy
Bob Newhart	St. Ignatius College Prep
Jackie Onassis	Miss Porter's

Robert Oppenheimer	Fieldston School
Gregory Peck	St. John's Military Academy
Anthony Perkins	Brooks School
George Plimpton	Phillips Exeter
Cole Porter	Worcester Academy
Vincent Price	Saint Louis Country Day
Nancy Reagan	Sidwell Friends
Christopher Reeve	Princeton Day School
Lee Remick	Miss Hewitt's
Elliot Richardson	Milton Academy
Joan Rivers	Adelphi Academy
Pat Robertson	McCallie School
Cesar Romero	Collegiate
Andy Rooney	Albany Academy
Franklin D. Roosevelt	Groton
John Rubinstein	Collegiate
Robert Ryan	Loyola Academy
J.D. Salinger	McBurney School, Valley Forge Military Academy
Boz Scaggs	St. Mark's–Texas
James Schlesinger	Horace Mann
George P. Schultz	Loomis
Randolph Scott	Woodberry Forest
John Scully	Buckley School, St. Mark's
Frank Serpico	St. Francis Prep
Shah of Iran	Le Rosey
H. Sargent Shriver	Canterbury School
Carly Simon	Riverdale Country Day
Alan Simpson	Cranbrook School
Grace Slick	Castilleja
James Spader	Andover
Sylvester Stallone	Charlotte Hall
Elizabeth Cady Stanton	Emma Willard
George Steinbrenner	Culver Military Academy
John Paul Stevens	U. of Chicago Lab School
Adlai E. Stevenson	Choate
Parker Stevenson	Brooks School
James Stewart	Mercersburg
Brandon Stoddard	Deerfield
Oliver Stone	Trinity, Hill School
Elizabeth Swados	Buffalo Seminary
Brandon Tartikoff	Lawrenceville
James Taylor	Milton Academy
Garry Trudeau	St. Paul's
Margaret Truman	Gunston School
Ted Turner	Georgia Military Academy
Peter Ustinov	Westminster School, U.K.
Garrick Utley	U. of Chicago Lab School
Brenda Vaccaro	Hockaday
Cyrus Vance	Kent
Gore Vidal	Phillips Exeter

Barbara Walters	Birch Wathen, Fieldston
Sam Waterston	Groton
Sigourney Weaver	Ethel Walker
Daniel Webster	Phillips Exeter
Lowell Weicker	Lawrenceville
Bruce Weitz	Ransom–Everglades
Theodore White	Boston Latin
Bud Wilkinson	Shattuck Academy
Robin Williams	Detroit Country Day
Treat Williams	Kent
Sloan Wilson	Ransom–Everglades
Tom Wolfe	St. Christopher's
Darryl F. Zanuck	Page Military Academy
Richard Zanuck	Harvard School
Stephanie Zimbalist	Foxcroft

★ Famous Military Academy Attendees ★

Alexander Haig (government official)	West Point
Frank Borman (astronaut)	West Point
James E. Carter (U.S. President)	Annapolis
Harry Chapin (singer)	Air Force Academy
Merian C. Cooper (movie producer)	Annapolis
George Custer (U.S. general)	West Point
Dwight D. Eisenhower (U.S. President)	West Point
R. Buckminster Fuller (inventor; designer)	Annapolis
Timothy Leary (counterculture leader; professor)	West Point
David Niven (actor)	Sandhurst
H. Ross Perot (entrepreneur)	Annapolis
John Phillips (singer)	Annapolis
Edgar Allan Poe (writer)	West Point
Jody Powell (presidential advisor)	Air Force Academy
Anastasio Somoza (Nicaraguan leader)	West Point
Stansfield Turner (CIA head)	Annapolis
James Whistler (painter)	West Point

Kareem Abdul-Jabbar	UCLA
Edward Albee	Trinity College
Eddie Albert	U. of Minnesota
Alan Alda	Fordham U.
Jane Alexander	Sarah Lawrence
Woody Allen	NYU, City College of N.Y.
Herb Alpert	U. of Southern California
Robert Altman	U. of Missouri
Don Ameche	Loras College, Marquette, Georgetown
Laurie Anderson	Barnard
Cleveland Amory	Harvard
Dana Andrews	Sam Houston State
Ann-Margret	Northwestern
Alan Arkin	Bennington, L.A. City College
Arthur Ashe	UCLA
Elizabeth Ashley	Louisiana State U.
Ed Asner	U. of Chicago
Burt Bacharach	McGill U.
F. Lee Bailey	Harvard, Boston U. Law
Martin Balsam	New School for Social Research
Richard Barthelmess	Trinity College
Dave Barry	Haverford
Orson Bean	Harvard
Warren Beatty	Northwestern
Saul Bellow	Northwestern
John Belushi	U. of Wisconsin, U. of Illinois, College of DuPage
Peter Benchley	Harvard
Richard Benjamin	Northwestern
Candice Bergen	U. of Pennsylvania
Leonard Bernstein	Harvard
Charles Bickford	MIT
David Birney	Dartmouth
Karen Black	Northwestern
Sidney Blackmer	U. of North Carolina
Larry Blyden	U. of Houston
Erma Bombeck	U. of Dayton
Pat Boone	Columbia
Tom Bosley	De Paul
Charles Boyer	Sorbonne
Peter Boyle	LaSalle College
Charles Brackett	Williams, Harvard Law
Tom Brokaw	U. of South Dakota
Mel Brooks	Brooklyn College
Roscoe Lee Browne	Lincoln U., Middleburg, Columbia
Anita Bryant	Northwestern
William F. Buckley, Jr.	Yale

Carol Burnett	UCLA
Raymond Burr	Stanford, Columbia, U. of California
Richard Burton	Oxford
Barbara Bush	Smith
George Bush	Yale
James Caan	Hofstra
Frank Capra	Calif. Institute of Technology
David Carradine	San Francisco State College
Keith Carradine	Colorado State College
Johnny Carson	U. of Nebraska
James E. Carter	U.S. Naval Academy
John Cassavetes	Mohawk College, Colgate
Dick Cavett	Yale, Yale Drama
Richard Chamberlain	Pomona
Carol Channing	Bennington
Harry Chapin	U.S. Air Force Academy, Cornell
Chevy Chase	Haverford, Bard
Julia Child	Smith
Julie Christie	Brighton Technical College
Dane Clark	Cornell, St. Johns
Jill Clayburgh	Sarah Lawrence
James Coburn	L.A. City College
Dabney Coleman	U. of Texas Law
Stephen Collins	Amherst
Jimmy Connors	UCLA
Robert Conrad	Northwestern
Bert Convy	UCLA
Rita Coolidge	Florida State U.
Gary Cooper	Wesleyan (Montana), Grinnell
Merian C. Cooper	U.S. Naval Academy
Francis Ford Coppola	Hofstra
Roger Corman	Stanford, Oxford
Bill Cosby	Temple, U. of Massachusetts (Ph.D.)
Howard Cosell	New York U. Law
Kevin Costner	U. of California, California State
Michael Crichton	Harvard
Donald Crisp	Oxford
Walter Cronkite	U. of Texas
Hume Cronyn	Ridley College, McGill
Bing Crosby	Gonzaga
James Daly	Cornell
Tyne Daly	Brandeis
William Daniels	Northwestern
Ted Danson	Stanford, Carnegie Mellon
Tony Danza	U. of Dubuque
Howard Da Silva	Carnegie Tech
John Davidson	Denison
Geena Davis	Boston U.
Mac Davis	Emory U.

James Dean	UCLA
Fred de Cordova	Northwestern, Harvard
Ruby Dee	Hunter College
John Denver	Texas Tech
Bruce Dern	U. of Pennsylvania
Neil Diamond	New York U.
Angie Dickinson	Glendale College
Phyllis Diller	Bluffton College
Richard Dix	Northwestern
Phil Donahue	Notre Dame
Michael Douglas	U. of Calif. (Santa Barbara)
Hugh Downs	Bluffton College
Alfred Drake	Brooklyn College
Peter Duchin	Yale
Patrick Duffy	U. of Washington
Olympia Dukakis	Boston U.
Faye Dunaway	U. of Florida
Mildred Dunnock	Goucher, Columbia
Christopher Durang	Harvard
Dan Duryea	Cornell
Nancy Dussault	Northwestern
Bob Dylan	U. of Minnesota
Clint Eastwood	L.A. City College
Vince Edwards	Ohio State U.
Michael Eisner	Denison
Julius Erving	U. of Massachusetts
Tom Ewell	U. of Wisconsin
Nanette Fabray	L.A. City College
Peter Falk	Hamilton, New School, Syracuse
Farrah Fawcett	U. of Texas
Tovah Feldshuh	Sarah Lawrence, U. of Minnesota
Roberta Flack	Howard U.
Henry Fonda	U. of Minnesota
Jane Fonda	Vassar
Peter Fonda	U. of Omaha
Harrison Ford	Ripon
Paul Ford	Dartmouth
Ruth Ford	U. of Mississippi
John Forsythe	U. of North Carolina
Jodie Foster	Yale
David Frost	Cambridge
Art Garfunkel	Columbia
John Gavin	Stanford
Ben Gazzara	City College of N.Y.
Will Geer	U. of Chicago, Columbia
Phyllis George	North Texas State College
Richard Gere	U. of Massachusetts
Alice Ghostley	U. of Oklahoma
Charles Gibson	Princeton
Lorne Greene	Queen's U. (Ontario)
Dick Gregory	Southern Illinois U.

Merv Griffin	San Mateo Jr. College, Stanford, U. of San Francisco
Tammy Grimes	Stephens College
George Grizzard	U. of North Carolina
Charles Grodin	U. of Miami
John Guare	Yale Drama
Bryant Gumbel	Bates College
Moses Gunn	U. of Kansas
Fred Gwynne	Harvard
Jean Hagen	Northwestern
Uta Hagen	U. of Wisconsin
Arsenio Hall	Kent State
Halston	U. of Indiana
Mark Hamill	L.A. City College
Tom Hanks	California State U.
Darryl Hannah	UCLA
Ann Harding	Bryn Mawr
Emmylou Harris	U. of North Carolina
Julie Harris	Yale Drama
Rex Harrison	Liverpool College
David Hartman	Duke
Goldie Hawn	American U.
Leland Hayward	Princeton
Van Heflin	U. of Oklahoma, Yale Drama
Hugh Hefner	U. of Illinois
Katharine Hepburn	Bryn Mawr
Charlton Heston	Northwestern
Arthur Hill	U. of British Columbia
George Roy Hill	Yale, Trinity (Dublin)
Pat Hingle	U. of Texas
Dustin Hoffman	Santa Monica College
Hal Holbrook	Denison U.
William Holden	Pasadena College
Ron Holgate	Northwestern
Earl Holliman	Louisiana State U., UCLA
Edward Everett Horton	Columbia
John Houseman	Clifton College (U.K.)
Ken Howard	Amherst, Yale Drama
Jeffrey Hunter	Northwestern
William Hurt	Tufts
Lauren Hutton	U. of South Florida, Sophie Newcomb
Martha Hyer	Northwestern
Julio Iglesias	Cambridge U.
Rex Ingram	Northwestern Medical
Albert Innaurato	Yale Drama
Burl Ives	Eastern Illinois State Teachers College
Kate Jackson	U. of Mississippi, Birmingham U.
Sam Jaffe	City College of N.Y., Columbia
Mick Jagger	London School of Economics

Tama Janowitz	Hollins College, Yale Drama
Bruce Jenner	San José State College
James Earl Jones	U. of Michigan
Victor Jory	U. of California
Madeline Kahn	Hofstra
Casey Kasem	Wayne State U.
Elia Kazan	Williams, Yale Drama
Stacy Keach	U. of Calif. (Berkeley), Yale Drama
Michael Keaton	Kent State U.
Arthur Kennedy	Carnegie Tech
Walter Kerr	Northwestern
Larry Kert	L.A. City College
Richard Kiley	Loyola U.
Billy Jean King	UCLA
Perry King	Yale
Henry Kissinger	Harvard
Robert Klein	Alfred U., Yale Drama
Kevin Kline	Indiana U.
Jack Klugman	Carnegie Tech
Howard Koch	Columbia Law
Norman Krasna	Brooklyn Law, St. John's
Kris Kristofferson	Pomona, Oxford
John Lahr	Yale, Oxford
Burt Lancaster	New York U.
Frank Langella	Syracuse
Louise Lasser	Brandeis
Tom Laughlin	U. of Indiana, U. of Minnesota
Linda Lavin	William and Mary
Cloris Leachman	Northwestern
Spike Lee	New York U.
Jack Lemmon	Harvard
Jay Leno	Emerson College
David Letterman	Ball State
Huey Lewis	Cornell
John Lithgow	Harvard
John Davis Lodge	Harvard Law
Ali MacGraw	Wellesley
Fred MacMurray	Carroll College
Kevin McCarthy	Georgetown
Jay McInerney	Williams, Syracuse
Ed McMahon	Catholic U.
Norman Mailer	Harvard
Lee Majors	Eastern Kentucky State College, U. of Indiana
Terence Malick	Harvard
Albert Malitz	Columbia, Yale Drama
Delbert Mann	Vanderbilt, Yale Drama
Garry Marshall	Northwestern
Penny Marshall	U. of New Mexico
Steve Martin	UCLA

Marsha Mason	Webster College
Johnny Mathis	San Francisco State College
Ralph Meeker	Northwestern
Adolph Menjou	Cornell
Burgess Meredith	Amherst
Gary Merrill	Bowdoin, Trinity
Bette Midler	U. of Hawaii
Donna Mills	U. of Illinois
Sherrill Milnes	Drake
George Montgomery	U. of Montana
Ralph Morgan	Columbia Law
Toni Morrison	Howard U., Cornell
Zero Mostel	City College of N.Y., New York U.
Bill Moyers	U. of Texas, Southwestern Theological Seminary
Richard Mulligan	Maryknoll Junior Seminary, Columbia
George Murphy	Yale
Tony Musante	Oberlin
Jim Nabors	U. of Alabama
Ralph Nader	Princeton, Harvard Law
Joe Namath	U. of Alabama
Mildred Natwick	Bryn Mawr
Patricia Neal	Northwestern
Tom Neal	Northwestern, Harvard Law
Bob Newhart	Loyola U.
Paul Newman	Kenyon, Yale Drama
Mike Nichols	U. of Chicago
Jack Nicklaus	Ohio State U.
Leonard Nimoy	Antioch, Boston College
David Niven	Sandhurst Military Academy (U.K.)
Richard M. Nixon	Whittier College, Duke Law
Lloyd Nolan	Stanford
Nick Nolte	Pasadena City College
Deborah Norville	U. of Georgia
Carrie Nye	Yale Drama
Pat O'Brien	Marquette
Carroll O'Connor	National U. (Dublin), U. of Montana
Jacqueline Kennedy Onassis	Vassar
Jerry Orbach	U. of Illinois, Northwestern
Fess Parker	U. of Texas, U. of Southern California
Estelle Parsons	Connecticut College, Boston U. Law
Mandy Patinkin	U. of Kansas
Jane Pauley	U. of Indiana
John Payne	Roanoke College
Gregory Peck	U. of California (Berkeley)

George Peppard	Purdue, Carnegie Tech
Anthony Perkins	Rollins College, Columbia
Brock Peters	U. of Chicago, City College of N.Y.
Lou Diamond Phillips	U. of Texas
Ben Piazza	Princeton
Suzanne Pleshette	Finch, Syracuse
George Plimpton	Harvard
Vincent Price	Yale, U. of London
Gilda Radner	U. of Michigan
Charlotte Rae	Northwestern
Bob Rafelson	Dartmouth
Bonnie Raitt	Radcliffe
Tony Randall	Northwestern
Dan Rather	Sam Houston State Teachers College
Nancy Reagan	Smith College
Ronald Reagan	Eureka College
Harry Reasoner	Stanford, U. of Minnesota
Robert Redford	U. of Colorado, Pratt Institute
Christopher Reeve	Cornell
Charles Nelson Reilly	U. of Connecticut
Burt Reynolds	Florida State College
Charlie Rich	U. of Arkansas
John Ritter	U. of Southern California
Tex Ritter	U. of Texas, Northwestern Law
Geraldo Rivera	U. of Arizona, Brooklyn Law
Joan Rivers	Barnard
Tony Roberts	Northwestern
Cliff Robertson	Antioch
Paul Robeson	Rutgers, Columbia Law
Marcia Rodd	Northwestern
Mr. (Fred) Rogers	Dartmouth, Rollins
Kenny Rogers	U. of Houston
Linda Ronstadt	U. of Arizona
Richard Roundtree	Southern Illinois U.
Gena Rowlands	U. of Wisconsin
Barbara Rush	U. of California
Robert Ryan	Dartmouth
Boris Sagal	Yale Drama
Raymond St. Jacques	Yale
Gene Saks	Cornell
Soupy Sales	Marshall College
Telly Savalas	Columbia
Jessica Savitch	Ithaca College
Diane Sawyer	Wellesley
Franklin Schaffner	Franklin and Marshall, Columbia Law
Roy Scheider	Franklin and Marshall
Maximilian Schell	U. of Zurich, U. of Munich
Martin Scorsese	New York U.
George C. Scott	U. of Missouri

Willard Scott	American U.
Tom Seaver	U. of Southern California
Jean Seberg	Iowa State U.
George Segal	Haverford, Columbia
Rod Serling	Antioch
Gene Shalit	U. of Illinois
Omar Sharif	Victoria College
Irwin Shaw	Brooklyn College
Ann Sheridan	North Texas State Teachers College
Brooke Shields	Princeton
Talia Shire	Yale Drama
Dinah Shore	Vanderbilt
Ron Silver	U. of Buffalo, St. John's
Frank Silvera	Northwestern Law
Carly Simon	Sarah Lawrence
Neil Simon	New York U.
Paul Simon	Queens College
O.J. Simpson	U. of Southern California
Grace Slick	Finch College
Everett Sloan	U. of Pennsylvania
Jaclyn Smith	Trinity College (Texas)
Kent Smith	Harvard
Liz Smith	U. of Texas
Tom and Dick Smothers	San José State College
Tom Snyder	Marquette
Suzanne Somers	Lone Mountain College
Stephen Sondheim	Williams
Steven Spielberg	California State College (Long Beach)
Robert Stack	U. of Southern California
Leslie Stahl	Wheaton College
Sylvester Stallone	U. of Miami
Lionel Stander	U. of North Carolina
Gloria Steinem	Smith
Craig Stevens	U. of Kansas
James Stewart	Princeton
Oliver Stone	Yale, New York U.
Peter Stone	Yale Drama
Meryl Streep	Vassar, Dartmouth, Yale Drama
Barbra Streisand	Yeshiva
Donald Sutherland	U. of Toronto
Marlo Thomas	U. of Southern California
Cheryl Tiegs	California State U. (L.A.)
Lily Tomlin	Wayne State U.
Rip Torn	Texas A & M, U. of Texas
Tom Tryon	Yale
Sonny Tufts	Yale
Tommy Tune	Lon Morris College, U. of Texas, U. of Houston
Kathleen Turner	U. of Maryland

John Updike	Harvard
Rudy Vallee	U. of Maine, Yale
Robert Vaughn	U. of Minnesota, L.A. State College, U. of Southern California
Jon Voight	Catholic U.
Mike Wallace	U. of Michigan
Eli Wallach	U. of Texas, City College of N.Y.
Barbara Walters	Sarah Lawrence
Andy Warhol	Carnegie Tech
Sam Waterston	Yale
John Wayne	U. of Southern California
Fritz Weaver	U. of Chicago
James Whitmore	Yale
Richard Widmark	Lake Forest College
Gene Wilder	U. of Iowa
Cindy Williams	L.A. City College
Robin Williams	College of Marin
Fred Williamson	Northwestern
Henry Winkler	Emerson College, Yale Drama
Jonathan Winters	Kenyon
Tom Wolfe	Washington & Lee, Yale
Joanne Woodward	Louisiana State U.
Monty Woolley	Yale, Harvard
Michael York	Oxford
Franco Zeffirelli	U. of Florence
Efrem Zimbalist, Jr.	Yale

Alumni of the American Academy of Dramatic Arts:
★ The "Harvard" of Acting Schools ★

After Harvard professor Franklin Haven Sargent's recommendation to create a drama department at Harvard was ignored, Sargent started his own drama school, the Lyceum Theatre School for Acting in New York in 1884. Now known as the American Academy of Dramatic Arts, it is the oldest school of professional dramatic training in the English-speaking world. Its alumni have been nominated for over 75 Oscars, 58 Tonys, and 92 Emmys! Here are a few of AADA's graduates:

Lauren Bacall	Eileen Brennan	Hume Cronyn
Jim Backus	Geraldine Brooks	Robert Cummings
Conrad Bain	Dale Carnegie	Cecil B. De Mille
Anne Bancroft	John Cassavetes	William Devane
Diana Barrymore	Diane Cilento	Danny De Vito

Colleen Dewhurst
Kirk Douglas
Vince Edwards
Florence Eldridge
James Farentino
Gail Fisher
Martin Gabel
Lynda Day George
Ruth Gordon
David Hartman
Florence Henderson
Judd Hirsch
Sterling Holloway
David Huddleston
Kate Jackson
Allen Jenkins
Jennifer Jones
Garson Kanin

Grace Kelly
Ron Leibman
Sam Levene
Cleavon Little
Marion Lorne
Barton MacLane
Melanie Mayron
Guthrie McClintic
Dina Merrill
Elizabeth
   Montgomery
Agnes Moorehead
Don Murray
Pat O'Brien
Tom Poston
William Powell
Robert Redford
Don Rickles

Thelma Ritter
Jason Robards, Sr.
Jason Robards, Jr.
Eric Roberts
Edward G. Robinson
Rosalind Russell
Gary Sandy
John Savage
John Saxon
Joseph Schildkraut
Ezra Stone
Renée Taylor
Spencer Tracy
Claire Trevor
Robert Walker
Peter Weller
James Whitmore, Jr.

★ Second City Graduates ★

Founded in Chicago in 1959 by Paul Sills and Bernie Sahlins, the Second City improvisational comedy troupe became a basic training base for many present-day actors and comedians. Its forerunners, the Playwrights' Theater Club and The Compass Players, included such notables as Mike Nichols, Elaine May, Edward Asner, Jerry Stiller, and Anne Meara.

Alan Alda
Jane Alexander
Alan Arkin
Ed Asner
Dan Aykroyd
Jim Belushi
John Belushi
Shelley Berman
Peter Boyle
John Candy
Severn Darden
Paul Dooley
Brian Doyle-Murray
Robin Duke

Andrew Duncan
Joe Flaherty
Mary Gross
Valerie Harper
Barbara Harris
Tim Kazurinsky
Robert Klein
Zohra Lampert
Ron Leibman
Eugene Levy
Shelley Long
Andrea Martin
Elaine May
Paul Mazursky

Anne Meara
Bill Murray
Mike Nichols
Tom O'Horgan
Gilda Radner
Harold Ramis
Joan Rivers
Paul Sand
Avery Schreiber
Martin Short
David Steinberg
Jerry Stiller
Richard Thomas
Larry Tucker

Lawyers Who Became Famous
in Other Careers

★ _____ ★

Mel Allen (sports announcer)
Charles Brackett (producer/
    screenwriter)
Rossano Brazzi (actor)
Michael Cacoyannis (movie
    director)
Hoagy Carmichael
    (songwriter)
John Cleese (comic actor)
Howard Cosell (sports
    commentator)
Erle Stanley Gardner (author)
Romain Gary (author)

Julio Iglesias (singer)
Meir Kahane (rabbi, Jewish
    Defense League founder)
Leo McCarey (movie director)
Ozzie Nelson (actor)
James Pike (clergyman)
Otto Preminger (movie
    director)
Quentin Reynolds (author)
Geraldo Rivera (TV
    personality)
Murray Schisgal (playwright)
John van Druten (playwright)

Note: Bing Crosby, George S. Kaufman, Estelle Parsons, and Cole Porter studied law but never received degrees.

Doctors Who Became Famous
in Other Careers

★ _____ ★

Michael Crichton (writer,
    movie director)
Armand Hammer
    (entrepreneur)
Somerset Maugham (author)
Jonathan Miller (director,
    writer)

Michael Myers (actor, *Good-
    bye Columbus*)
Frank Slaughter (author)
Jules Stein (MCA founder)
William Carlos Williams (poet)

Dentists Who Became Famous
in Other Careers

★ _____ ★

Edgar Buchanan (actor)
Zane Grey (author)

Allan Jones (singer)
Cary Middlecoff (golfer)

LOVE,
MARRIAGE,
AND SEX

★ Never Married ★

Edward Albee
Kay Ballard
Warren Beatty
Jacqueline Bisset
Beulah Bondi
Truman Capote
Richard Chamberlain
Wilt Chamberlain
Charley Chase
Julie Christie
Montgomery Clift
James Coco
Roy Cohn
Aaron Copland
Greta Garbo
Terri Garr
Sir John Gielgud
Lillian Gish
Sharon Gless
Virginia Grey

Halston
Edward Everett
  Horton
Tab Hunter
Anjelica Huston
Lauren Hutton
Derek Jacobi
Madeline Kahn
Diane Keaton
Swoosie Kurtz
Carl Laemmle, Jr.
Richard Lewis
Paul Lynde
Jackie Mason
Johnny Mathis
Roddy McDowall
Donna Mills
Sal Mineo
Jim Nabors
Ralph Nader

Ramon Novarro
Rudolf Nureyev
Al Pacino
Bernadette Peters
Rex Reed
Cesar Romero
Linda Ronstadt
Yves St. Laurent
Lizabeth Scott
Mack Sennett
Stephen Sondheim
Gloria Steinem
Betty Thomas
Lily Tomlin
John Travolta
Gore Vidal
Andy Warhol
Clifton Webb
Franco Zeffirelli

★ Celebrities Who Married the Greatest Number of Times ★

"Marriage is the most licentious of human institutions—that is the secret of its popularity."

George Bernard Shaw

No. of Times Married		No. of Times Married	
Tommy Manville	13	Rex Harrison	6
Lash LaRue	10	Dick Haymes	6
Cher's mother	8	DeWolf Hopper	6
Zsa Zsa Gabor	8	Larry King	6
Stan Laurel	8	Hedy Lamarr	6
Alan Jay Lerner	8	Jerry Lee Lewis	6
Marie McDonald	8	Norman Mailer	6
Mickey Rooney	8	Rue McClanahan	6
Artie Shaw	8	Jennifer O'Neill	6
Barbara Hutton	7	Martha Raye	6
Elizabeth Taylor	7	Lili St. Cyr	6
Lana Turner	7	Gloria Swanson	6
Louis Armstrong	6	Constance Bennett	5
Ingmar Bergman	6	Corinne Calvet	5
George Brent	6	Xavier Cugat	5

No. of Times Married		No. of Times Married	
Robert Cummings	5	John Loder	5
Arlene Dahl	5	John Osbourne	5
Henry Fonda	5	Richard Pryor	5
George Foreman	5	Claude Rains	5
Pauline Frederick	5	Ginger Rogers	5
Clark Gable	5	Elliot Roosevelt	5
Cary Grant	5	George C. Scott	5
Leo Gorcey	5	Roger Vadim	5
Rita Hayworth	5	Johnny Weissmuller	5
John Huston	5	Tammy Wynette	5
Betty Hutton	5	Gig Young	5
Curt Jurgens	5		

Celebrities Who Married the Same Person Twice

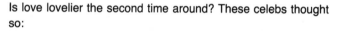

Is love lovelier the second time around? These celebs thought so:

Desi Arnaz and Lucille Ball
Milton Berle and
    Joyce Mathews
Richard Burton and Elizabeth
    Taylor
David Carradine and Gail
    Carradine
Jon Hall and Racquel Torres
Freddie Karger and
    Jane Wyman
Don Johnson and Melanie
    Griffith
Stan Laurel [eight marriages
    to four wives!]
George Metalious and Grace
    Metalious

Carroll O'Connor and Nancy
    Fields
George Peppard and
    Elizabeth Ashley
Bobby Riggs and Priscilla
    Wheelan
William Saroyan and Carol
    Saroyan
George C. Scott and Colleen
    Dewhurst
Neil Simon and Diane Lander
Dick Smothers and Linda
    Smothers
Robert Wagner and Natalie
    Wood

Short Marriages

*"I know a lot of people didn't expect our
relationship to last—but we've just celebrated
our two months' anniversary."*
Britt Ekland

	Length of Time Married
Tommy Manville and Sunny Ainsworth	1 day
Rudolph Valentino and Jean Acker	1 day
Buck Owens and Jana Grief	2 days
Dennis Hopper and Michelle Phillips	8 days
Patty Duke and Michael Tell	13 days
Germaine Greer and Paul De Feu	3 weeks
Katharine Hepburn and Ludlow Ogden Smith	3 weeks
Carole Landis and Irving Wheeler	3 weeks
Ethel Merman and Ernest Borgnine	3 weeks
Gig Young and Kim Schmidt	3 weeks
Gloria Swanson and Wallace Beery	3 weeks
Debra Paget and Budd Boetticher	22 days
Leif Erickson and Maggie Hayes	1 month
Burt Lancaster and June Ernst	1 month
Sammy Davis, Jr. and Loray White	2 months
Carole Landis and Willis Hunt, Jr.	2 months
Porfirio Rubirosa and Barbara Hutton	11 weeks
Loni Anderson and first husband	3 months
Michael Bennett and Donna McKechnie	3 months
James Caan and Sheila Ryan	3 months
Diahann Carroll and Freddie Glusman	3 months
Richard Pryor and Flynn Belaise	4 months
James Woods and Sarah Owen	4 months
Ava Gardner and Artie Shaw	7 months
Emmylou Harris and Paul Kennerly	1 year
Barry and Susan Manilow	1 year
Elaine May and Sheldon Harnick	1 year
Joni and Chuck Mitchell	1 year
Dinah Shore and Maurice Smith	1 year
Suzanne and Bruce Somers	1 year
Loretta Young and Grant Withers	1 year
Ava Gardner and Mickey Rooney	16 months
Marisa Berenson and Jim Randall	18 months
Angela Lansbury and Richard Cromwell	18 months
Rosanna Arquette and James Newton Howard	20 months
Victoria Jackson and Christopher Skinner	20 months
Redd Foxx and Yun Chi Chung	2 years
Kate Jackson and David Greenwald	2 years
Dudley Moore and Suzy Kendall	2 years

	Length of Time Married
Nick Nolte and Becky Linger	2 years
Gilda Radner and G.E. Smith	2 years
Jason Robards, Jr. and Rachel Taylor	2 years
Paul Simon and Carrie Fisher	2 years
Jaclyn Smith and Dennis Cole	2 years

★ Long Show-Biz Marriages ★

	Year(s) Married
James and "Bill" Cagney	1922–86
Alfred and Alma Hitchcock	1926–80
George Burns and Gracie Allen	1926–64
Henny and Sadie Youngman	1928
Ray and Gwendolyn Bolger	1929–87
Lawrence and Fern Welk	1930
Gene and Ina Mae Autry	1932
Joel McCrea and Francis Dee	1933–89
Perry and Roselle Como	1933
Robert and Betty Young	1933
Bob and Dolores Hope	1934
Danny and Rose Marie Thomas	1936
Karl and Mona Malden	1938
Lloyd and Dorothy Bridges	1939
Harry and Eileen Morgan	1939
Danny Kaye and Sylvia Fine	1940–87
Robert and Dorothy Mitchum	1940
Paul and Lynne Harvey	1940
Robert and Catherine Preston	1940
Tony and Florence Randall	1941
Richard and Ora Jane Widmark	1942
Hume Cronyn and Jessica Tandy	1942
Ruth Gordon and Garson Kanin	1942–85
Mike and Genevieve Douglas	1943
Sid and Florence Caesar	1943
Federico Fellini and Giulietta Masina	1943
John and Julie Forsythe	1943
Carl and Estelle Reiner	1943
Hugh and Ruth Downs	1944
Charlton and Lydia Heston	1944
Gene and Betty Barry	1944
Conrad and Monica Bain	1945
Dennis and Geraldine Weaver	1945
Eddie and Margo Albert	1945
George and Helen Segal	1946
Alan and Jeannette King	1947
Henry and Virginia Mancini	1947
Ralph and Alice Bellamy	1949

	Year(s) Married
James and Gloria Stewart	1949
Angela Lansbury and Peter Shaw	1949
Jimmy and Mary Dean	1950
George Roy and Helen Hill	1951
Carroll and Nancy O'Connor	1951
Ronald and Nancy Reagan	1952
Victor and Sarabel Borge	1953
Larry and Maj Hagman	1954
Leonard and Sandi Nimoy	1954
Kirk and Anne Douglas	1954
Anne Meara and Jerry Stiller	1954
Gregory and Veronique Peck	1955
Robert and Rosemarie Stack	1956
James and Lois Garner	1956
Carol Channing and Charles Lowe	1956
Alan and Arlene Alda	1957
Steve Lawrence and Eydie Gormé	1957
Paul Newman and Joanne Woodward	1958
Hal and Frances Linden	1958
Joel and Jo Grey	1958
Sydney and Claire Pollack	1958
Bert and Monica Convy	1959
Edward and Nancy Lou Asner	1959
Walter and Carol Matthau	1959
Helen Gurley Brown and David Brown	1959
Laurence Olivier and Joan Plowright	1960–89
Gene and Jeanne Kelly	1960
Telly and Katherine Savalas	1960
Martin and Janet Sheen	1961
Jack Lemmon and Felicia Farr	1962
Bob and Virginia Newhart	1963
Paul and Anne Anka	1963
Mel Brooks and Anne Bancroft	1964
Dom and Carol DeLuise	1965
Anthony and Iolanda Quinn	1966

HONORABLE MENTION: Jerry and Patti Lewis were divorced in 1980 after 36 years of marriage.

★ Famous Homosexual Men ★

Horatio Alger	Montgomery Clift
Hans Christian Andersen	Jean Cocteau
W.H. Auden	Roy Cohn
Brendan Behan	Noël Coward
Malcolm Boyd	Leonardo Da Vinci
Truman Capote	Harvey Fierstein

E.M. Forster
Jean Genet
André Gide
Allen Ginsberg
Halston
Dag Hammarskjöld
Keith Haring
Lorenz Hart
Rock Hudson
Christopher Isherwood
John Maynard Keynes
Charles Laughton
T.E. Lawrence ("Lawrence of
    Arabia")
Liberace
Paul Lynde
Robert Mapplethorpe
Christopher Marlowe

Merle Miller
John Milton
Vaslav Nijinsky
Ramon Novarro
Pier Paolo Pasolini
Cole Porter
Marcel Proust
Arthur Rimbaud
Algernon Swinburne
Peter Ilyich Tchaikovsky
Bill Tilden
Paul Verlaine
Andy Warhol
Clifton Webb
Walt Whitman
Oscar Wilde
Tennessee Williams
Ludwig Wittgenstein

★ # Famous Lesbians ★

Willa Cather
Janis Joplin
Kate Millet
Victoria Sackville-West
Sappho

Bessie Smith
Gertrude Stein
Alice B. Toklas
Virginia Woolf

Sex Quotations:
★ # What the Famous Have Said ★

Woody Allen. "I'm a practicing heterosexual, but bisexuality immediately doubles your chances for a date on a Saturday night."

Tallulah Bankhead. "I've tried several varieties of sex. The conventional position makes me claustrophobic and the others give me a stiff neck or lockjaw."

Anita Bryant. "I don't hate homosexuals. I love homosexuals. It's the sin of homosexuality I hate."

Yul Brynner. "Girls have an unfair advantage over men: if they can't get what they want by being smart, they can get it by being dumb."

Truman Capote. "The good thing about masturbation is that you don't have to dress up for it."

Johnny Carson. "When turkeys mate they think of swans."

James E. "Jimmy" Carter. "I've looked on a lot of women with lust. I've committed adultery in my heart many times. . . . Christ says, don't consider yourself better than someone else because one guy screws a whole bunch of women while the other guy is loyal to his wife."

Cher. "My rule of thumb, and it's never failed me, is if a man's a good kisser, he's a great f***er."

Quentin Crisp. "For flavor, instant sex will never supercede the stuff you have to peel and cook."

Rodney Dangerfield. "If it weren't for pickpockets I'd have no sex life at all."

Harvey Fierstein. "I've been in love with 100 men and slept with a few thousand. Now [1983] I look upon that as promiscuous and very stupid."

Zsa Zsa Gabor. "It's never easy keeping your husband happy. It's much easier to make someone else's husband happy."

Cary Grant. "The best exercise I know of is making love."

Xaviera Hollander. "My method is basically the same as Masters and Johnson, only they charge thousands of dollars and it's called therapy. I charge fifty dollars and it's called prostitution."

Mick Jagger. "All dancing is a replacement for sex."

Alfred Kinsey. "The only unnatural sex act is that which you cannot perform."

Sophia Loren. "Sex appeal is 50 percent what you've got and 50 percent what people think you've got."

Norman Mailer. "A little bit of rape is good for a man's soul."

Marcello Mastroianni. "Once they call you a 'Latin Lover,' you're in real trouble. Women expect an Oscar performance in bed."

Walter Matthau. "The first girl you go to bed with is always pretty."

Henry Miller. "To enter life by way of the vagina is as good a way as any."

Desmond Morris. "Sex is one of the great pleasures of life. I think sex is lovely, just as I enjoy eating, drinking and sleeping. I am against all inhibitions and taboos about them."

Peter O'Toole. "The nicest asses in the world [are in] Ireland. Irish women still are carrying water on their heads and carrying their husbands home from pubs and such things are the greatest posture builders in the world."

Roman Polanski. "First comes my love of my work but secondary to the creation itself is the need to get laid."

Leontyne Price. "A healthy sex life—best thing in the world for a woman's voice."

Ayn Rand. "A man's sexual choice is the result and sum of his fundamental convictions. Tell me what a man finds sexually attractive and I will tell you his entire philosophy of life."

Harold Robbins. "I personally guarantee my readers that everything that has ever been done [sexually] in my books, I have done. The amazing thing is, very few people believe me."

Sophocles. "The eyes of men love to pluck the blossoms— from the faded flowers they turn away."

Gloria Steinem. "A woman reading Playboy feels a little like a Jew reading a Nazi manual."

Lily Tomlin. "There will be sex after death—we just won't be able to feel it."

Andy Warhol. "Sex is the biggest nothing of our time."

PHYSICAL
ATTRIBUTES

Famous People Who
Have Had Plastic Surgery

★ ★

Loni Anderson	Breast reduction
Ursula Andress	Breast reduction
Paul Anka	Nose job, hair transplant
Bea Arthur	Face-lift
Jean-Pierre Aumont	Face-lift
Lauren Bacall	Face-lift
Tammy Faye Bakker	Breast enlargement
Lucille Ball	Face-lift
Rona Barrett	Nose job
Milton Berle	Nose job
Fanny Brice	Nose job
Dyan Cannon	Face-lift
Truman Capote	Face-lift
Rosalyn Carter	Eyelid lift
Cher	All of the above and below!
Montgomery Clift	Facial reconstruction after accident
Gary Cooper	Face-lift
Bud Cort	Facial reconstruction after accident
Joan Crawford	Face-lift
Vic Damone	Nose job
Bette Davis	Jaw reconstruction, face-lift
Bo Derek	Breast enlargement, nose job
Marlene Dietrich	Face-lift
Phyllis Diller	All of the above and below!
Kirk Douglas	Face-lift
Hugh Downs	Hair transplant
Barbara Eden	Nose job
Nanette Fabray	Nose enlargement
Morgan Fairchild	Breast enlargement
Rhonda Fleming	Nose job
Henry Fonda	Face-lift
Jane Fonda	Eyelid lift, breast enlargement
Betty Ford	Face-lift
Connie Francis	Nose job
Annette Funicello	Nose job
Eva Gabor	Nose job
Zsa Zsa Gabor	Nose job
Mitzi Gaynor	Nose job
David Geffen	Nose job
Jackie Gleason	Face-lift
Lee Grant	Nose job

Juliette Greco	Nose job
Jennifer Grey	Nose job
Joel Grey	Nose job
Melanie Griffith	Breast enlargement
Joan Hackett	Nose job
Jessica Hahn	Breast enlargement
Mark Hamill	Facial reconstruction after accident
George Hamilton	Nose job
Rita Hayworth	Face-lift
Mariel Hemingway	Breast enlargement
Rock Hudson	Eyelid lift
Iman	Breast enlargement
Janet Jackson	Breast enlargement, facial work
Latoya Jackson	Nose job
Michael Jackson	Face-lift, nose job, etc.— the "works"!
Elton John	Hair transplant
Al Jolson	Nose job
Carolyn Jones	Nose job
Michael Keaton	Hair transplant
Alan King	Nose job
Cheryl Ladd	Nose job
Carole Landis	Nose job
Michael Landon	Ears pinned back
Liberace	Face-lifts
Carole Lombard	Facial reconstruction
Dean Martin	Face-lift, nose job
Melanie Mayron	Nose job, facial reconstruction
Maureen McGovern	Nose job
Cameron Mitchell	Nose job
Marilyn Monroe	Nose job
Rita Moreno	Nose job
Brigitte Nielsen	Breast enlargement
Merle Oberon	Facial reconstruction after accident
Jackie Onassis	Face-lift
Christina Onassis	Nose job
Peter O'Toole	Nose job
Jack Palance	Facial reconstruction after accident
Dolly Parton	Breast reshaping
Mary Pickford	Face-lift
Suzanne Pleshette	Nose job
Elvis Presley	Face-lift, eyelid lift
Juliet Prowse	Breast enlargement, face-lift
Robin Quivers	Breast reduction
George Raft	Ears pinned back

Debbie Reynolds	Face-lift
Joan Rivers	Face-lift, nose job, breast enlargement
Jason Robards, Jr.	Facial reconstruction after accident
Edward G. Robinson	Facial reconstruction after accident
Diana Ross	Nose job
Vidal Sassoon	Face-lift
Jessica Savitch	Nose job
Talia Shire	Nose job
Dinah Shore	Nose job
Frank Sinatra	Face-lift, hair transplant
Nancy Sinatra	Nose job
Liz Smith	Face-lift
Sissy Spacek	Nose job
Barbara Stanwyck	Face-lift
Jan Sterling	Nose job
Jill St. John	Nose job
Rod Stewart	Nose job
Sting	Nose job
Elizabeth Taylor	Face-lift
Marlo Thomas	Nose job
Lana Turner	Face-lift
Bobby Van	Nose job
Vera-Ellen	Nose job
Barbara Walters	Face-lift
Raquel Welch	"Most of the above"
Marie Wilson	Nose job
Dana Wynter	Nose job
Jackie Zeman	Breast enlargement

Famous People Who
★ **Have Not Had Nose Jobs** ★

If there were an award for those stalwart celebrities who achieved fame in spite of their schnozzolas, here are some world-class winners:

Tony Bennett	Judd Hirsch	Barbra Streisand
Jimmy Durante	Dustin Hoffman	Danny Thomas
Jamie Farr	Karl Malden	

Tattoos were formerly only for drunken sailors and marines, but are now chic in celebrity circles. Here are a few of the celebrities who have tattoos, not all of which are in good taste or readily visible:

Celebrity	Description and Location of Tattoo(s)
Gregg Allman	A coyote on his forearm
Kenneth Anger	The name "Lucifer" on his chest
Joan Baez	A flower on the small of her back
Pearl Bailey	A heart on her thigh
Roseanne Barr	The name "Tom" on her derrière. (Her husband, Tom Arnold, has "Rosie" on his derrière and her portrait on the left side of his chest!)
Orson Bean	A rose on his wrist
Glen Campbell	A dagger on his arm
Cher	A flower design (Japanese chrysanthemum) on her derrière; a flower near her left ankle; also has designs on her lower abdomen and arms.
Sean Connery	"Mum & Dad" and "Scotland Forever" on his forearm
Tony Danza	The words "Keep on Truckin' " and a cartoon of a man on his right shoulder
Johnny Depp	"Winona Forever" (his girlfriend, actress Winona Ryder) on his right shoulder; an Indian chief (he's part Cherokee) just below; his mother's name, "Betty Sue," on his left arm above the bicep
Marianne Faithfull	A swallow on her right thumb
Peter Fonda	Dolphins on one of his shoulders; three stars on his inner forearm
Whoopi Goldberg	A Charles Schulz Woodstock (cartoon bird) on her left breast
Barry Goldwater	Four dots and a half circle on his left hand (worn by the Smoki people, a non-Indian group in Prescott, Arizona—he is an honorary chief)
Charles Gordone	Flowers on his shoulder
Melanie Griffith	A tiny yellow pear on her left buttock
Daryl Hall	A seven-pointed star on his shoulder
Janis Joplin	A heart on one of her breasts; a filigree bracelet around her wrist
Lorenzo Lamas	A Harley Davidson emblem on his right shoulder
John Cougar Mellencamp	A woman with long, dark hair on his right shoulder

Celebrity	Description and Location of Tattoo(s)
Robert Mitchum	An obscene word on his arm
Ozzy Osbourne	Lots of tattoos!
Sean Penn	The name "Madonna" on his right arm
Anita Pointer	A flower on her wrist
Michael J. Pollard	A heart with a girl's name on his shoulder
Kirby Puckett	The name "Kirby" on his arm
Oliver Reed	An unusual tattoo on his private parts!
George Shultz	A Princeton tiger on his derrière
Gene Simmons	A rose on his arm
Ringo Starr	A half-moon and shooting star on his arm
Lee Trevino	The name "Ann" on his right forearm
Mike Tyson	The name "Mike" on his right bicep
Flip Wilson	A winged number "13" and a cross on his upper forearm

Famous Men Who Wear Toupees or Have Had Hair Transplants

★ ★

Brian Aherne
Steve Allen
Paul Anka
  (transplant)
Fred Astaire
Tony Bennett
Jack Benny
Humphrey Bogart
Charles Boyer
Lee J. Cobb
Sean Connery
Gary Cooper
Howard Cosell
Bing Crosby
Brian Donleavy
Hugh Downs
  (transplant)

Henry Fonda
Rex Harrison
Paul Harvey
Van Heflin
Charlton Heston
Elton John
  (transplant)
Gene Kelly
Fred MacMurray
Fredric March
Ray Milland
Robert Montgomery
David Niven
Laurence Olivier
Jack Paar
George Raft
Charles Nelson Reilly

Carl Reiner
Rob Reiner
Burt Reynolds
Peter Sellers
Richard Simmons
  (transplant)
Paul Simon
Frank Sinatra
  (transplant)
Rod Steiger
James Stewart
Franchot Tone
Andy Warhol
John Wayne

Celebrity Lefties

★ ★

Eddie Albert
June Allyson
Earl Anthony
Dan Aykroyd
F. Lee Bailey
Robert Blake
Bill Bradley

Lenny Bruce
McGeorge Bundy
Carol Burnett
George Burns
George Bush
Ruth Buzzi
Sid Caesar

Vicki Carr
Jack Carter
Peggy Cass
Charlie Chaplin
Prince Charles
Natalie Cole
Chuck Connors

Angel Cordero
Olivia De Havilland
Albert De Salvo
John Dillinger
Robert Dole
Richard Dreyfuss
Bob Dylan
Albert Einstein
Queen Elizabeth
W.C. Fields
Peter Fonda
Gerald Ford
Henry Ford II
Allen Funt
Judy Garland
Errol Garner
Euell Gibbons
Paul Michael Glaser
George Gobel
Betty Grable
Cary Grant
Peter Graves
Dorothy Hamill
Rex Harrison
Goldie Hawn
Isaac Hayes
Joey Heatherton
Jimi Hendrix
Ben Hogan*
    (played righty)
Rock Hudson
Daniel Inouye
Kate Jackson

Bruce Jenner
Hamilton Jordan
Gabe Kaplan
Danny Kaye
Caroline Kennedy
Graham Kerr
Phyllis Kirk
Michael Landon
Hope Lange
Peter Lawford
Cloris Leachman
Hal Linden
Cleavon Little
Paul McCartney
Robert McNamara
Kristy McNichol
Steve McQueen
Marcel Marceau
Harpo Marx
Marsha Mason
Bill Mauldin
Anne Meara
James Michener
Ray Milland
Johnny Miller*
    (plays righty)
Marilyn Monroe
Robert Morse
Edward R. Murrow
LeRoy Neiman
Anthony Newley
Kim Novak
Ryan O'Neal

Estelle Parsons
Pelé
Pablo Picasso
Cole Porter
Robert Preston
Richard Pryor
Robert Redford
Don Rickles
Nelson Rockefeller
Bobby Rydell
Eva Marie Saint
Wally Schirra
Jean Seberg
Dick Smothers
Mark Spitz
Ringo Starr
Rod Steiger
Casey Stengel
Terry Thomas
Tiny Tim
Rip Torn
Brenda Vaccaro
Karen Valentine
Rudy Vallee
Dick Van Dyke
John Weitz
Jessamyn West
James Whitmore
Paul Williams
Joanne Woodward
Keenan Wynn

*Played golf righty.

★ Heavyweights ★

Fatty Arbuckle
Roseanne Barr
James Beard
Brendan Behan
Marlon Brando
    (on occasion!)
Victor Buono
Raymond Burr
John Candy

Dom De Luise
King Farouk
Billy Gilbert
Jackie Gleason
John Goodman
Sydney Greenstreet
Oliver Hardy
Al Hirt
Burl Ives

Herman Kahn
Zero Mostel
Paul Prudhomme
Walter Slezak
William Taft
Fats Waller
Orson Welles
Paul Whiteman

Celebrities with Physical Ailments or Disabilities

★ _____ ★

Kaye Ballard	Deaf in one ear
Walter Brennan	No teeth
Truman Capote	Lisp
Richard Condon	Stutter
Hume Cronyn	Blind in one eye
Bing Crosby	Colorblind
Marion Davies	Stutter
Sammy Davis, Jr.	Blind in one eye
Sandy Duncan	Blind in one eye
Deanna Durbin	Withered arm
Peter Falk	Blind in one eye
John Ford	Blind in one eye
Rex Harrison	Blind in one eye
James Earl Jones	Once had a stutter
Madeline Kahn	Lisp
Stacy Keach	Harelip
Alan Jay Lerner	Blind in one eye
Harold Lloyd	Missing two fingers on right hand
Marilyn Monroe	Stammer
Dudley Moore	Clubfoot
Paul Newman	Colorblind
Jack Nicklaus	Colorblind
Jack Paar	Stammer, once had a stutter
Charles Nelson Reilly	Lisp
Fred ("Mr.") Rogers	Colorblind
Ned Rorem	Lisp
Harold Russell	Missing both hands
Norma Shearer	Cross-eyed
James Stewart	An engaging stammer
Mel Tillis	Stutter
Raoul Walsh	Blind in one eye
Barbara Walters	Lisp, mispronounces Rs and over-pronounces Gs

★ # Heights of Famous Women ★

_____

	Height		Height
Julia Child	6′2″	Susan Anton	5′11½″
Geena Davis	6′	Jerry Hall	5′11″
Dian Fossey	6′	Vanessa Redgrave	5′11″
Margaux Hemingway	6′	Carly Simon	5′11″
Brigitte Nielsen	6′	Toni Tennille	5′11″
Brooke Shields	6′	Bea Arthur	5′10″

	Height		Height
Princess Diana	5'10"	Joanne Woodward	5'7"
Cheryl Tiegs	5'10"	Tammy Wynette	5'7"
Anjelica Huston	5'9½"	Ellen Burstyn	5'6½"
Kate Jackson	5'9½"	Diana Lynn	5'6½"
Lauren Bacall	5'9"	Shirley MacLaine	5'6½"
Marisa Berenson	5'9"	Anne Murray	5'6½"
Candice Bergen	5'9"	Jane Alexander	5'6"
Christy Brinkley	5'9"	Elizabeth Ashley	5'6"
Natalie Cole	5'9"	Lucille Ball	5'6"
Faye Dunaway	5'9"	Theda Bara	5'6"
Angela Lansbury	5'9"	Diahann Carroll	5'6"
Ali MacGraw	5'9"	Joan Collins	5'6"
Diane Sawyer	5'9"	Doris Day	5'6"
Lily Tomlin	5'9"	Farrah Fawcett	5'6"
Carol Channing	5'8½"	Crystal Gayle	5'6"
Cher	5'8½"	Lillian Gish	5'6"
Jill Clayburgh	5'8½"	Goldie Hawn	5'6"
Sophia Loren	5'8½"	Glenda Jackson	5'6"
Gloria Steinem	5'8¼"	Billy Jean King	5'6"
Anne Bancroft	5'8"	Penny Marshall	5'6"
Rita Coolidge	5'8"	Sandra Day	
Linda Evans	5'8"	O'Connor	5'6"
Ella Fitzgerald	5'8"	Victoria Principal	5'6"
Greta Garbo	5'8"	Gilda Radner	5'6"
Phyllis George	5'8"	Susan Sarandon	5'6"
Lauren Hutton	5'8"	Elizabeth Taylor	5'6"
Cybill Shepherd	5'8"	Twiggy	5'6"
Jean Stapleton	5'7¾"	Leslie Uggams	5'6"
Jessica Lange	5'7½"	Racquel Welch	5'6"
Julie Andrews	5'7"	Vanessa Williams	5'6"
Jacqueline Bisset	5'7"	Jane Wyman	5'6"
Carol Burnett	5'7"	Marilyn Monroe	5'5½"
Princess Caroline	5'7"	Moira Shearer	5'5½"
Julie Christie	5'7"	Suzanne Somers	5'5½"
Jane Fonda	5'7"	Abigail Van Buren	5'5½"
Aretha Franklin	5'7"	Kaye Ballard	5'5"
Audrey Hepburn	5'7"	Joan Caulfield	5'5"
Madeline Kahn	5'7"	Sandy Dennis	5'5"
Diane Keaton	5'7"	Angie Dickinson	5'5"
Ruby Keeler	5'7"	Marlene Dietrich	5'5"
Jacqueline Kennedy	5'7"	Chris Evert	5'5"
Cloris Leachman	5'7"	Lola Folana	5'5"
Peggy Lee	5'7"	Tammy Grimes	5'5"
Melina Mercouri	5'7"	Lena Horne	5'5"
Rosalind Russell	5'7"	Dorothy Lamour	5'5"
Grace Slick	5'7"	Marjorie Main	5'5"
Donna Summer	5'7"	Sarah Miles	5'5"
Meryl Streep	5'7"	Olivia Newton-John	5'5"
Gene Tierney	5'7"	Ginger Rogers	5'5"

	Height		Height
Jessica Savitch	5′5″	Imogene Coca	5′3″
Lizabeth Scott	5′5″	Bette Davis	5′3″
Dinah Shore	5′5″	Bo Derek	5′3″
Marlo Thomas	5′5″	Alice Faye	5′3″
Ann-Margret	5′4¾″	Judy Garland	5′3″
Jeanne Crain	5′4½″	Dorothy Hamill	5′3″
Tatum O'Neal	5′4½″	Deborah Harry	5′3″
Diana Ross	5′4½″	Miriam Hopkins	5′3″
Barbra Streisand	5′4½″	Cyndi Lauper	5′3″
Brigitte Bardot	5′4″	Bernadette Peters	5′3″
Debby Boone	5′4″	Diane Von	
Anita Bryant	5′4″	Fürstenberg	5′3″
Claudette Colbert	5′4″	Loretta Young	5′3″
Linda Darnell	5′4″	Carole Lombard	5′2½″
Catherine Deneuve	5′4″	Paula Abdul	5′2″
Phyllis Diller	5′4″	Debbie Allen	5′2″
Mia Farrow	5′4″	Linda Blair	5′2″
Roberta Flack	5′4″	Sally Field	5′2″
Paulette Goddard	5′4″	Eva Gabor	5′2″
Eydie Gormé	5′4″	Sonja Henie	5′2″
Lee Grant	5′4″	Veronica Lake	5′2″
Valerie Harper	5′4″	Carmen Miranda	5′2″
Florence Henderson	5′4″	Priscilla Presley	5′2″
Katharine Hepburn	5′4″	Joan Rivers	5′2″
Betty Hutton	5′4″	Linda Ronstadt	5′2″
Gladys Knight	5′4″	Natalie Wood	5′2″
Cheryl Ladd	5′4″	Connie Francis	5′1½″
Madonna	5′4″	Sally Struthers	5′1½″
Melissa Manchester	5′4″	Petula Clark	5′1″
Liza Minnelli	5′4″	Ruby Dee	5′1″
Yoko Ono	5′4″	Sheena Easton	5′1″
Patti Page	5′4″	Carrie Fisher	5′1″
Lilli Palmer	5′4″	Bette Midler	5′1″
Nancy Reagan	5′4″	Debbie Reynolds	5′1″
Lee Remick	5′4″	Geraldine Chaplin	5′1″
Romy Schneider	5′4″	Patty Duke	5′
Sylvia Sidney	5′4″	Janet Gaynor	5′
Maggie Smith	5′4″	Margaret Hamilton	5′
Tina Turner	5′4″	Helen Hayes	5′
Barbara Walters	5′4″	Dolly Parton	5′
Mae West	5′4″	Molly Picon	5′
Cindy Williams	5′4″	Pia Zadora	5′
Debra Winger	5′4″	Estelle Getty	4′11″
Shelley Winters	5′4″	Gloria Swanson	4′11″
Shirley Temple Black	5′3½″	Charlene Tilton	4′11″
Clara Bow	5′3½″	Nancy Walker	4′11″
Peggy Fleming	5′3½″	Linda Hunt	4′9″
Betty Grable	5′3½″	Ruth Westheimer	4′7″
Erma Bombeck	5′3″		

Heights of Famous Men

Name	Height
Kareem Abdul-Jabbar	7′3″
Richard "Jaws" Kiel	7′2″
Michael Crichton	6′9″
Richard Moll	6′8″
James Arness	6′6″
Tommy Tune	6′6″
Abe Vigoda	6′6″
Lowell Weicker	6′6″
Bill Bradley	6′5″
Fred Gwynne	6′5″
David Hartman	6′5″
Sterling Hayden	6′5″
Ken Howard	6′5″
Bowie Kuhn	6′5″
Howard Stern	6′5″
Idi Amin	6′4″
Chevy Chase	6′4″
Clint Eastwood	6′4″
John Gavin	6′4″
Jeff Goldblum	6′4″
Lou Gossett	6′4″
Garrison Keillor	6′4″
Harvey Korman	6′4″
Kenny Loggins	6′4″
Ed McMahon	6′4″
Ralph Nader	6′4″
Gregory Peck	6′4″
George Plimpton	6′4″
Christopher Reeve	6′4″
Robert Ryan	6′4″
Tom Selleck	6′4″
Tom Snyder	6′4″
Donald Sutherland	6′4″
John Wayne	6′4″
Orson Welles	6′3½″
Danny Aiello	6′3″
Muhammad Ali	6′3″
James Beard	6′3″
Gary Cooper	6′3″
Jimmy Dean	6′3″
James Dickey	6′3″
Michael Eisner	6′3″
John Frankenheimer	6′3″
James Garner	6′3″
Elliot Gould	6′3″
Charlton Heston	6′3″
Rock Hudson	6′3″
Stephen King	6′3″
John V. Lindsay	6′3″
Barry Manilow	6′3″
Victor McLaglen	6′3″
Peter O'Toole	6′3″
Vincent Price	6′3″
Michael Redgrave	6′3″
George Sanders	6′3″
Willard Scott	6′3″
MacLean Stevenson	6′3″
James Stewart	6′3″
James Taylor	6′3″
Fritz Weaver	6′3″
Steve Allen	6′2½″
Howard Cosell	6′2½″
Lee Marvin	6′2½″
Victor Mature	6′2½″
Spiro Agnew	6′2″
Alan Alda	6′2″
Cleveland Amory	6′2″
Richard Boone	6′2″
David Brenner	6′2″
Jeff Bridges	6′2″
David Brinkley	6′2″
Michael Caine	6′2″
Louis Calhern	6′2″
Johnny Cash	6′2″
James Coburn	6′2″
Sean Connery	6′2″
Bruce Dern	6′2″
Melvyn Douglas	6′2″
Vince Edwards	6′2″
Peter Fonda	6′2″
Bob Geldof	6′2″
Rev. Billy Graham	6′2″
Gene Hackman	6′2″
Marvin Hamlisch	6′2″
William Hurt	6′2″
Jesse Jackson	6′2″
Michael Jackson	6′2″
Edward Kennedy	6′2″
Burt Lancaster	6′2″
Lee Majors	6′2″
Walter Matthau	6′2″

	Height		Height
Roger Moore	6'2"	Ronald Reagan	6'1"
Jim Nabors	6'2"	George Segal	6'1"
Joe Namath	6'2"	O.J. Simpson	6'1"
Wayne Newton	6'2"	Dick Van Dyke	6'1"
Sidney Poitier	6'2"	Jon Voight	6'1"
Freddie Prinze	6'2"	Herb Alpert	6'
Arnold		Don Ameche	6'
Schwarzenegger	6'2"	Eddy Arnold	6'
Henny Youngman	6'2"	Burt Bacharach	6'
Ralph Bellamy	6'1½"	Jean-Paul Belmondo	6'
Daniel Day-Lewis	6'1½"	Bill Blass	6'
Patrick Duffy	6'1½"	Pat Boone	6'
Lorne Greene	6'1½"	Sid Caesar	6'
Neil Simon	6'1½"	Glen Campbell	6'
Anthony Perkins	6'1½"	David Carradine	6'
Famous Amos	6'1"	John Chancellor	6'
Arthur Ashe	6'1"	Ray Charles	6'
Dan Aykroyd	6'1"	Roy Clark	6'
Warren Beatty	6'1"	Bill Cosby	6'
William F. Buckley,		Walter Cronkite	6'
Jr.	6'1"	Phil Donahue	6'
Keith Carradine	6'1"	Sam Donaldson	6'
Richard Chamberlain	6'1"	Kirk Douglas	6'
Bill Cosby	6'1"	Keir Dullea	6'
Kevin Costner	6'1"	Robert Duvall	6'
Neil Diamond	6'1"	Federico Fellini	6'
Errol Flynn	6'1"	Albert Finney	6'
Henry Fonda	6'1"	John Forsythe	6'
Harrison Ford	6'1"	David Frost	6'
Clark Gable	6'1"	Boy George	6'
Art Garfunkel	6'1"	Robert Goulet	6'
Cary Grant	6'1"	Arlo Guthrie	6'
Charles Grodin	6'1"	Richard Harris	6'
Halston	6'1"	Pat Hingle	6'
Rex Harrison	6'1"	Pope John Paul	6'
Jim Henson	6'1"	Tom Jones	6'
Engelbert		Danny Kaye	6'
Humperdinck	6'1"	Stacy Keach	6'
Lee Iacocca	6'1"	Kevin Kline	6'
Julio Iglesias	6'1"	David Letterman	6'
Timothy Hutton	6'1"	Jerry Lewis	6'
Waylon Jennings	6'1"	Liberace	6'
James Earl Jones	6'1"	Hal Linden	6'
Robert Mitchum	6'1"	Rich Little	6'
Graham Nash	6'1"	Fred MacMurray	6'
Edwin Newman	6'1"	Dean Martin	6'
Mike Nichols	6'1"	Lee Marvin	6'
Ryan O'Neal	6'1"	Bill Murray	6'
Basil Rathbone	6'1"	Nick Nolte	6'

	Height		Height
George Peppard	6′	Ingmar Bergman	5′10½″
Tyrone Power	6′	James Caan	5′10½″
Richard Pryor	6′	Alex Haley	5′10½″
Dan Rather	6′	Henry Kissinger	5′10½″
Ralph Richardson	6′	Steve Miller	5′10½″
Lionel Richie	6′	Laurence Olivier	5′10½″
John Ritter	6′	Steven Spielberg	5′10½″
Yves Saint Laurent	6′	Spencer Tracy	5′10½″
Telly Savalas	6′	Tony Bennett	5′10″
Maximilian Schell	6′	Robby Benson	5′10″
Paul Scofield	6′	Frank Borman	5′10″
George C. Scott	6′	Marlon Brando	5′10″
Gene Shalit	6′	Maurice Chevalier	5′10″
Daniel J. Travanti	6′	Eric Clapton	5′10″
John Travolta	6′	Alice Cooper	5′10″
Gore Vidal	6′	Albert Finney	5′10″
Robert Wagner	6′	Alec Guinness	5′10″
Tom Wolfe	6′	Gregory Hines	5′10″
Stevie Wonder	6′	Bob Hope	5′10″
Michael York	6′	Mel Gibson	5′10″
Robert Young	6′	Merv Griffin	5′10″
Peter Ustinov	5′11½″	Ron Howard	5′10″
Alan Bates	5′11″	Mick Jagger	5′10″
Orson Bean	5′11″	Louis Jourdan	5′10″
Charles Bronson	5′11″	Gene Kelly	5′10″
Prince Charles	5′11″	Jack Klugman	5′10″
Mike Douglas	5′11″	Ted Knight	5′10″
Johnny Carson	5′11″	Jack Lemmon	5′10″
David Frost	5′11″	Steve McQueen	5′10″
Ben Gazzara	5′11″	Roger Miller	5′10″
Arsenio Hall	5′11″	Eddie Murphy	5′10″
George Hamilton	5′11″	Rudolf Nureyev	5′10″
Don Johnson	5′11″	Carroll O'Connor	5′10″
Kris Kristofferson	5′11″	Anthony Quinn	5′10″
Michael Landon	5′11″	Robert Redford	5′10″
E.G. Marshall	5′11″	Rex Reed	5′10″
Johnny Mathis	5′11″	Roy Rogers	5′10″
Rod McKuen	5′11″	Sylvester Stallone	5′10″
Ricardo Montalban	5′11″	Rod Steiger	5′10″
George Murphy	5′11″	Robert Vaughn	5′10″
Randy Newman	5′11″	Mike Wallace	5′10″
Burt Reynolds	5′11″	Jonathan Winters	5′10″
Cliff Robertson	5′11″	Joey Bishop	5′9½″
Omar Sharif	5′11″	David Bowie	5′9½″
Robert Shaw	5′11″	John Denver	5′9½″
Lewis Stone	5′11″	Michael Douglas	5′9½″
Mr. T	5′11″	Steve Martin	5′9½″
Ted Turner	5′11″	Bruce Springsteen	5′9½″
Richard Widmark	5′11″	Edward Asner	5′9″

	Height		Height
Fred Astaire	5'9"	Humphrey Bogart	5'7"
F. Lee Bailey	5'9"	Dick Cavett	5'7"
George Burns	5'9"	Garry Moore	5'7"
George Carlin	5'9"	Al Pacino	5'7"
John Cassavetes	5'9"	Claude Rains	5'7"
Joe Cocker	5'9"	Edward G. Robinson	5'7"
James Dean	5'9"	Kenny Rogers	5'7"
Robert De Niro	5'9"	Casey Kasem	5'6½"
Richard Gere	5'9"	Henry Winkler	5'6½"
Giancarlo Giannini	5'9"	Woody Allen	5'6"
Calvin Klein	5'9"	Paul Anka	5'6"
Ted Koppel	5'9"	Perry Como	5'6"
Stanley Kubrick	5'9"	Bob Dylan	5'6"
Steve Lawrence	5'9"	Peter Falk	5'6"
George Lucas	5'9"	Dustin Hoffman	5'6"
Marcello Mastroianni	5'9"	Neil Sedaka	5'6"
Paul McCartney	5'9"	Vidal Sassoon	5'6"
Paul Newman	5'9"	Andy Williams	5'6"
Jack Nicholson	5'9"	Darryl F. Zanuck	5'6"
Jason Robards, Jr.	5'9"	George Gobel	5'5½"
Sting	5'9"	John Tower	5'5½"
Oskar Werner	5'9"	Peter Lorre	5'5"
Gene Wilder	5'9"	Charles Manson	5'5"
Richard Dreyfuss	5'8½"	Rod Serling	5'5"
George Harrison	5'8½"	Alan Ladd	5'4½"
Anthony Newley	5'8½"	Robert Blake	5'4"
Frank Sinatra	5'8½"	Mel Brooks	5'4"
Andy Warhol	5'8½"	Michael J. Fox	5'4"
Louis Armstrong	5'8"	Norman Mailer	5'4"
Matthew Broderick	5'8"	Roman Polanski	5'4"
Dick Clark	5'8"	Charles Aznavour	5'3"
Redd Foxx	5'8"	Sammy Davis, Jr.	5'3"
Mark Hamill	5'8"	Mickey Rooney	5'3"
Hugh Hefner	5'8"	Prince	5'2½"
Elton John	5'8"	Buckminster Fuller	5'2"
Billy Joel	5'8"	Michael Korda	5'2"
Chuck Mangione	5'8"	Dudley Moore	5'2"
Robert Morse	5'8"	Paul Simon	5'2"
Willie Nelson	5'8"	Paul Williams	5'2"
Bob Newhart	5'8"	Danny De Vito	5'
Lou Rawls	5'8"	Willie Shoemaker	4'11"
Tony Randall	5'8"	Gary Coleman	4'7"
Ringo Starr	5'8"	David Rappaport	3'11"
Robin Williams	5'8"	Johnny Roventini	3'11"
Lee Trevino	5'7½"	Hervé Villechaize	3'10"
Rod Stewart	5'7½"	Emmanuel Lewis	3'7"
Mikhail		Michu	2'9"
Baryshnikov	5'7"	Kenny Baker	2'8"

Warning: The heights of famous people are often exaggerated. Use these figures with caution!

HOLLYWOOD

★ Second-Generation Hollywood Types ★

If movie-making is so rough, why are so many second- and third-generation show-biz kids going into it? The answer is easy: It is great on the ego, and $1,000,000 a movie certainly beats working for the post office.

Parents	Children or Grandchildren*
Eddie Albert	Edward Albert
Robert Alda	Alan Alda
Alan Arkin	Adam Arkin
Desi Arnaz, Lucille Ball	Luci Arnaz, Desi Arnaz, Jr.
John Barrymore	John Barrymore, Jr.; Drew Barrymore
Noah Beery	Noah Beery, Jr.
Ed Begley	Ed Begley, Jr.
Richard Bennett	Constance, Joan, and Barbara Bennett
Edgar Bergen	Candice Bergen
Ingrid Bergman, Roberto Rossellini	Isabella Rossellini
Pat Boone	Debby Boone
Helen Broderick	Broderick Crawford
James Brolin	John Brolin
Lloyd Bridges	Jeff and Beau Bridges
John Carradine	David and Keith Carradine
Johnny Cash	Roseanne Cash
Lon Chaney	Lon Chaney, Jr.
Charlie Chaplin	Geraldine Chaplin
Nat King Cole	Natalie Cole
Robert Conrad	Christian and Shane Conrad
Francis Coppola	Sofia Coppola
Tony Curtis, Janet Leigh	Jamie Lee Curtis
Dom DeLuise	Peter DeLuise
Bruce Dern	Laura Dern
Kirk Douglas	Michael Douglas
Patty Duke, John Astin	Mackenzie Astin
Douglas Fairbanks	Douglas Fairbanks, Jr.
John Farrow, Maureen O'Sullivan	Mia Farrow
Eddie Fisher, Debbie Reynolds	Carrie Fisher
Henry Fonda	Jane and Peter Fonda

*Where both children and grandchildren are indicated, they are separated by a semicolon.

Parents	Children or Grandchildren*
Judy Garland, Vincente Minnelli	Liza Minnelli
Judy Garland, Sid Luft	Lorna Luft
Lee Grant	Dinah Manoff
Joel Grey	Jennifer Grey
Allan Hale	Allan Hale, Jr.
Jack Haley	Jack Haley, Jr.
Helen Hayes	James MacArthur
Tippi Hedren	Melanie Griffith
Walter Huston	John Huston; Anjelica Huston
Jim Hutton	Timothy Hutton
Robert Keith	Brian Keith
Alan Ladd	Alan Jr. and David Ladd
Jack Lemmon	Chris Lemmon
John Lennon	Julian Lennon
Viveca Lindfors	Kris Tabori
Gene Lockhart	June Lockhart
Jayne Mansfield	Mariska Hargitay
Mary Martin	Larry Hagman
Walter Matthau	Charles Matthau
John Mills	Hayley and Juliet Mills
Robert Mitchum	Jim Mitchum
Robert Montgomery	Elizabeth Montgomery
Zero Mostel	Josh Mostel
Ozzie and Harriet Nelson	Ricky and David Nelson
Ricky Nelson	Tracy Nelson and The Nelsons (Matthew and Gunnar)
Ryan O'Neal	Tatum O'Neal
Gordon Parks	Gordon Parks, Jr.
Osgood Perkins	Anthony Perkins
John Phillips	Mackenzie Phillips
John and Michelle Phillips	Chynna Phillips
Christopher Plummer, Tammy Grimes	Amanda Plummer
Tyrone Power, Sr.	Tyrone Power
Richard Pryor	Rain Pryor
John Raitt	Bonnie Raitt
Michael Redgrave	Vanessa, Lynn, and Corin Redgrave
Carl Reiner	Rob Reiner
Jason Robards	Jason Jr. and Sam Robards
Bing Russell	Kurt Russell
Martin Sheen	Charlie Sheen and Emilio Estevez
Stella Stevens	Andrew Stevens
Lee Strasberg	Susan Strasberg
Donald Sutherland	Keifer Sutherland

*Where both children and grandchildren are indicated, they are separated by a semicolon.

Parents	Children or Grandchildren*
Danny Thomas	Marlo Thomas
John Wayne	Patrick, Michael, and Ethan Wayne
Pat Weaver	Sigourney Weaver
Raquel Welch	Tahnee Welch
Brian Wilson	Carnie and Wendy Wilson
Ed Wynn	Keenan Wynn
Frank Zappa	Dweezil and Moon Unit Zappa
Efrem Zimbalist, Jr.	Stephanie Zimbalist

*Where both children and grandchildren are indicated, they are separated by a semicolon.

★ Ronald Reagan's Leading Ladies ★

Not every actress can say she has played opposite a President of the United States, but here are some who can:

	Movie
Jane Wyman*	*Brother Rat* (1938)
Margaret Lindsay	*Hell's Kitchen* (1939)
Ann Sheridan	*Angels Wash Their Faces* (1939)
Jane Wyman	*Brother Rat and a Baby* (1940)
Jane Wyman	*An Angel From Texas* (1940)
Jane Wyman	*Tugboat Annie Sails Again* (1940)
Olivia De Havilland	*Santa Fe Trail* (1940)
Laraine Day	*The Bad Man* (1941)
Priscilla Lane	*Million Dollar Baby* (1941)
Ann Sheridan	*King's Row* (1942)
Ann Sheridan	*Juke Girl* (1942)
Joan Leslie	*This Is the Army* (1943)
Alexis Smith	*Stallion Road* (1947)
Shirley Temple	*That Hagen Girl* (1947)
Viveca Lindfors	*Night Unto Night* (1949)
Virginia Mayo	*The Girl From Jones Beach* (1949)
Patricia Neal	*John Loves Mary* (1949)
Patricia Neal	*The Hasty Heart* (1950)
Ruth Hussey	*Louisa* (1950)
Ginger Rogers	*Storm Warning* (1951)
Doris Day	*Storm Warning* (1951)
Diana Lynn	*Bedtime for Bonzo* (1951)
Rhonda Fleming	*The Last Outpost* (1951)
Rhonda Fleming	*Hong Kong* (1951)
Virginia Mayo	*She's Working Her Way Through College* (1952)

*Reagan's first wife.

Movie

Doris Day	*The Winning Team* (1952)
Rhonda Fleming	*Tropic Zone* (1953)
Dorothy Malone	*Law and Order* (1953)
Barbara Stanwyck	*Cattle Queen of Montana* (1954)
Rhonda Fleming	*Tennessee's Partner* (1954)
Nancy Davis**	*Hellcats of the Navy* (1957)
Angie Dickinson	*The Killers* (1964)

**Reagan's second wife.

★ Highest-Paid Entertainers ★

		Yearly Gross Income
1.	Bill Cosby	$57,500,000
2.	Michael Jackson	$50,000,000
3.	The Rolling Stones	$44,000,000
4.	Steven Spielberg	$43,500,000
5.	New Kids on the Block	$39,000,000
6.	Oprah Winfrey	$34,000,000
7.	Sylvester Stallone	$31,500,000
8.	Madonna	$31,000,000
9.	Arnold Schwarzenegger	$27,500,000
10.	Charles M. Schulz	$27,000,000
11.	Johnny Carson	$25,000,000
12.	Jack Nicholson	$25,000,000
13.	Eddie Murphy	$24,000,000
14.	Paul McCartney	$22,500,000
15.	Julio Iglesias	$22,000,000
16.	Bruce Willis	$18,000,000
17.	The Who	$17,500,000
18.	Sean Connery	$17,500,000
19.	Bon Jovi	$17,500,000
20.	Prince	$17,500,000
21.	Michael J. Fox	$16,500,000
22.	Billy Joel	$16,000,000
23.	Aerosmith	$15,500,000
24.	Pink Floyd	$15,000,000
25.	The Grateful Dead	$15,000,000
26.	Janet Jackson	$15,000,000
27.	Siegfried & Roy	$14,000,000
28.	Frank Sinatra	$13,500,000
29.	Tom Cruise	$13,000,000
30.	U-2	$12,500,000
31.	Michael Douglas	$12,000,000
32.	Andrew Lloyd Webber	$12,000,000
33.	Paula Abdul	$11,500,000

34. Stephen King	$11,000,000
35. Harrison Ford	$11,000,000
36. Jim Davis	$10,500,000
37. Mel Gibson	$10,000,000
38. Cameron Mackintosh	$10,000,000
39. George Michael	$9,000,000
40. Guns N' Roses	$8,500,000

Source: Forbes magazine, October 1, 1990. Based on average of 1989 and 1990 incomes.

Actors Who Have Directed
★ at Least One* Movie ★

Movie(s)

Alan Alda	*The Four Seasons* (1981)
Alan Arkin	*Little Murders* (1971)
Richard Attenborough	*Oh! What a Lovely War* (1969); *Gandhi* (1982)
Dan Aykroyd	*Nothing But Trouble* (1991)
Lionel Barrymore	*Confession* (1929)
Warren Beatty	*Reds* (1981); *Dick Tracy* (1990)
Richard Benjamin	*My Favorite Year* (1982)
Marlon Brando	*One-Eyed Jacks* (1960)
Albert Brooks	*Defending One's Life* (1991)
Richard Burton	*Dr. Faustus* (1967) co-director
James Caan	*Hide in Plain Sight* (1980)
James Cagney	*Short Cut to Hell* (1958)
Dyan Cannon	*The End of Innocence* (1991)
William Conrad	*Two on a Guillotine* (1964)
Ricardo Cortez	*City Girl* (1938)
Kevin Costner	*Dances With Wolves* (1990)
John Derek	*Once Before I Die* (1966); *Tarzan* (1981)
Kirk Douglas	*Scalawag* (1973); *Posse* (1975)
Clint Eastwood	*Play Misty for Me* (1971); *Breezy* (1973)
José Ferrer	*The Shrike* (1954)
Mel Ferrer	*Girl of the Limberlost* (1945)
Albert Finney	*Charlie Bubbles* (1968)
Peter Fonda	*The Hired Hand* (1971)
Jodie Foster	*Little Man Tate* (1991)
Al Freeman, Jr.	*A Fable* (1971)
Lee Grant	*Tell Me a Riddle* (1980)

*If the actor directed more than one movie, not all are shown. Those movies listed are either directorial debuts or representative.

	Movie(s)
Laurence Harvey	*The Ceremony* (1963)
David Hemmings	*Running Scared* (1972)
Paul Henreid	*For Men Only* (1951)
Charlton Heston	*Antony and Cleopatra* (1971)
Dennis Hopper	*Easy Rider* (1968)
Leslie Howard	*Pygmalion* (1938)
Ron Howard	*Splash* (1984); *Cocoon* (1985)
Burt Lancaster	*The Kentuckian* (1955)
Charles Laughton	*Night of the Hunter* (1955)
Jack Lemmon	*Kotch* (1971)
Jerry Lewis	*One More Time* (1971)
Peter Lorre	*Die Verlorene Ehre der Katharina Blum* (1950)
Ida Lupino	*Not Wanted* (1949)
Roddy McDowall	*Tam Lin* (1970)
Karl Malden	*Time Limit* (1957)
Penny Marshall	*Big* (1988); *Awakenings* (1990)
Walter Matthau	*Gangster Story* (1960)
Burgess Meredith	*The Yin and the Yang* (1970)
Ray Milland	*A Man Alone* (1955)
John Mills	*Sky West and Crooked* (1956)
George Montgomery	*Samar* (1962)
Robert Montgomery	*The Lady in the Lake* (1946)
Anthony Newley	*Can Hieronymous Merkin . . . (etc.)* (1969)
Paul Newman	*Rachel, Rachel* (1968); *Sometimes a Great Notion* (1971)
Jack Nicholson	*Drive, He Said* (1970); *The Two Jakes* (1990)
Edmund O'Brien	*Shield for Murder* (1954) co-director
Dennis O'Keefe	*The Diamond Wizard* (1954)
Laurence Olivier	*Hamlet* (1948)
Sidney Poitier	*A Warm December* (1973); *Stir Crazy* (1980)
Dick Powell	*Split Second* (1953)
Anthony Quinn	*The Buccaneer* (1959)
Robert Redford	*Ordinary People* (1980); *The Milagro Beanfield War* (1986)
Rob Reiner	*This Is Spinal Tap* (1984); *The Princess Bride* (1987)
Ralph Richardson	*Home at Seven* (1952)
Cliff Robertson	*J.W. Coop* (1972)
Peter Sellers	*Mr. Topaze* (1961)
Martin Sheen	*Gates* (1991)
Frank Sinatra	*None But the Brave* (1965)
Barbra Streisand	*Yentl* (1983)
Peter Ustinov	*School for Secrets* (1946)

	Movie(s)
John Wayne	*The Green Berets* (1968)
Cornel Wilde	*Storm Fear* (1955); *The Naked Prey* (1966)
Mai Zetterling	*The War Game* (1962); *Night Games* (1966)

Directors Who Have Appeared
★   in Movies   ★

	Movie(s)
Robert Aldrich	*The Big Knife* (1955)
Woody Allen	*What's New Pussycat* (1965); *The Front* (1976); and many others
Ingmar Bergman	*Waiting Woman* (1952)
Peter Bogdanovich	*Targets* (1968)
Frank Borzage	*Jeanne Eagels* (1957)
Claude Chabrol	*Les Biches* (1968); *The Road to Corinth* (1967)
Jean Cocteau	*Orphée* (1950); *Le Testament d'Orphée* (1959)
Roger Corman	*Silence of the Lambs* (1991)
Jules Dassin	*Rififi* (1955); *Never On Sunday* (1960)
Cecil B. De Mille	*Sunset Boulevard* (1950) and others
Samuel Fuller	*House of Bamboo* (1955)
Alfred Hitchcock	(12-frame cameos in almost every movie he directed)
John Huston	*The Treasure of the Sierra Madre* (1947); *The List of Adrian Messenger* (1963); *The Cardinal* (1963); *Winter Kills* (1979)
Joseph Losey	*The Intimate Stranger* (1956)
Paul Mazursky	(makes cameo appearances in most movies that he directs, à la Alfred Hitchcock)
Roman Polanski	*When Angels Fall* (1959); *Chinatown* (1974)
Sydney Pollack	*Tootsie* (1982)
Nicholas Ray	*55 Days in Peking* (1963)
Jean Renoir	*The Human Beast* (1938); *Rules of the Game* (1939)
Tony Richardson	*Tom Jones* (1963)
Martin Scorsese	*Cannonball* (1976); *Raging Bull* (1980); *Taxi Driver* (1976); and others

	Movie(s)
Preston Sturges	*Sullivan's Travels* (1941); *Paris Holiday* (1958)
François Truffaut	*The Wild Child* (1970); *Day for Night* (1973); *Close Encounters of the Third Kind* (1977)
King Vidor	*Our Daily Bread* (1934)
Erich von Stroheim	*La Grande Illusion* (1937); *Sunset Boulevard* (1950); and many others

★ Actors Who Debuted at a Late Age ★

	Age	Movie
Chief Dan George	70	*Smith!* (1969)
John Houseman	62	*Seven Days in May* (1964)
Sydney Greenstreet	61	*The Maltese Falcon* (1941)
Charles Coburn	56	*Boss Tweed* (1933)
S.Z. Sakall	55	*It's a Date* (1940)
George Arliss	53	*The Devil* (1921)
Florence Bates	49	*The Man in Blue* (1937)
Dame May Whitty	49	*Enoch Arden* (1914)
Monty Woolley	49	*Live, Love and Learn* (1937)
Margaret Rutherford	44	*Talk of the Devil* (1936)
Barry Fitzgerald	42	*Juno and the Paycock* (1930)
Edmund Gwenn	41	*The Real Thing At Last* (1916)
Will Sampson	40	*One Flew Over the Cuckoo's Nest* (1975)

★ Non-Actors Who Have Appeared in Movies ★

	Movie(s)
Julian Bond	*Greased Lightning* (1977)
Jimmy Breslin	*If Ever I See You Again* (1978)
Truman Capote	*Murder by Death* (1976)
Johnny Carson	*Looking for Love* (1965)
Pablo Casals	*Windjammer* (1958)
Howard Cosell	*Bananas* (1971)
Dionne Quintuplets	*Reunion* (1936); *The Country Doctor* (1936); *Quintupland* (1938); others
Everett Dirksen	*The Monitors* (1969)

Red Foley	*Sing a Song for Heaven's Sake* (1966)
Rube Goldberg	*He Danced Himself to Death* (1914)
Abel Green	*Copacabana* (1947)
Oscar Hammerstein II	*Main Street to Broadway* (1953)
Gabriel Heatter	*Champagne for Caesar* (1950); *The Day the Earth Stood Still* (1951)
Ben Hecht	*The Scoundrel* (1935)
Harry Houdini	*The Master Mystery* (1918) serial; *The Grim Game* (1919); *Terror Island* (1920)
Chet Huntley	*I Cheated the Law* (1949); *Cry Terror* (1958)
William Inge	*Splendor in the Grass* (1961)
Janis Joplin	*Petulia* (1968); *Big Brother* (1968)
Estes Kefauver	*The Captive City* (1952)
Dorothy Kilgallen	*Sinner Take Tall* (1936); *Pajama Party* (1964)
Jerzy Kosinski	*Reds* (1981)
John V. Lindsay	*Rosebud* (1975)
Frank Loesser	*Red, Hot and Blue* (1949)
Frankie Lymon	*Mister Rock and Roll* (1957)
Moms Mabley	*Emperor Jones* (1970); *It's Your Thing* (1970)
Charles MacArthur	*Crime Without Passion* (1934); *Scoundrel* (1936)
Bernarr Macfadden	*Building of the Health of a Nation* series (1915); *The Wrongdoers* (1925)
Norman Mailer	*Wild 90* (1967); *Maidstone* (1969); *Ragtime* (1981)
Somerset Maugham	*Quartet* (1948); *Trio* (1950); *Encore* (1951)
Elsa Maxwell	*Hotel for Women* (1939); *Public Deb No. 1* (1940); *Stage Door Canteen* (1943)
Jimmy McHugh	*The Helen Morgan Story* (1957)
Glenn Miller	*Orchestra Wives* (1942), *Sun Valley Serenade* (1942)
Jim Morrison	*Machine Gun McCain* (1970)
Edward R. Murrow	*Around the World in 80 Days* (1956)
Alfred Newman	*They Shall Have Music* (1939)
Ignace Paderewski	*Moonlight Sonata* (1937)
Westbrook Pegler	*Madison Square Garden* (1937)

	Movie(s)
Pablo Picasso	*La Vie Commence Demain* (1952); *Orphée* (1950); *La Testament d'Orphée* (1959)
Wiley Post	*Air Hawks* (1935)
Joe Pyne	*Mother Goose a Go-Go* (1966); *The Love-Ins* (1967)
Mike Romanoff	*Arch of Triumph* (1948); *Von Ryan's Express* (1965); *Tony Rome* (1967); *Lady in Cement* (1968)
Robert Ruark	*Target Earth* (1955)
Damon Runyon	*Madison Square Garden* (1932)
Erich Segal	*Without Apparent Motive* (1972)
Rod Serling	*The Outer Space Connection* (1975)
George Bernard Shaw	*Masks and Faces* (1918)
Bill Stern	*Pride of the Yankees* (1942); *Stage Door Canteen* (1943)
Mrs. Tom Thumb	*The Lilliputian's Courtship* (1915)
Countess Tolstoy	*George Robey's Day Off* (1918)
Leon Trotsky	*My Official Wife* (1914)

Note: Fidel Castro, contrary to other reports, never appeared as an extra in any Hollywood movie.

Athletes Who Have Appeared
★ in Movies ★

	Sport	Movie Credit(s) (Partial)
Kareem Abdul-Jabbar	Basketball	*Airplane* (1980)
Muhammad Ali	Boxing	*The Greatest* (1977); "Freedom Road" (1979), TV miniseries
Max Baer	Boxing	*The Prizefighter and the Lady* (1933); *The Harder They Fall* (1956)
Buddy Baer	Boxing	*Jack and the Beanstalk* (1952); *Snow White and the Three Stooges* (1961)
Bruce Bennett	Discus	*The New Adventures of Tarzan* (1935); *The Treasure of the Sierra Madre* (1947)
Johnny Mack Brown	Football	*Billy the Kid* (1933); *Ride 'Em Cowboy* (1941)
Jim Brown	Football	*Rio Conchos* (1964); *The Dirty Dozen* (1967)

	Sport	Movie Credit(s) (Partial)
Ty Cobb	Baseball	*The Ninth Inning* (1942)
Chuck Connors	Baseball, basketball	*Pat and Mike* (1952); "The Rifleman" TV series (1958–63)
Buster Crabbe	Swimming	*Tarzan the Fearless* (1933); *Flash Gordon* serials (1930s); *Buck Rogers* serials (1930s)
Lou Gehrig	Baseball	*Rawhide* (1938); *The Ninth Inning* (1942)
Mark Harmon	Football	*Summer School* (1987); *The Presidio* (1988); plus many TV appearances
Bruce Jenner	Decathlon	*Can't Stop the Music* (1980)
Alex Karras	Football	*Blazing Saddles* (1974); "Babe" (1977) TV movie; "Webster" TV series (1980s)
Canada Lee	Boxing	*Lifeboat* (1943); *Cry, the Beloved Country* (1952)
Gus Lesnevitch	Boxing	*Requiem for a Heavyweight* (1962)
Sonny Liston	Boxing	*Harlow* (1965); *Head* (1968)
Joe Namath	Football	*C.C. Rider & Company* (1970); *The Last Rebel* (1971); TV and summer stock appearances
Jackie Robinson	Baseball	*The Jackie Robinson Story* (1950)
Maxie Rosenbloom	Boxing	*Mr. Broadway* (1933)
Barney Ross	Boxing	*Requiem for a Heavyweight* (1962); *The Doctor and the Playgirl* (1965)
Babe Ruth	Baseball	*Headin' Home* (1920); *Babe Come Home* (1927); *Pride of the Yankees* (1942)
O.J. Simpson	Football	"Roots" (1976) TV miniseries; *The Towering Inferno* (1974); *Naked Gun* (1988)
Casey Stengel	Baseball	*Safe at Home* (1941)
Woody Strode	Football	*The Ten Commandments* (1956); *Sergeant Rutledge* (1960); *The Professionals* (1966)

	Sport	Movie Credit(s) (Partial)
Jim Thorpe	Football	*White Eagle* (1932); *Big City* (1937); *Outlaw Trail* (1944); *Wagonmaster* (1950)
Johnny Weissmuller	Swimming	*Tarzan the Ape Man* (1932) and many other Tarzan movies through 1948
Fred Williamson	Football	*M*A*S*H* (1970); *Boss Nigger* (1975)
Babe Didrikson Zaharias	Golf	*Pat and Mike* (1952)

Actors Who Have Appeared
★ in Drag in Movies ★

	Movie
Lionel Barrymore	*The Devil Doll* (1936)
Jack Benny	*Charley's Aunt* (1941)
Helmut Berger	*The Damned* (1969)
Ray Bolger	*Where's Charlie?* (1948)
Joe E. Brown	*Shut My Big Mouth* (1942)
Eddie Cantor	*Ali Baba Goes to Town* (1937)
Charlie Chaplin	*A Woman* (1915)
Jean Cocteau	*Orphée* (1950)
Lee J. Cobb	*In Like Flint* (1967)
James Coco	*The Wild Party* (1975)
Robbie Coltrane	*Nuns on the Run* (1990)
Lou Costello	*Lost in a Harem* (1944)
Tim Curry	*The Rocky Horror Picture Show* (1974)
Tony Curtis	*Some Like It Hot* (1959)
Billy De Wolfe	*Isn't It Romantic?* (1948)
Melvyn Douglas	*The Amazing Mr. Williams* (1939)
Harvey Fierstein	*Torch Song Trilogy* (1988)
Preston Foster	*Up the River* (1930)
Cary Grant	*I Was a Male War Bride* (1949)
Alec Guinness	*Kind Hearts and Coronets* (1949); *The Comedians* (1967)
Bob Hope	*The Princess and the Pirate* (1944)
Dustin Hoffman	*Tootsie* (1983)
Eric Idle	*Nuns on the Run* (1990)
Stan Laurel	*Jitterbugs* (1943)
Jack Lemmon	*Some Like It Hot* (1959)

	Movie
Oscar Levant	*The I Don't Care Girl* (1953)
Jerry Lewis	*At War With the Army* (1950)
John Lithgow	*The World According to Garp* (1982)
Matthew Modine	*Private School* (1983)
Dudley Moore	*Bedazzled* (1968)
Jack Oakie	*Let's Go Native* (1930)
William Powell	*Love Crazy* (1941)
Tony Perkins	*Psycho* (1960)
Robert Preston	*Victor/Victoria* (1982)
Charles Ruggles	*Charley's Aunt* (1930)
George Sanders	*The Kremlin Letter* (1969)
Michel Serrault	*La Cage aux Folles* (1979); *La Cage aux Folles II* (1981)
Alistair Sim	*The Belles of St. Trinian's* (1954); *Blue Murder at St. Trinian's* (1958)
Arthur Treacher	*Up the River* (1930)
David Wayne	*The I Don't Care Girl* (1953)

Actresses Who Have Appeared as Men in Movies

★   ★

	Movie
Julie Andrews	*Victor, Victoria* (1982)
Annabella	*Wings of the Morning* (1937)
Louise Brooks	*Beggars of Life* (1936)
Doris Day	*Calamity Jane* (1953)
Marlene Dietrich	*Seven Sinners* (1940)
Frances Farmer	*Badlands of Dakota* (1941)
Signe Hasso	*Where There's Life* (1947)
Katharine Hepburn	*Sylvia Scarlett* (1935)
Miriam Hopkins	*She Loves Me Not* (1934)
Linda Hunt	*The Year of Living Dangerously* (1983)
Merle Oberon	*A Song to Remember* (1945)
Maureen O'Hara	*At Sword's Point* (1952)
Jean Peters	*Anne of the Indies* (1952)
Barbra Streisand	*Yentl* (1983)
Shirley Temple	*Rebecca of Sunnybrook Farm* (1938)
Lupe Velez	*Honolulu Lu* (1941)
Raquel Welch	*Myra Breckinridge* (1970)

Movie-Star Autograph Values

	Price (Item)
Marilyn Monroe	$15,000 (handwritten letter)
	3,000 (signed photo)
	750 (signature)
Greta Garbo	10,000 (handwritten letter)
	5,000 (signed photo)
	2,000 (signature)
Clark Gable	3,500 (handwritten letter)
	3,000 (signed photo)
Lon Chaney, Sr.	2,000 (signed photo)
W.C. Fields	1,500 (signed photo)
Bela Lugosi	1,000 (signed photo)
Rudolph Valentino	750 (signed photo)
Errol Flynn	500 (signed photo)
Elvis Presley	250 (signed photo)
Marlon Brando	250 (signed photo)
Frank Sinatra	200 (signed photo)
Liz Taylor	150 (signed photo)
Clint Eastwood	100 (signed photo)
Liberace	100 (signed photo)
Paul Newman	60 (signed photo)

Source: Charles Hamilton, autograph expert.

Celebrity Autobiographies

Edie Adams	*Sing a Pretty Song* (1990) with Robert Windeler
Brian Aherne	*A Proper Job* (1969)
June Allyson	*June Allyson* (1982)
Desi Arnaz	*A Book* (1975)
Elizabeth Ashley	*Actress: Postcards from the Road* (1978)
Fred Astaire	*Steps in Time* (1960)
Mary Astor	*My Story* (1959); *A Life on Film* (1971)
Jean-Pierre Aumont	*Sun and Shadow* (1977)
Lauren Bacall	*By Myself* (1979)
Carroll Baker	*Baby Doll* (1983)
Roseanne Barr	*Stand Up: My Life as a Woman* (1989)
Rona Barrett	*Miss Rona* (1974)
Diana Barrymore	*Too Much Too Soon* (1958)
Ethel Barrymore	*Memories* (1956)
John Barrymore	*Confessions of an Actor* (1926)

Anne Baxter	*Intermission* (1976)
Orson Bean	*Too Much Is Not Enough* (1988)
Priscilla Beaulieu	*Elvis and Me* (1985) with Sandra Harmon
Joan Bennett	*The Bennett Playbill* (1970) with Louis Kibbee
Jack Benny	*Sunday Nights at Seven* (1990) with Joan Benny
Ingrid Bergman	*Ingrid Bergman: My Story* (1980)
Milton Berle	*Milton Berle* (1974) with Haskel Frankel; *B.S. I Love You* (1987)
Charles Bickford	*Bulls, Balls, Bicycles and Actors* (1965)
Shirley Temple Black	*Child Star* (1988)
Claire Bloom	*Limelight and After* (1982)
Dirk Bogarde	*A Postillion Struck by Lightning* (1977)
David Brenner	*Soft Pretzels with Mustard* (1983)
Louise Brooks	*Lulu in Hollywood* (1982)
Joe E. Brown	*Laughter Is a Wonderful Thing* (1959)
Billie Burke	*With a Feather on My Nose* (1949); *With a Powder on My Nose* (1959)
George Burns	*Living It Up* (1976); *Gracie: A Love Story* (1988); *All My Best Friends* (1989)
Abe Burrows	*Honest Abe* (1980)
Sid Caesar	*Where Have I Been?* (1982) with Bill Davidson
James Cagney	*Cagney by Cagney* (1976)
Sammy Cahn	*I Should Care* (1974)
Cab Calloway	*Of Minnie the Moocher and Me* (1976)
Frank Capra	*The Name Above the Title* (1971)
Kitty Carlisle Hart	*Kitty* (1988)
Hoagy Carmichael	*Washboard Blues* (1947)
Dick Cavett	*Cavett* (1974) with Christopher Porterfield
Marilyn Chambers	*Marilyn Chambers: My Story* (1975)
Charlie Chaplin	*My Trip Abroad* (1922); *My Wonderful Visit* (1930); *My Autobiography* (1964); *My Life in Pictures* (1974)
Cyd Charisse	*The Two of Us* (1976) with Tony Martin
Maurice Chevalier	*With Love* (1960); *I Remember It Well* (1972)
Rosemary Clooney	*This for Remembrance* (1977)
Joan Collins	*Past Imperfect* (1984)

Judy Collins	*Trust Your Heart* (1987)
Alice Cooper	*Me Alice* (1976)
Gladys Cooper	*Without Veils* (1953)
Roger Corman	*How I Made a Hundred Movies In Hollywood and Never Lost a Dime* (1990)
Joseph Cotten	*Vanity Will Get You Somewhere* (1987)
Noël Coward	*President Indicative* (1937); *Middle East Diary* (1945); *Future Indefinite* (1954)
Cheryl Crawford	*One Naked Individual* (1977)
Christina Crawford	*Mommie Dearest* (1978)
Joan Crawford	*A Portrait of Joan* (1962)
Bing Crosby	*Call Me Lucky* (1953)
Marion Davies	*The Times We Had* (1975)
Bette Davis	*The Lonely Life* (1962); *This 'N That* (1987) with Michael Herskowitz
Sammy Davis, Jr.	*Yes I Can* (1966); *Why Me?* with Jane and Burt Boyar (1989)
Doris Day	*Doris Day: Her Own Story* (1976) with A.E. Hotchner
Laraine Day	*Day With the Giants* (1952)
Yvonne De Carlo	*Yvonne: An Autobiography* (1987)
Olivia De Havilland	*Every Frenchman Has One* (1960)
Cecil B. De Mille	*An Autobiography* (1960)
Edward Dmytryk	*It's a Helluva Life But Not a Bad Living* (1979)
Phil Donahue	*Donahue* (1980)
Kirk Douglas	*The Ragman's Son* (1988)
Melvyn Douglas	*See You at the Movies* (1987)
Hugh Downs	*Yours Truly, Hugh Downs* (1960)
Marie Dressler	*My Own Story* (1934)
Patty Duke	*Anna: The Autobiography of Patty Duke* (1987)
Britt Ekland	*True Britt* (1980)
Frances Farmer	*Will There Ever Be a Morning?* (1972)
Gracie Fields	*Sing as We Go* (1960)
W.C. Fields	*W.C. Fields by Himself* (1973)
Errol Flynn	*Beam Ends* (1934); *My Wicked, Wicked Ways* (1959)
Henry Fonda	*Fonda: My Life* (1981) with Howard Teichmann
Joan Fontaine	*No Bed of Roses* (1978)
Arlene Francis	*Arlene Francis* (1978) with Florence Rome

Joe Franklin	*A Gift for People* (1978)
Eva Gabor	*Orchids and Salami* (1954)
Ava Gardner	*Ava: My Story* (1990)
William Gargan	*Why Me?* (1969)
Tay Garnett	*Light Your Torches and Pull Up Your Tights* (1973) with Fredda Dudley Balling
John Gielgud	*Early Stages* (1938); *Distinguished Company* (1972); *Gielgud: An Actor and His Time* (1980)
Lillian Gish	*The Movies, Mr. Griffith & Me* (1969)
Ruth Gordon	*Myself Among Others* (1970); *My Side* (1976)
Leo Gorcey	*Dead End Yells, Wedding Bells, Cockle Shells and Dizzy Spells* (1967)
Sheilah Graham	*Beloved Infidel* (1958); *A College of One* (1967); *Confessions of a Hollywood Gossip Columnist* (1968); *A State of Heart* (1972)
Stewart Granger	*Sparks Fly Upward* (1981)
Rocky Graziano	*Somebody Up There Likes Me* (1955); *Somebody Down There Likes Me, Too* (1981) with Ralph Corsel
Merv Griffin	*Merv* (1979) with Peter Barsocchino
Alec Guinness	*Blessings in Disguise* (1986)
Cedric Hardwicke	*A Victorian in Orbit* (1961)
Rex Harrison	*Rex* (1975); *A Damned Serious Business* (1990)
Moss Hart	*Act One* (1958)
June Havoc	*Early Havoc* (1960)
Jack Hawkins	*Anything For a Quiet Life* (1974)
Helen Hayes	*Letters to Mary Catherine Hayes Brown* (1940); *On Reflection* (1960); *A Gift of Joy* (1965); *Loving Life* (1987) with Marion Gladney; *Where the Truth Lies* (1988)
Brooke Hayward	*Haywire* (1977)
Ben Hecht	*A Child of the Century* (1954); *Gaily Gaily* (1963)
Lillian Hellman	*An Unfinished Woman* (1969); *Pentimento* (1973); *Scoundrel Time* (1976)
Katharine Hepburn	*The Making of the African Queen* (1987); *Me* (1991)

Charlton Heston	*The Actor's Life* (1976)
Stanley Holloway	*Wiv a Little Bit of Luck* (1969)
Bob Hope	*Have Tux Will Travel* (1958); *I Owe Russia $2,000* (1963); *The Road to Hollywood* (1977); and others
Hedda Hopper	*From Under My Hat* (1952); *The Whole Truth and Nothing But* (1963)
Lena Horne	*In Person* (1950); *Lena* (1966) with Richard Schickel
John Houseman	*Run-Through* (1972); *Front and Center* (1979); *Final Dress* (1983)
John Huston	*John Huston: An Open Book* (1980)
George Jessel	*So Help Me* (1943); *This Way, Miss* (1955); *The World I Live In* (1975)
Shirley Jones	*Martin and Shirley* (1990) with Marty Ingels and Mickey Hershkowitz
Curt Jurgens	*Sixty and Not Yet Wise* (1973)
Garson Kanin	*Hollywood* (1974)
Buster Keaton	*My Wonderful World of Slapstick* (1962)
Klaus Kinski	*All I Need Is Love* (1988)
Gelsey Kirkland	*Dancing on My Grave* (1986) with Greg Lawrence
Veronica Lake	*Veronica* (1968)
Hedy Lamarr	*Ecstasy and Me* (1967)
Jesse Lasky	*I Blow My Own Horn* (1958)
Jesse Lasky, Jr.	*Whatever Happened to Hollywood?* (1973)
Gertrude Lawrence	*A Star Danced* (1949)
Gypsy Rose Lee	*Gypsy* (1957)
Christopher Lee	*Tall, Dark and Gruesome* (1977)
Mervyn LeRoy	*Mervyn LeRoy: Take One* (1974) with Dick Kleiner
Oscar Levant	*A Smattering of Ignorance* (1944); *Memoirs of an Amnesiac* (1965)
Liberace	*Liberace* (1973)
Margaret Lockwood	*Lucky Star* (1955)
Josh Logan	*Josh* (1976)
Anita Loos	*A Girl Like I* (1966); *Kiss Hollywood Good-Bye* (1974); *A Cast of Thousands* (1977)
Sophia Loren	*Sophia: Living and Loving* (1979) with A.E. Hotchner
Linda Lovelace	*Out of Bondage* (1986) with Mike McGrady

Shirley MacLaine	*Don't Fall Off the Mountain* (1970); *You Can Get There From Here* (1975); *Out On a Limb* (1983); and others
Ali MacGraw	*Moving Pictures* (1991)
Henry Mancini	*Did They Mention the Music?* (1990)
Mary Martin	*My Heart Belongs* (1976)
Groucho Marx	*Groucho and Me* (1959); *Memoirs of a Mangy Lover* (1964); *The Groucho Letters* (1967)
Harpo Marx	*Harpo Speaks!* (1961)
Raymond Massey	*When I Was Young* (1976); *A Hundred Different Lives* (1979)
Mercedes McCambridge	*The Two of Us* (1961)
Tim McCoy	*Tim McCoy Remembers the West* (1977) with Ronald McCoy
Rod McKuen	*Finding My Father* (1976)
Ed McMahon	*Here's Ed* (1976) with Carroll Carroll
Adolphe Menjou	*It Took Nine Tailors* (1952)
Melina Mercouri	*I Was Born Greek* (1971)
Ethel Merman	*Who Could Ask for Anything More?* (1956)
Gary Merrill	*Bette, Rita and the Rest of My Life* (1989)
Ray Milland	*Wide-Eyed in Babylon* (1974)
Ann Miller	*Miller's High Life* (1974)
Vincente Minnelli	*I Remember It Well* (1974) with Hector Arce
Marilyn Monroe	*My Story* (1974)
Robert Morley	*Robert Morley: A Reluctant Autobiography* (1966) with Sewell Stokes
George Murphy	*Say, Didn't You Use to Be George Murphy?* (1970)
Hildegarde Neff	*The Gift Horse* (1971); *The Verdict* (1975)
Pola Negri	*Memories of a Star* (1970)
Ozzie Nelson	*Ozzie* (1973)
Cathleen Nesbitt	*A Little Love and Good Company* (1973)
Leonard Nimoy	*I Am Not Spock* (1975)
David Niven	*The Moon's a Balloon* (1972); *Bring on the Empty Horses* (1975)
Pat O'Brien	*Wind at My Back* (1963)
Laurence Olivier	*Confessions of an Actor* (1983)

Jack Paar	*I Kid You Not* (1959) with John Reddy; *My Saber Is Bent* (1961) with John Reddy
Lilli Palmer	*Change Lobsters and Dance* (1975)
Joe Pasternak	*Easy the Hard Work* (1956)
John Phillips	*Papa John* (1986) with Jim Jerome
Mary Pickford	*Sunshine and Shadow* (1955)
Sidney Poitier	*This Life* (1980)
Otto Preminger	*Preminger: An Autobiography* (1977)
Anthony Quinn	*Original Sin* (1972)
Gilda Radner	*It's Always Something* (1989)
Tony Randall	*Which Reminds Me* (1989) with Michael Mindlin
Basil Rathbone	*In and Out of Character* (1956)
Nancy Reagan	*My Turn* (1989) with William Novak
Ronald Reagan	*Where's the Rest of Me?* (1965); *An American's Story* (1991)
Liz Renay	*My Face for the World to See* (1971)
Jean Renoir	*Renoir: My Life and My Films* (1974)
Debbie Reynolds	*Debbie* (1988) with David Patrick Columbia
Paul Robeson	*Here I Stand* (1958)
Edward G. Robinson	*All My Yesterdays* (1973)
Mickey Rooney	*I.E.* (1965)
Lillian Roth	*I'll Cry Tomorrow* (1954)
Philip Roth	*The Facts* (1990)
Rosalind Russell	*Life Is a Banquet* (1977) with Chris Chase
Margaret Rutherford	*An Autobiography* (1972)
S.Z. Sakall	*The Story of Cuddles* (1953)
George Sanders	*Memoirs of a Professional Cad* (1960)
Joseph Schildkraut	*My Father and I* (1959)
Budd Schulberg	*Moving Pictures: Memories of a Hollywood Prince* (1981)
Mack Sennett	*The King of Comedy* (1954)
Omar Sharif	*The Eternal Males* (1976) with Marie-Therese Guinchard
Simone Signoret	*Nostalgia Isn't What It Used to Be* (1978)
Phil Silvers	*The Laugh Is on Me* (1973)
Walter Slezak	*What Time's the Next Swan?* (1962)
Donald Ogden Stewart	*By a Stroke of Luck* (1975)
Gloria Swanson	*Swanson on Swanson* (1980)

Danny Thomas	*Make Room for Danny* (1991) with Bill Davidson
Gene Tierney	*Self-Portrait* (1978) with Mickey Herskowitz
Lana Turner	*Lana: The Lady, the Legend, the Truth* (1982)
Liv Ullman	*Changing* (1976)
Peter Ustinov	*Dear Me* (1977)
Rudy Vallee	*Let the Chips Fall . . .* (1975)
Roger Vadim	*Bardot Deneuve Fonda* (1986)
King Vidor	*A Tree Is a Tree* (1953)
Josef von Sternberg	*Fun in a Chinese Laundry* (1965)
Raoul Walsh	*Each Man in His Own Time* (1974)
Andy Warhol	*The Andy Warhol Diaries* (1989)
Jack Warner	*My First Hundred Years in Hollywood* (1965) with Dean Jennings
Ethel Waters	*His Eye Is on the Sparrow* (1953)
Johnny Weissmuller	*Water, World and Weissmuller* (1967)
William Wellman	*A Short Time for Insanity* (1974)
Mae West	*Goodness Had Nothing to Do With It* (1959); *Life, Sex and ESP* (1975)
Emlyn Williams	*George* (1961); *Emlyn* (1974)
Tennessee Williams	*Memoirs* (1975)
Walter Winchell	*Winchell Exclusive* (1975)
Shelley Winters	*Shelley: Also Known as Shirley* (1980); *Shelley II* (1988)
Tammy Wynette	*Stand By Your Man* (1979)
Keenan Wynn	*Ed Wynn's Son* (1960)
Loretta Young	*The Things I Had to Learn* (1962)
Henny Youngman	*Take My Wife . . . Please* (1973)
Adolph Zukor	*The Public Is Never Wrong* (1953)

AWARDS AND HONORS

Best Actor	Movie
1928 Emil Jannings	*The Way of All Flesh; The Last Command*
1929 Warner Baxter	*In Old Arizona*
1930 George Arliss	*Disraeli*
1931 Lionel Barrymore	*A Free Soul*
1932 Fredric March	*Dr. Jekyll and Mr. Hyde*
Wallace Beery	*The Champ*
1933 Charles Laughton	*The Private Life of Henry VIII*
1934 Clark Gable	*It Happened One Night*
1935 Victor McLaglen	*The Informer*
1936 Paul Muni	*The Story of Louis Pasteur*
1937 Spencer Tracy	*Captains Courageous*
1938 Spencer Tracy	*Boys Town*
1939 Robert Donat	*Goodbye, Mr. Chips*
1940 James Stewart	*The Philadelphia Story*
1941 Gary Cooper	*Sergeant York*
1942 James Cagney	*Yankee Doodle Dandy*
1943 Paul Lukas	*Watch on the Rhine*
1944 Bing Crosby	*Going My Way*
1945 Ray Milland	*The Lost Weekend*
1946 Fredric March	*The Best Years of Our Lives*
1947 Ronald Colman	*A Double Life*
1948 Laurence Olivier	*Hamlet*
1949 Broderick Crawford	*All the King's Men*
1950 José Ferrer	*Cyrano de Bergerac*
1951 Humphrey Bogart	*The African Queen*
1952 Gary Cooper	*High Noon*
1953 William Holden	*Stalag 17*
1954 Marlon Brando	*On the Waterfront*
1955 Ernest Borgnine	*Marty*
1956 Yul Brynner	*The King and I*
1957 Alec Guinness	*The Bridge on the River Kwai*
1958 David Niven	*Separate Tables*
1959 Charlton Heston	*Ben-Hur*
1960 Burt Lancaster	*Elmer Gantry*
1961 Maximilian Schell	*Judgment at Nuremberg*
1962 Gregory Peck	*To Kill a Mockingbird*
1963 Sidney Poitier	*Lilies of the Field*
1964 Rex Harrison	*My Fair Lady*
1965 Lee Marvin	*Cat Ballou*
1966 Paul Scofield	*A Man for All Seasons*
1967 Rod Steiger	*In the Heat of the Night*
1968 Cliff Robertson	*Charly*
1969 John Wayne	*True Grit*
1970 George C. Scott	*Patton*
1971 Gene Hackman	*The French Connection*

Best Actor	Movie
1972 Marlon Brando	*The Godfather*
1973 Jack Lemmon	*Save the Tiger*
1974 Art Carney	*Harry and Tonto*
1975 Jack Nicholson	*One Flew Over the Cuckoo's Nest*
1976 Peter Finch	*Network*
1977 Richard Dreyfuss	*The Goodbye Girl*
1978 Jon Voight	*Coming Home*
1979 Dustin Hoffman	*Kramer vs. Kramer*
1980 Robert De Niro	*Raging Bull*
1981 Henry Fonda	*On Golden Pond*
1982 Ben Kingsley	*Gandhi*
1983 Robert Duvall	*Tender Mercies*
1984 F. Murray Abraham	*Amadeus*
1985 William Hurt	*Kiss of the Spider Woman*
1986 Paul Newman	*The Color of Money*
1987 Michael Douglas	*Wall Street*
1988 Dustin Hoffman	*Rain Man*
1989 Daniel Day-Lewis	*My Left Foot*
1990 Jeremy Irons	*Reversal of Fortune*

Best Actress	Movie
1928 Janet Gaynor	*Seventh Heaven; Street Angel; Sunrise*
1929 Mary Pickford	*Coquette*
1930 Norma Shearer	*The Divorcée*
1931 Marie Dressler	*Min and Bill*
1932 Helen Hayes	*The Sin of Madelon Claudet*
1933 Katharine Hepburn	*Morning Glory*
1934 Claudette Colbert	*It Happened One Night*
1935 Bette Davis	*Dangerous*
1936 Luise Rainer	*The Great Ziegfeld*
1937 Luise Rainer	*The Good Earth*
1938 Bette Davis	*Jezebel*
1939 Vivien Leigh	*Gone With the Wind*
1940 Ginger Rogers	*Kitty Foyle*
1941 Joan Fontaine	*Suspicion*
1942 Greer Garson	*Mrs. Miniver*
1943 Jennifer Jones	*The Song of Bernadette*
1944 Ingrid Bergman	*Gaslight*
1945 Joan Crawford	*Mildred Pierce*
1946 Olivia De Havilland	*To Each His Own*
1947 Loretta Young	*The Farmer's Daughter*
1948 Jane Wyman	*Johnny Belinda*
1949 Olivia De Havilland	*The Heiress*
1950 Judy Holliday	*Born Yesterday*
1951 Vivien Leigh	*A Streetcar Named Desire*
1952 Shirley Booth	*Come Back, Little Sheba*
1953 Audrey Hepburn	*Roman Holiday*

Best Actress	Movie
1954 Grace Kelly	*The Country Girl*
1955 Anna Magnani	*The Rose Tattoo*
1956 Ingrid Bergman	*Anastasia*
1957 Joanne Woodward	*The Three Faces of Eve*
1958 Susan Hayward	*I Want to Live!*
1959 Simone Signoret	*Room at the Top*
1960 Elizabeth Taylor	*Butterfield 8*
1961 Sophia Loren	*Two Women*
1962 Anne Bancroft	*The Miracle Worker*
1963 Patricia Neal	*Hud*
1964 Julie Andrews	*Mary Poppins*
1965 Julie Christie	*Darling*
1966 Elizabeth Taylor	*Who's Afraid of Virginia Woolf?*
1967 Katharine Hepburn	*Guess Who's Coming to Dinner*
1968 Katharine Hepburn	*The Lion in Winter*
Barbra Streisand	*Funny Girl*
1969 Maggie Smith	*The Prime of Miss Jean Brodie*
1970 Glenda Jackson	*Women in Love*
1971 Jane Flonda	*Klute*
1972 Liza Minnelli	*Cabaret*
1973 Glenda Jackson	*A Touch of Class*
1974 Ellen Burstyn	*Alice Doesn't Live Here Anymore*
1975 Louise Fletcher	*One Flew Over the Cuckoo's Nest*
1976 Faye Dunaway	*Network*
1977 Diane Keaton	*Annie Hall*
1978 Jane Fonda	*Coming Home*
1979 Sally Field	*Norma Rae*
1980 Sissy Spacek	*Coal Miner's Daughter*
1981 Katharine Hepburn	*On Golden Pond*
1982 Meryl Streep	*Sophie's Choice*
1983 Shirley MacLaine	*Terms of Endearment*
1984 Sally Field	*Places in the Heart*
1985 Geraldine Page	*The Trip to Bountiful*
1986 Marlee Matlin	*Children of a Lesser God*
1987 Cher	*Moonstruck*
1988 Jodie Foster	*The Accused*
1989 Jessica Tandy	*Driving Miss Daisy*
1990 Kathy Bates	*Misery*

Best Supporting Actor	Movie
1936 Walter Brennan	*Come and Get It*
1937 Joseph Schildkraut	*The Life of Émile Zola*
1938 Walter Brennan	*Kentucky*
1939 Thomas Mitchell	*Stagecoach*
1940 Walter Brennan	*The Westerner*
1941 Donald Crisp	*How Green Was My Valley*
1942 Van Heflin	*Johnny Eager*

Best Supporting Actor — Movie

Year	Best Supporting Actor	Movie
1943	Charles Coburn	*The More the Merrier*
1944	Barry Fitzgerald	*Going My Way*
1945	James Dunn	*A Tree Grows in Brooklyn*
1946	Harold Russell	*The Best Years of Our Lives*
1947	Edmund Gwenn	*Miracle on 34th Street*
1948	Walter Huston	*The Treasure of the Sierra Madre*
1949	Dean Jagger	*Twelve O'Clock High*
1950	George Sanders	*All About Eve*
1951	Karl Malden	*A Streetcar Named Desire*
1952	Anthony Quinn	*Viva Zapata!*
1953	Frank Sinatra	*From Here to Eternity*
1954	Edmond O'Brien	*The Barefoot Contessa*
1955	Jack Lemmon	*Mister Roberts*
1956	Anthony Quinn	*Lust for Life*
1957	Red Buttons	*Sayonara*
1958	Burl Ives	*The Big Country*
1959	Hugh Griffith	*Ben-Hur*
1960	Peter Ustinov	*Spartacus*
1961	George Chakiris	*West Side Story*
1962	Ed Begley	*Sweet Bird of Youth*
1963	Melvyn Douglas	*Hud*
1964	Peter Ustinov	*Topkapi*
1965	Martin Balsam	*A Thousand Clowns*
1966	Walter Matthau	*The Fortune Cookie*
1967	George Kennedy	*Cool Hand Luke*
1968	Jack Albertson	*The Subject Was Roses*
1969	Gig Young	*They Shoot Horses, Don't They?*
1970	John Mills	*Ryan's Daughter*
1971	Ben Johnson	*The Last Picture Show*
1972	Joel Grey	*Cabaret*
1973	John Houseman	*The Paper Chase*
1974	Robert De Niro	*The Godfather, Part II*
1975	George Burns	*The Sunshine Boys*
1976	Jason Robards, Jr.	*All the President's Men*
1977	Jason Robards, Jr.	*Julia*
1978	Christopher Walken	*The Deer Hunter*
1979	Melvyn Douglas	*Being There*
1980	Timothy Hutton	*Ordinary People*
1981	Sir John Gielgud	*Arthur*
1982	Louis Gossett, Jr.	*An Officer and a Gentleman*
1983	Jack Nicholson	*Terms of Endearment*
1984	Haing S. Ngor	*The Killing Fields*
1985	Don Ameche	*Cocoon*
1986	Michael Caine	*Hannah and Her Sisters*
1987	Sean Connery	*The Untouchables*
1988	Kevin Kline	*A Fish Called Wanda*
1989	Denzel Washington	*Glory*
1990	Joe Pesci	*Goodfellas*

Best Supporting Actress	Movie
1936 Gale Sondergaard	*Anthony Adverse*
1937 Alice Brady	*In Old Chicago*
1938 Fay Bainter	*Jezebel*
1939 Hattie McDaniel	*Gone With the Wind*
1940 Jane Darwell	*The Grapes of Wrath*
1941 Mary Astor	*The Great Lie*
1942 Teresa Wright	*Mrs. Miniver*
1943 Katina Paxinou	*For Whom the Bell Tolls*
1944 Ethel Barrymore	*None But the Lonely Heart*
1945 Anne Rever	*National Velvet*
1946 Anne Baxter	*The Razor's Edge*
1947 Celeste Holm	*Gentleman's Agreement*
1948 Claire Trevor	*Key Largo*
1949 Mercedes McCambridge	*All the King's Men*
1950 Josephine Hull	*Harvey*
1951 Kim Hunter	*A Streetcar Named Desire*
1952 Gloria Grahame	*The Bad and the Beautiful*
1953 Donna Reed	*From Here to Eternity*
1954 Eva Marie Saint	*On the Waterfront*
1955 Jo Van Fleet	*East of Eden*
1956 Dorothy Malone	*Written on the Wind*
1957 Miyoshi Umeki	*Sayonara*
1958 Wendy Hiller	*Separate Tables*
1959 Shelley Winters	*The Diary of Anne Frank*
1960 Shirley Jones	*Elmer Gantry*
1961 Rita Moreno	*West Side Story*
1962 Patty Duke	*The Miracle Worker*
1963 Margaret Rutherford	*The V.I.P.s*
1964 Lila Kedrova	*Zorba the Greek*
1965 Shelley Winters	*A Patch of Blue*
1966 Sandy Dennis	*Who's Afraid of Virginia Woolf?*
1967 Estelle Parsons	*Bonnie and Clyde*
1968 Ruth Gordon	*Rosemary's Baby*
1969 Goldie Hawn	*Cactus Flower*
1970 Helen Hayes	*Airport*
1971 Cloris Leachman	*The Last Picture Show*
1972 Eileen Heckart	*Butterflies Are Free*
1973 Tatum O'Neal	*Paper Moon*
1974 Ingrid Bergman	*Murder on the Orient Express*
1975 Lee Grant	*Shampoo*
1976 Beatrice Straight	*Network*
1977 Vanessa Redgrave	*Julia*
1978 Maggie Smith	*California Suite*
1979 Meryl Streep	*Kramer vs. Kramer*
1980 Mary Steenburgen	*Melvin and Howard*
1981 Maureen Stapleton	*Reds*
1982 Jessica Lange	*Tootsie*
1983 Linda Hunt	*The Year of Living Dangerously*
1984 Dame Peggy Ashcroft	*A Passage to India*

Best Supporting Actress	Movie
1985 Anjelica Huston	*Prizzi's Honor*
1986 Dianne Wiest	*Hannah and Her Sisters*
1987 Olympia Dukakis	*Moonstruck*
1988 Geena Davis	*The Accidental Tourist*
1989 Brenda Fricker	*My Left Foot*
1990 Whoopi Goldberg	*Ghost*

Best Director	Movie
1928 Frank Borzage	*Seventh Heaven*
Lewis Milestone	*Two Arabian Nights*
1929 Frank Lloyd	*The Divine Lady*
1930 Lewis Milestone	*All Quiet on the Western Front*
1931 Norman Taurog	*Skippy*
1932 Frank Borzage	*Bad Girl*
1933 Frank Lloyd	*Cavalcade*
1934 Frank Capra	*It Happened One Night*
1935 John Ford	*The Informer*
1936 Frank Capra	*Mr. Deeds Goes to Town*
1937 Leo McCarey	*The Awful Truth*
1938 Frank Capra	*You Can't Take It With You*
1939 Victor Fleming	*Gone With the Wind*
1940 John Ford	*The Grapes of Wrath*
1941 John Ford	*How Green Was My Valley*
1942 William Wyler	*Mrs. Miniver*
1943 Michael Curtiz	*Casablanca*
1944 Leo McCarey	*Going My Way*
1945 Billy Wilder	*The Lost Weekend*
1946 Wiliam Wyler	*The Best Years of Our Lives*
1947 Elia Kazan	*Gentleman's Agreement*
1948 John Huston	*The Treasure of the Sierra Madre*
1949 Joseph L. Mankiewicz	*A Letter to Three Wives*
1950 Joseph L. Mankiewicz	*All About Eve*
1951 George Stevens	*A Place in the Sun*
1952 John Ford	*The Quiet Man*
1953 Fred Zinnemann	*From Here to Eternity*
1954 Elia Kazan	*On the Waterfront*
1955 Delbert Mann	*Marty*
1956 George Stevens	*Giant*
1957 David Lean	*The Bridge on the River Kwai*
1958 Vincente Minnelli	*Gigi*
1959 William Wyler	*Ben-Hur*
1960 Billy Wilder	*The Apartment*
1961 Robert Wise and Jerome Robbins	*West Side Story*
1962 David Lean	*Lawrence of Arabia*
1963 Tony Richardson	*Tom Jones*
1964 George Cukor	*My Fair Lady*
1965 Robert Wise	*The Sound of Music*

Best Director	Movie
1966 Fred Zinnemann	*A Man for All Seasons*
1967 Mike Nichols	*The Graduate*
1968 Sir Carol Reed	*Oliver!*
1969 John Schlesinger	*Midnight Cowboy*
1970 Franklin J. Schaffner	*Patton*
1971 William Friedkin	*The French Connection*
1972 Bob Fosse	*Cabaret*
1973 George Roy Hill	*The Sting*
1974 Francis Ford Coppola	*The Godfather, Part II*
1975 Milos Forman	*One Flew Over the Cuckoo's Nest*
1976 John G. Avildsen	*Rocky*
1977 Woody Allen	*Annie Hall*
1978 Michael Cimino	*The Deer Hunter*
1979 Robert Benton	*Kramer vs. Kramer*
1980 Robert Redford	*Ordinary People*
1981 Warren Beatty	*Reds*
1982 Richard Attenborough	*Gandhi*
1983 James L. Brooks	*Terms of Endearment*
1984 Milos Forman	*Amadeus*
1985 Sydney Pollack	*Out of Africa*
1986 Oliver Stone	*Platoon*
1987 Bernardo Bertolucci	*The Last Emperor*
1988 Barry Levinson	*Rain Man*
1989 Oliver Stone	*Born on the Fourth of July*
1990 Kevin Costner	*Dances With Wolves*

Youngest and Oldest Oscar Winners

★   ★

Youngest Best Actor	Richard Dreyfuss (age 29) *The Goodbye Girl* (1977)
Youngest Best Actress	Janet Gaynor (age 22) *Seventh Heaven* (1928)
Youngest Best Supporting Actor	Timothy Hutton (age 19) *Ordinary People* (1980)
Youngest Best Supporting Actress	Tatum O'Neal (age 10) *Paper Moon* (1973)
Oldest Best Actor	Henry Fonda (age 76) *On Golden Pond* (1981)
Oldest Best Actress	Jessica Tandy (age 80) *Driving Miss Daisy* (1989)
Oldest Best Supporting Actor	George Burns (age 80) *The Sunshine Boys* (1975)
Oldest Best Supporting Actress	Peggy Ashcroft (age 77) *Passage to India* (1984)

Well-Known Actors Who
Never Won an Oscar

★   ★

Actor	No. of Oscar Nominations
Richard Burton	7
Peter O'Toole	7
Charles Boyer	4
Montgomery Clift	4
Claude Rains	4
Kirk Douglas	3
William Powell	3
James Dean	2
John Garfield	2
Cary Grant	2
Edward G. Robinson	0

Note: Several of the above-mentioned actors won special or honorary Oscars, e.g., Charles Boyer (1942), Cary Grant (1969), and Edward G. Robinson (1972).

Well-Known Actresses Who
Never Won an Oscar

★   ★

Actress	No. of Oscar Nominations
Deborah Kerr	6
Thelma Ritter	6
Rosalind Russell	5
Agnes Moorehead	4
Barbara Stanwyck	4
Greta Garbo	3
Gloria Swanson	3
Ruth Chatterton	2
Judy Garland	2
Liv Ullman	2
Marlene Dietrich	1

Note: Judy Garland won a special Oscar in 1939; Greta Garbo won an honorary Oscar in 1954; and Barbara Stanwyck won an honorary Oscar in 1981.

Tony Awards Winners— Broadway's Oscars

★ ★

The Tony Awards, Broadway's answer to the Oscars, were named after Antoinette Perry (1888–1946), the actress/producer/ director who was Chairman of the Board and Secretary of the American Theatre Wing, which established the awards in her honor. Originally the voters were members of the Board of the American Theatre Wing, but in 1954 eligibility was expanded to include members of the governing boards of the Actors' Equity Association, the Dramatists Guild, the Society of Stage Directors and Choreographers, and the United Scenic Artists, members of the League of New York Theatres and Producers, and members of the press—approximately 560 people. The first awards were given at a dinner on Easter Sunday, April 6, 1947, at the Waldorf-Astoria Hotel in New York City.

Best Actor in a Dramatic Role	Play
1947 José Ferrer	*Cyrano de Bergerac*
Fredric March	*Years Ago*
1948 Henry Fonda	*Mister Roberts*
Paul Kelly	*Command Decision*
Basil Rathbone	*The Heiress*
1949 Rex Harrison	*Anne of the Thousand Days*
1950 Sidney Blackmer	*Come Back, Little Sheba*
1951 Claude Rains	*Darkness at Noon*
1952 José Ferrer	*The Shrike*
1953 Tom Ewell	*The Seven Year Itch*
1954 David Wayne	*The Teahouse of the August Moon*
1955 Alfred Lunt	*Quadrille*
1956 Paul Muni	*Inherit the Wind*
1957 Fredric March	*Long Day's Journey Into Night*
1958 Ralph Bellamy	*Sunrise at Campobello*
1959 Jason Robards, Jr.	*The Disenchanted*
1960 Melvyn Douglas	*The Best Man*
1961 Zero Mostel	*Rhinoceros*
1962 Paul Scofield	*A Man for All Seasons*
1963 Arthur Hill	*Who's Afraid of Virginia Woolf?*
1964 Alec Guinness	*Dylan*
1965 Walter Matthau	*The Odd Couple*
1966 Hal Holbrook	*Mark Twain Tonight*
1967 Paul Rogers	*The Homecoming*
1968 Martin Balsam	*You Know I Can't Hear You When the Water's Running*
1969 James Earl Jones	*The Great White Hope*
1970 Fritz Weaver	*Child's Play*
1971 Brian Bedford	*The School for Wives*
1972 Cliff Gorman	*Lenny*

Best Actor in a Dramatic Role   **Play**

1973 Alan Bates   *Butley*
1974 Michael Moriarty   *Find Your Way Home*
1975 John Kani   *Sizwe Banzi*
     Winston Ntshona   *The Island*
1976 John Wood   *Travesties*
1977 Al Pacino   *The Basic Training of Pavlo Hummel*

1978 Barnard Hughes   *Da*
1979 Tom Conti   *Whose Life Is It, Anyway?*
1980 John Rubinstein   *Children of a Lesser God*
1981 Ian McKellen   *Amadeus*
1982 Roger Rees   *The Life and Adventures of Nicholas Nickleby*

1983 Harvey Fierstein   *Torch Song Trilogy*
1984 Jeremy Irons   *The Real Thing*
1985 Derek Jacobi   *Much Ado About Nothing*
1986 Judd Hirsch   *I'm Not Rappaport*
1987 James Earl Jones   *Fences*
1988 Ron Silver   *Speed-The-Plow*
1989 Philip Bosco   *Lend Me a Tenor*
1990 Robert Morse   *Tru*
1991 Nigel Hawthorne   *Shadowlands*

Best Actress in a Dramatic Role   **Play**

1947 Ingrid Bergman   *Joan of Lorraine*
     Helen Hayes   *Happy Birthday*
1948 Judith Anderson   *Medea*
     Katherine Cornell   *Antony and Cleopatra*
     Jessica Tandy   *A Streetcar Named Desire*
1949 Martita Hunt   *The Madwoman of Chaillot*
1950 Shirley Booth   *Come Back, Little Sheba*
1951 Uta Hagen   *The Country Girl*
1952 Julie Harris   *I Am a Camera*
1953 Shirley Booth   *Time of the Cuckoo*
1954 Audrey Hepburn   *Ondine*
1955 Nancy Kelly   *The Bad Seed*
1956 Julie Harris   *The Lark*
1957 Margaret Leighton   *Separate Tables*
1958 Helen Hayes   *Time Remembered*
1959 Gertrude Berg   *A Majority of One*
1960 Anne Bancroft   *The Miracle Worker*
1961 Joan Plowright   *A Taste of Honey*
1962 Margaret Leighton   *The Night of the Iguana*
1963 Uta Hagen   *Who's Afraid of Virginia Woolf?*
1964 Sandy Dennis   *Any Wednesday*
1965 Irene Worth   *Tiny Alice*
1966 Rosemary Harris   *The Lion in Winter*
1967 Beryl Reid   *The Killing of Sister George*
1968 Zoe Caldwell   *The Prime of Miss Jean Brodie*

Best Actress in a Dramatic Role   **Play**

1969 Julie Harris   *Forty Carats*
1970 Tammy Grimes   *Private Lives*
1971 Maureen Stapleton   *The Gingerbread Lady*
1972 Sada Thompson   *Twigs*
1973 Julie Harris   *The Last of Mrs. Lincoln*
1974 Colleen Dewhurst   *A Moon for the Misbegotten*
1975 Ellen Burstyn   *Same Time, Next Year*
1976 Irene Worth   *Sweet Bird of Youth*
1977 Julie Harris   *The Belle of Amherst*
1978 Jessica Tandy   *The Gin Game*
1979 Constance Cummings   *Wings*
        Carole Shelley   *The Elephant Man*
1980 Phyllis Frelich   *Children of a Lesser God*
1981 Jane Lapotaire   *Piaf*
1982 Zoe Caldwell   *Medea*
1983 Jessica Tandy   *Foxfire*
1984 Glenn Close   *The Real Thing*
1985 Stockard Channing   *Joe Egg*
1986 Lily Tomlin   *The Search for Signs of Intelligent
                              Life in the Universe*
1987 Linda Lavin   *Broadway Bound*
1988 Joan Allen   *Burn This*
1989 Pauline Collins   *Shirley Valentine*
1990 Maggie Smith   *Lettice and Lovage*
1991 Mercedes Ruehl   *Lost in Yonkers*

Best Actor in a Musical   **Play**

1948 Paul Hartman   *Angel in the Wings*
1949 Ray Bolger   *Where's Charley?*
1950 Ezio Pinza   *South Pacific*
1951 Robert Alda   *Guys and Dolls*
1952 Phil Silvers   *Top Banana*
1953 Thomas Mitchell   *Hazel Flagg*
1954 Alfred Drake   *Kismet*
1955 Walter Slezak   *Fanny*
1956 Ray Walston   *Damn Yankees*
1957 Rex Harrison   *My Fair Lady*
1958 Robert Preston   *The Music Man*
1959 Richard Kiley   *Redhead*
1960 Jackie Gleason   *Take Me Along*
1961 Richard Burton   *Camelot*
1962 Robert Morse   *How to Succeed in Business
                              Without Really Trying*
1963 Zero Mostel   *A Funny Thing Happened on the
                              Way to the Forum*
1964 Bert Lahr   *Foxy*
1965 Zero Mostel   *Fiddler on the Roof*
1966 Richard Kiley   *Man of La Mancha*
1967 Robert Preston   *I Do! I Do!*
1968 Robert Goulet   *The Happy Time*

Best Actor in a Musical — Play

Year	Actor	Play
1969	Jerry Orbach	*Promises, Promises*
1970	Cleavon Little	*Purlie*
1971	Hal Linden	*The Rothschilds*
1972	Phil Silvers	*A Funny Thing Happened on the Way to the Forum*
1973	Ben Vereen	*Pippin*
1974	Christopher Plummer	*Cyrano*
1975	John Cullum	*Shenandoah*
1976	George Rose	*My Fair Lady*
1977	Barry Bostwick	*The Robber Bridegroom*
1978	John Cullum	*On the Twentieth Century*
1979	Len Cariou	*Sweeney Todd*
1980	Jim Dale	*Barnum*
1981	Kevin Kline	*The Pirates of Penzance*
1982	Ben Harney	*Dreamgirls*
1983	Tommy Tune	*My One and Only*
1984	George Hearn	*La Cage aux Folles*
1985	(no award)	
1986	George Rose	*The Mystery of Edwin Drood*
1987	Robert Lindsay	*Me and My Girl*
1988	Michael Crawford	*The Phantom of the Opera*
1989	Jason Alexander	*Jerome Robbins's Broadway*
1990	James Naughton	*City of Angels*
1991	Jonathan Pryce	*Miss Saigon*

Best Actress in a Musical — Play

Year	Actress	Play
1948	Grace Hartman	*Angel With Wings*
1949	Nanette Fabray	*Love Life*
1950	Mary Martin	*South Pacific*
1951	Ethel Merman	*Call Me Madam*
1952	Gertrude Lawrence	*The King and I*
1953	Rosalind Russell	*Wonderful Town*
1954	Dolores Gray	*Carnival in Flanders*
1955	Mary Martin	*Peter Pan*
1956	Gwen Verdon	*Damn Yankees*
1957	Judy Holliday	*Bells Are Ringing*
1958	Thelma Ritter	*New Girl in Town*
	Gwen Verdon	*New Girl in Town*
1959	Gwen Verdon	*Redhead*
1960	Mary Martin	*The Sound of Music*
1961	Elizabeth Seal	*Irma La Douce*
1962	Anna Maria Alberghetti	*Carnival*
	Diahann Carroll	*No Strings*
1963	Vivien Leigh	*Tovarich*
1964	Carol Channing	*Hello, Dolly!*
1965	Liza Minnelli	*Flora, the Red Menace*
1966	Angela Lansbury	*Mame*
1967	Barbara Harris	*The Apple Tree*
1968	Patricia Routledge	*Darling of the Day*
	Leslie Uggams	*Hallelujah, Baby!*

Best Actress in a Musical	Play
1969 Angela Lansbury	Gypsy
1970 Lauren Bacall	Applause
1971 Helen Gallagher	No, No, Nanette
1972 Alexis Smith	Follies
1973 Glynis Johns	A Little Night Music
1974 Virginia Capers	Raisin
1975 Angela Lansbury	Gypsy
1976 Donna McKechnie	A Chorus Line
1977 Dorothy Loudon	Annie
1978 Liza Minnelli	The Act
1979 Angela Lansbury	Sweeney Todd
1980 Patti LuPone	Evita
1981 Lauren Bacall	Woman of the Year
1982 Jennifer Holliday	Dreamgirls
1983 Natalia Makarova	On Your Toes
1984 Chita Rivera	The Rink
1985 (no award)	
1986 Bernadette Peters	Song & Dance
1987 Maryann Plunkett	Me and My Girl
1988 Joanna Gleason	Into the Woods
1989 Ruth Brown	Black and Blue
1990 Tyne Daly	Gypsy
1991 Lea Salonga	Miss Saigon

Best Supporting or Featured Actress in a Dramatic Role	Play
1947 Patricia Neal	Another Part of the Forest
1948 (no award)	
1949 Shirley Booth	Goodby, My Fancy
1950 (no award)	
1951 Maureen Stapleton	The Rose Tattoo
1952 Marian Winters	I Am a Camera
1953 Beatrice Straight	The Crucible
1954 Jo Van Fleet	The Trip to Bountiful
1955 Patricia Jessel	Witness for the Prosecution
1956 Una Merkel	The Ponder Heart
1957 Peggy Cass	Auntie Mame
1958 Anne Bancroft	Two for the Seesaw
1959 Julie Newmar	The Marriage-Go-Round
1960 Anne Revere	Toys in the Attic
1961 Colleen Dewhurst	All the Way Home
1962 Elizabeth Ashley	Take Her, She's Mine
1963 Sandy Dennis	A Thousand Clowns
1964 Barbara Loden	After the Fall
1965 Alice Ghostley	The Sign in Sidney Brustein's Window
1966 Zoe Caldwell	Slapstick Tragedy
1967 Marian Seldes	A Delicate Balance
1968 Zena Walker	Joe Egg
1969 Jane Alexander	The Great White Hope
1970 Blythe Danner	Butterflies Are Free

Best Supporting or Featured Actress in a Dramatic Role

	Play
1971 Rae Allen	*And Miss Reardon Drinks a Little*
1972 Elizabeth Wilson	*Sticks and Bones*
1973 Leora Dana	*The Last of Mrs. Lincoln*
1974 Frances Sternhagen	*The Good Doctor*
1975 Rita Moreno	*The Ritz*
1976 Shirley Knight	*Kennedy's Children*
1977 Trazana Beverley	*For Colored Girls Who Have Considered Suicide When the Rainbow Is Enuf*
1978 Ann Wedgeworth	*Chapter Two*
1979 Joan Hickson	*Bedroom Farce*
1980 Dinah Manoff	*I Ought to Be in Pictures*
1981 Swoosie Kurtz	*Fifth of July*
1982 Amanda Plummer	*Agnes of God*
1983 Judith Ivey	*Steaming*
1984 Christine Baranski	*The Real Thing*
1985 Judith Ivey	*Hurlyburly*
1986 Swoosie Kurtz	*The House of Blue Leaves*
1987 Mary Alice	*Fences*
1988 L. Scott Caldwell	*Joe Turner's Come and Gone*
1989 Christine Baranski	*Rumors*
1990 Margaret Tyzack	*Lettice and Lovage*
1991 Irene Worth	*Lost in Yonkers*

Best Supporting or Featured Actor in a Dramatic Role

	Play
1949 Arthur Kennedy	*Death of a Salesman*
1950 (no award)	
1951 Eli Wallach	*The Rose Tattoo*
1952 John Cromwell	*Point of No Return*
1953 John Williams	*Dial M for Murder*
1954 John Kerr	*Tea and Sympathy*
1955 Francis L. Sullivan	*Witness for the Prosecution*
1956 Ed Begley	*Inherit the Wind*
1957 Frank Conroy	*The Potting Shed*
1958 Henry Jones	*Sunrise at Campobello*
1959 Charlie Ruggles	*The Pleasure of His Company*
1960 Roddy McDowall	*The Fighting Cock*
1961 Martin Gabel	*Big Fish, Little Fish*
1962 Walter Matthau	*A Shot in the Dark*
1963 Alan Arkin	*Enter Laughing*
1964 Hume Cronyn	*Hamlet*
1965 Jack Albertson	*The Subject Was Roses*
1966 Patrick Magee	*Marat/Sade*
1967 Ian Holm	*The Homecoming*
1968 James Patterson	*The Birthday Party*
1969 Al Pacino	*Does a Tiger Wear a Necktie?*
1970 Ken Howard	*Child's Play*
1971 Paul Sand	*Story Theatre*
1972 Vincent Gardenia	*The Prisoner of Second Avenue*

Best Supporting or Featured Actor in a Dramatic Role

	Play
1973 John Lithgow	*The Changing Room*
1974 Ed Flanders	*A Moon for the Misbegotten*
1975 Frank Langella	*Seascape*
1976 Edward Herrmann	*Mrs. Warren's Profession*
1977 Jonathan Pryce	*Comedians*
1978 Lester Rawlins	*Da*
1979 Michael Gough	*Bedroom Farce*
1980 David Rounds	*Mornings at Seven*
1981 Brian Backer	*The Floating Light Bulb*
1982 Zakes Mokae	*Master Harold . . . and the Boys*
1983 Matthew Broderick	*Brighton Beach Memoirs*
1984 Joe Mantegna	*Glengarry Glen Ross*
1985 Barry Miller	*Biloxi Blues*
1986 John Mahoney	*The House of Blue Leaves*
1987 John Randolph	*Broadway Bound*
1988 B.D. Wong	*M. Butterfly*
1989 Boyd Gaines	*The Heidi Chronicles*
1990 Charles Durning	*Cat on a Hot Tin Roof*
1991 Kevin Spacey	*Lost in Yonkers*

Best Supporting or Featured Actor in a Musical

	Play
1947 David Wayne	*Finian's Rainbow*
1948 (no award)	
1949 (no award)	
1950 Myron McCormick	*South Pacific*
1951 Russell Nype	*Call Me Madam*
1952 Yul Brynner	*The King and I*
1953 Hiram Sherman	*Two's Company*
1954 Harry Belafonte	*John Murray Anderson's Almanac*
1955 Cyril Ritchard	*Peter Pan*
1956 Russ Brown	*Damn Yankees*
1957 Sydney Chaplin	*Bells Are Ringing*
1958 David Burns	*The Music Man*
1959 Russell Nype	*Goldilocks*
Cast	*La Plume de Ma Tante*
1960 Tom Bosley	*Fiorello!*
1961 Dick Van Dyke	*Bye, Bye Birdie*
1962 Charles Nelson Reilly	*How to Succeed in Business Without Really Trying*
1963 David Burns	*A Funny Thing Happened on the Way to the Forum*
1964 Jack Cassidy	*She Loves Me*
1965 Victor Spinetti	*Oh! What a Lovely War*
1966 Frankie Michaels	*Mame*
1967 Joel Grey	*Cabaret*
1968 Hiram Sherman	*How Now, Dow Jones*
1969 Ronald Holgate	*1776*
1970 René Auberjonois	*Coco*

Best Supporting or Featured Actor in a Musical

	Play
1971 Keene Curtis	*The Rothschilds*
1972 Larry Blyden	*A Funny Thing Happened on the Way to the Forum*
1973 George S. Irving	*Irene*
1974 Tommy Tune	*Seesaw*
1975 Ted Rose	*The Wiz*
1976 Sammy Williams	*A Chorus Line*
1977 Lenny Baker	*I Love My Wife*
1978 Kevin Kline	*On the Twentieth Century*
1979 Henderson Forsythe	*The Best Little Whorehouse in Texas*
1980 Mandy Patinkin	*Evita*
1981 Hinton Battle	*Sophisticated Ladies*
1982 Clevant Derricks	*Dreamgirls*
1983 Charles "Honi" Coles	*My One and Only*
1984 Hinton Battle	*The Tap Dance Kid*
1985 Ron Richardson	*Big River*
1986 Michael Rupert	*Sweet Charity*
1987 Michael Maguire	*Les Misérables*
1988 Bill McCutcheon	*Anything Goes*
1989 Scott Wise	*Jerome Robbins's Broadway*
1990 Michael Jeter	*Grand Hotel*
1991 Hinton Battle	*Miss Saigon*

Best Supporting or Featured Actress in a Musical

	Play
1950 Juanita Hall	*South Pacific*
1951 Isabel Bigley	*Guys and Dolls*
1952 Helen Gallagher	*Pal Joey*
1953 Sheila Bond	*Wish You Were Here*
1954 Gwen Verdon	*Can-Can*
1955 Carol Haney	*The Pajama Game*
1956 Lotte Lenya	*The Threepenny Opera*
1957 Edie Adams	*Li'l Abner*
1958 Barbara Cook	*The Music Man*
1959 Pat Stanley	*Goldilocks*
Cast	*La Plume de Ma Tante*
1960 Patricia Neway	*The Sound of Music*
1961 Tammy Grimes	*The Unsinkable Molly Brown*
1962 Phyllis Newman	*Subways Are for Sleeping*
1963 Anna Quayle	*Stop the World, I Want to Get Off*
1964 Tessie O'Shea	*The Girl Who Came to Supper*
1965 Maria Karnilova	*Fiddler on the Roof*
1966 Beatrice Arthur	*Mame*
1967 Peg Murray	*Cabaret*
1968 Lillian Hayman	*Hallelujah, Baby!*
1969 Marian Mercer	*Promises, Promises*
1970 Melba Moore	*Purlie*
1971 Patsy Kelly	*No, No, Nanette*

1972 Linda Hopkins	*Inner City*
1973 Patricia Elliot	*A Little Night Music*
1974 Janie Sell	*Over Here!*
1975 Dee Dee Bridgewater	*The Wiz*
1976 Carole Bishop	*A Chorus Line*
1977 Delores Hall	*Your Arm's Too Short to Box With God*
1978 Nell Carter	*Ain't Misbehavin'*
1979 Carlin Glynn	*The Best Little Whorehouse in Texas*
1980 Priscilla Lopez	*The Day in Hollywood/A Night in the Ukraine*
1981 Marilyn Cooper	*Woman of the Year*
1982 Liliane Montevecchi	*Nine*
1983 Betty Buckley	*Cats*
1984 Lila Kedrova	*Zorba*
1985 Leilani Jones	*Grind*
1986 Bebe Neuwirth	*Sweet Charity*
1987 Frances Ruffelle	*Les Misérables*
1988 Judy Kaye	*The Phantom of the Opera*
1989 Debbie Shapiro	*Jerome Rabbins's Broadway*
1990 Randy Graff	*City of Angels*
1991 Daisy Eagan	*The Secret Garden*

★ Kennedy Center Honorees ★

The John F. Kennedy Center for the Performing Arts in Washington, D.C. has honored the achievements of five distinguished contributors to the performing arts every year since 1978.

1978. Marian Anderson (contralto), Fred Astaire (dancer–actor), Richard Rodgers (composer), Arthur Rubinstein (pianist), George Balanchine (choreographer).

1979. Ella Fitzgerald (singer), Henry Fonda (actor), Martha Graham (dancer–choreographer), Tennessee Williams (playwright), Aaron Copland (composer).

1980 James Cagney (actor), Leonard Bernstein (composer–conductor), Agnes de Mille (choreographer), Lynn Fontanne (actress), Leontyne Price (soprano).

1981. Count Basie (jazz composer–pianist), Cary Grant (actor), Helen Hayes (actress), Jerome Robbins (choreographer), Rudolf Serkin (pianist).

1982. George Abbott (theater producer), Lillian Gish (actress), Benny Goodman (band leader–musician), Gene Kelly (dancer–actor), Eugene Ormandy (conductor).

1983. Katherine Dunham (dancer–choreographer), Elia Kazan (director–author), James Stewart (actor), Virgil Thomson (music critic–composer), Frank Sinatra (singer–actor).

1984. Lena Horne (singer), Danny Kaye (comedian–actor), Gian Carlo Menotti (composer), Arthur Miller (playwright), Isaac Stern (violinist).

1985. Merce Cunningham (dancer–choreographer), Irene Dunne (actress), Bob Hope (comedian), Alan Jay Lerner (lyricist–playwright), Frederick Lowe (composer), Beverly Sills (soprano).

1986. Lucille Ball (comedic actress–producer), Ray Charles (singer), Yehudi Menuhin (violinist), Anthony Tudor (choreographer), Hume Cronyn (actor), Jessica Tandy (actress).

1987. Perry Como (singer), Bette Davis (actress), Sammy Davis, Jr. (entertainer), Nathan Milstein (violinist), Alwin Nikolais (choreographer).

1988. Alvin Ailey (choregrapher), George Burns (comedian), Myrna Loy (actress), Alexander Schneider (violinist), Roger L. Stevens (theatrical producer and founding chairman of Kennedy Center).

1989. Harry Belafonte (singer–actor), Claudette Colbert (actress), Alexandra Danilova (ballerina), Mary Martin (actress), William Schuman (composer).

1990. Katharine Hepburn (actress), Dizzy Gillespie (jazz muscian–band leader), Risë Stevens (opera singer), Billy Wilder (movie director), Jule Styne (composer).

★ Honor Roll Members ★

Debbie Allen	Cum laude, Howard U.
Laurie Anderson	Magna cum laude, Barnard
Johnny Bench	Valedictorian, high school
Pat Boone	Magna cum laude, Columbia
Bill Bradley	President of student council, high school
Tom Brokaw	President of student council, high school
Helen Gurley Brown	President of scholastic society and honor roll, high school
Pat Buchanan	Cum laude, Georgetown
George Bush	President of senior class, Andover
Dick Cavett	President of student council; national honor society
Chevy Chase	Valedictorian, Dalton School

Michael Crichton	Summa cum laude, Harvard
Jerry Falwell	Valedictorian, high school
Jodie Foster	Magna cum laude, Yale
Connie Francis	Honor roll, high school
Betty Friedan	Summa cum laude, Smith
Crystal Gayle	National honor society, high school
Marvin Hamlisch	Cum laude, Queens College
Lee Iacocca	National honor society, high school
Henry Kissinger	Summa cum laude, Harvard
Don Knotts	President of high school class
Kris Kristofferson	High honors, Pomona College
Ann Landers	Honor roll, high school
Art Linkletter	Honor roll, high school
John Lithgow	Magna cum laude, Harvard
Shirley MacLaine	Honor roll, high school
Karl Malden	President of high school class
Bette Midler	President of high school class
Kate Millett	Magna cum laude, U. of Minnesota
Pat Nixon	Cum laude, U. of Southern California
Sylvia Porter	Magna cum laude, Hunter College
Rex Reed	Honor roll, high school
John Ritter	President of student council
Oral Roberts	President of high school class; honor roll
Fred "Mr." Rogers	President of student council; national honor society
Philip Roth	Magna cum laude, Bucknell
Pat Sajak	National honor society
Willard Scott	President of high school class
Rod Serling	Honor society, high school
Meryl Streep	National honor society, high school
Barbra Streisand	Honor roll, high school
Sally Struthers	Honor roll, high school
Marlo Thomas	3.8 average, U. of Southern California
Tom Tryon	Cum laude, Yale
John Updike	Summa cum laude, Harvard
Abigail Van Buren	Honor roll, high school
Sam Walton	President of student council
Richard Widmark	President of high school class
Oprah Winfrey	President of student council; honor society
Tom Wolfe	Cum laude, Washington & Lee

★   # Phi Beta Kappa Key Holders   ★

Phi Beta Kappa is an acronym from the Greek words *philosophia biou kybernētēs,* which mean "philosophy, the guide of life." The national honorary academic society was founded in 1776 at the College of William and Mary. Students who are elected to the society are usually in the top 5 percent or 10 percent of a given college's junior or senior class. Only about 15,000 students are elected each year, and there are about 400,000 living members. Here are over 60 well-known people who have been awarded the key to success—a Phi Beta Kappa key. Chapter and year of election are given in parentheses.

John Quincy Adams (Harvard 1787), U.S. President
Chester A. Arthur (Union College 1848), U.S. President
Louis Auchincloss (Yale 1938), Author
Leonard Bernstein (Harvard 1964), Composer, conductor
Harry Blackmun (Harvard 1929), Supreme Court justice
Daniel Boorstin (Harvard 1932), Librarian of Congress
David Boren (Yale 1961), U.S. Senator
MacGeorge Bundy (Yale 1938), Former government official
George Bush (Yale 1948), U.S. President
Glenn Close (William & Mary), Actress
Francis Ford Coppola (Hofstra), Movie director
Angela Davis (Brandeis 1965), Civil rights activist
Elizabeth Dole (Duke 1958), Government official
Elizabeth Drew (Wellesley 1957), Journalist
Cyndy Garvey (Michigan State), TV personality
Mark Goodson (U. of California 1936), TV producer
Ella Grasso (Mount Holyoke 1940), Governor of Connecticut
Meg Greenfield (Smith 1952), Journalist
Mark Hatfield (South Carolina), U.S. Senator
Christie Hefner (Brandeis 1973), Publisher
Joseph Heller (New York U. 1948), Writer
Evan Hunter (Hunter College 1950), Writer
Erica Jong (Barnard 1963), Writer
Henry Kissinger (Harvard 1949), Former government official
Juanita Kreps (Duke 1974), Former government official
William Kunstler (Yale 1941), Lawyer
Flora Lewis (UCLA 1941), Journalist
Richard G. Lugar (Denison 1953), U.S. Senator
Michael Milken (U. of California at Berkeley 1968), Junk bond
    king
Kate Millett (U. of Minnesota 1956), Women's rights activist
Daniel Moynihan (Harvard), U.S. Senator
Edmund Muskie (Bates 1936), Former U.S. Senator
Diana Nyad (Lake Forest College 1972), Olympic swimmer
Joyce Carol Oates (Syracuse 1959), Writer
Claude Pepper (U. of Alabama 1921), U.S. Representative
Samuel R. Pierce (Cornell 1943), Former government official
Sylvia Porter (Hunter 1931), Newspaper columnist
Lewis F. Powell (Washington & Lee 1929), Supreme Court
    justice
Larry Pressler (U. of South Dakota 1964), U.S. Senator
William H. Rehnquist (Stanford 1948), Supreme Court justice
Joan Rivers (Barnard), Comedienne
Paul Robeson (Rutgers 1919), Singer, actor

Theodore Roosevelt (Harvard), U.S. President
Dean Rusk (Dartmouth 1931), Former government official
Paul Sarbanes (Princeton 1954), U.S. Senator
Phyllis Schlafly (U. of Washington, MO 1944), Conservative
activist
James Schlesinger (Harvard 1949), Former government official
Patricia Schroeder (U. of Minnesota 1961), U.S. Representative
Richard Schweiker (Penn State 1950), Former government
official
William Shirer (Coe College 1952), Author
Hugh Sidey (Iowa State), Journalist
B.F. Skinner (Hamilton 1925), Psychologist
Eleanor Smeal (Duke 1961), Women's rights activist
Howard K. Smith (Tulane 1936), Journalist
William French Smith (UCLA 1939), Former government official
Stephen Sondheim (Williams 1949), Composer, lyricist
Gloria Steinem (Smith 1955), Women's rights activist
John Stennis (U. of Virginia 1928), U.S. Senator
John Paul Stevens (U. of Chicago 1941), Supreme Court justice
Potter Stewart (Yale 1937), Supreme Court justice
William Styron (Duke), Author
William H. Taft (Yale 1878), U.S. President
Lowell Thomas (U. of Denver 1944), Journalist
Lester Thurow (Williams), Economist
Franchot Tone (Cornell 1926), Actor
Daniel J. Travanti (U. of Wisconsin 1961), Actor
John Updike (Harvard 1953), Writer
Caspar Weinberger (Harvard 1938), Former government official
Byron R. White (U. of Colorado 1937), Supreme Court justice

Source: United Chapters of Phi Beta Kappa, 1811 Q Street N.W., Washington, D.C. 20009. Undated entries usually indicate that the recipients were awarded keys years after graduation.

★ Famous Rhodes Scholars ★

Cecil J. Rhodes, British diamond and gold-mining millionaire, left in his 1899 will a scholarship fund to allow British Commonwealth and American students to study at Oxford University for two or three years at the graduate level. The scholarship covers free tuition and living expenses to about 70 students a year. Awards are not based on need alone but are given to those scholar-atheletes who are not "merely bookworms" but who have a "fondness of manly [sic] outdoor sports" and have "the moral force of character and instincts to lead." Since 1975 the scholarships have also gone to women.

Carl Albert (U.S. Speaker of the House)
Daniel J. Boorstin (Librarian of Congress)
David Boren (U.S. Senator, Oklahoma)
John Brademas (New York U. president)
Bill Bradley (U.S. Senator, New Jersey)
Richard Celeste (Governor, Ohio)
Bill Clinton (Governor, Arkansas)
Charles Collingwood (TV journalist)
Pete Dawkins (U.S. Army General, retired)
Hedley Donovan (Publishing executive)
James Fallows (Writer)
J. William Fulbright (U.S. Senator, Arkansas)
Pat Haden (Pro football player; lawyer)
Michael Kinsley (Editor; writer)
Jonathan Kozol (Author; educator)
Kris Kristofferson (Singer; songwriter; actor)
Elliott Levitas (U.S. Representative, Georgia)
Richard Lugar (U.S. Senator, Indiana)
Terrence Malick (Director)
Willie Morris (Writer)
Larry Pressler (U.S. Senator, South Dakota)
Bernard W. Rogers (U.S. General; Supreme Allied Commander)
Dean Rusk (U.S. Secretary of State)
Paul Sarbanes (U.S. Senator, Maryland)
Adam Smith (Writer, né George J. Goodman)
Howard K. Smith (TV journalist)
Stansfield Turner (U.S. Admiral; head of CIA)
Lester Thurow (Economist)
Robert Penn Warren (Author)
Byron "Whizzer" White (Supreme Court justice)

Note: It has been said that John F. Kennedy appointed 11 Rhodes scholars in his administration.

Time Magazine's
 ★ "Man of the Year" Winners ★

Each year the editors of *Time* magazine select an individual (or individuals) who have had the greatest impact on the lives of Americans in the past year. The individuals, selected in early January, do not necessarily have a positive effect on history, as the presence of Adolf Hitler and Ayatollah Khomeini on the list suggests.

1927	Charles Lindbergh
1928	Walter P. Chrysler
1929	Owen D. Young
1930	Mahatma Gandhi

1931	Pierre Laval
1932	Franklin D. Roosevelt
1933	Hugh S. Johnson
1934	Franklin D. Roosevelt
1935	Haile Selassie
1936	Wallis Warfield Simpson
1937	General and Mme. Chiang Kai-shek
1938	Adolf Hitler
1939	Joseph Stalin
1940	Winston Churchill
1941	Franklin D. Roosevelt
1942	Joseph Stalin
1943	George C. Marshall
1944	Dwight D. Eisenhower
1945	Harry S. Truman
1946	James F. Byrnes
1947	George C. Marshall
1948	Harry S. Truman
1949	Winston Churchill
1950	American Fighting Man
1951	Mohammed Mossadegh
1952	Queen Elizabeth
1953	Konrad Adenauer
1954	John Foster Dulles
1955	Harlow Curtice
1956	Hungarian Freedom Fighter
1957	Nikita Khrushchev
1958	Charles De Gaulle
1959	Dwight D. Eisenhower
1960	15 U.S. Scientists—John F. Ender, Willard F. Libby, Linus C. Pauling, Isidor I. Rabi, Edward Teller, Joshua Lederberg, Donald A. Glaser, Robert B. Woodward, Charles Draper, William Shockley, Emilio G. Segre, Charles Townes, George W. Beadle, James A. van Allen, and Edward Purcell
1961	John F. Kennedy
1962	Pope John XXIII
1963	Martin Luther King, Jr.
1964	Lyndon B. Johnson
1965	General William Westmoreland
1966	Youth, Americans 25 and under
1967	Lyndon B. Johnson
1968	Apollo 8 Astronauts—William Anders, Frank Borman, and James Lovell
1969	The Middle Americans
1970	Willy Brandt
1971	Richard M. Nixon
1972	Richard M. Nixon and Henry Kissinger
1973	Judge John J. Sirica
1974	King Faisal of Saudi Arabia

1975	12 U.S. Women—Alison Cheek, Billie Jean King, Carla Hills, Jill Conway, Betty Ford, Susie Sharp, Barbara Jordan, Ella Grasso, Addie Wyatt, Susan Brownmiller, Carol Sutton, and Kathleen Byerly
1976	Jimmy Carter
1977	Anwar al-Sadat
1978	Ten Hsiao-p'ing
1979	Ayatollah Khomeini
1980	Ronald Reagan
1981	Lech Walesa
1982	The Computer (Machine of the Year)
1983	Ronald Reagan and Yuri Andropov
1984	Peter Ueberroth
1985	Den Xiaoping
1986	Corazon Aquino
1987	Mikhail Gorbachev
1988	Endangered Earth (Planet of the Year)
1989	Mikhail Gorbachev
1990	"Men of the Year: The Two George Bushes"

Source: Time magazine.

★ Miss America Winners ★

1921	Margaret Gorman, Washington, D.C.
1922	Mary Campbell, Columbus, OH
1923	(no pageant)
1924	Ruth Malcolmson, Philadelphia, PA
1925	Fay Lanphier, Oakland, CA
1926	Norma Smallwood, Tulsa, OK
1927	Lois Delaner, Joliet, IL
1928–32	(no pageants)
1933	Marion Bergeron, West Haven, CT
1934	(no pageant)
1935	Henrietta Leaver, Pittsburgh, PA
1936	Rose Coyle, Philadelphia, PA
1937	Bette Cooper, Bertrand Island, NJ
1938	Marilyn Meseke, Marion, OH
1939	Patricia Donnelly, Detroit, MI
1940	Frances Marie Burke, Philadelphia, PA
1941	Rosemary LaPlanche, Los Angeles, CA
1942	Jo-Carroll Dennison, Tyler, TX
1943	Jean Bartel, Los Angeles, CA
1944	Venus Ramey, Washington, D.C.
1945	Bess Myerson, New York, NY
1946	Marilyn Buferd, Los Angeles, CA
1947	Barbara Walker, Memphis, TN
1948	BeBe Shopp, Hopkins, MN
1949	Jacque Mercer, Litchfield, AZ

1950	(no pageant)
1951	Yolande Betbeze, Mobile, AL
1952	Coreen Kay Hutchins, Salt Lake City, UT
1953	Neva Jane Langley, Macon, GA
1954	Evelyn Margaret Ay, Ephrata, PA
1955	Lee Meriwether, San Francisco, CA
1956	Sharon Ritchie, Denver, CO
1957	Marian McKnight, Manning, SC
1958	Marilyn Van Derbur, Denver, CO
1959	Mary Ann Mobley, Brandon, MS
1960	Lynda Lee Mead, Natchez, MS
1961	Nancy Fleming, Montague, MI
1962	Maria Fletcher, Asheville, NC
1963	Jacquelyn Mayer, Sandusky, OH
1964	Donna Axum, El Dorado, AR
1965	Vonda Kay Van Dyke, Phoenix, AZ
1966	Deborah Irene Bryant, Overland Park, KS
1967	Jane Anne Jayroe, Laverne, OK
1968	Debra Dene Barnes, Moran, KS
1969	Judith Anne Ford, Belvidere, IL
1970	Pamela Anne Eldred, Birmingham, MI
1971	Phyllis Ann George, Denton, TX
1972	Laurie Lea Schaefer, Columbus, OH
1973	Terre Anne Meeuwsen, De Pere, WI
1974	Rebecca Ann King, Denver, CO
1975	Shirley Cothran, Fort Worth, TX
1976	Tawny Elaine Godin, Yonkers, NY
1977	Dorothy Kathleen Benham, Edina, MN
1978	Susan Perkins, Columbus, OH
1979	Kylene Baker, Roanoke, VA
1980	Cheryl Prewitt, Ackerman, MS
1981	Susan Powell, Elk City, OK
1982	Elizabeth Ward, Russellville, AR
1983	Debra Sue Maffett, Anaheim, CA
1984	Vanessa Williams,* Millwood, NY
	Suzette Charles, Mays Landing, NJ
1985	Sharlene Wells, Salt Lake City, UT
1986	Susan Akin, Meridian, MS
1987	Kellye Cash, Memphis, TN
1988	Kaye Lani Rae Rafko, Toledo, OH
1989	Gretchen Elizabeth Carlson, Anoka, MN
1990	Debbye Turner, Mexico, MO

*Resigned on July 23, 1984, after discovery that she had posed nude with another woman for *Penthouse* magazine.

Market Evaluations, Inc. rates celebrities according to their likability (or lack of it) and the public's familiarity with them. The likability and familiarity result in a "Q Rating."

Most Popular	% Familiar	Pos. Q Rating	Neg. Q Rating
Bill Cosby	92%	53%	11%
Mary Kate/Ashley Olsen	49	48	10
Steven Spielberg	76	45	8
Robin Williams	79	43	14
Michael Jordan	75	42	13
Michael J. Fox	87	41	11
Jack Nicholson	81	40	11
Tom Hanks	76	40	8
Dustin Hoffman	84	40	7
Park Overall	41	40	10
Betty White	85	40	11
Clint Eastwood	89	39	11
Carol Burnett	87	39	14

Least Popular	% Familiar	Neg. Q. Rating	Pos. Q. Rating
Leona Helmsley	51	80	2
Zsa Zsa Gabor	85	75	4
Morton Downey, Jr.	71	73	6
Don King	56	70	6
George Steinbrenner	48	58	5
Eva Gabor	76	53	7
Grace Jones	52	52	9
Brigitte Nielsen	55	51	8
Dr. Ruth Westheimer	71	49	9
Ron Reagan, Jr.	49	49	9
Robin Givens	66	48	9
Dick Cavett	68	43	7
Dr. Joyce Brothers	75	39	8

Postive Q Rating = $\dfrac{\text{\% Rating "One of My Favorites"}}{\text{Total Familiar}}$

Negative Q Rating = $\dfrac{\text{\% Rating "Fair" or "Poor"}}{\text{Total Familiar}}$

Source: Marketing Evaluations, Inc., Port Washington, NY 11050.

Most Popular Comedians

(According to Performer Q Ratings)

Comedian/Comedienne	Q Rating
1. Bill Cosby	53%
2. Robin Williams	43
3. Carol Burnett	39
4. George Burns	38
5. Billy Crystal	37
6. Damon Wayans	35
7. Keenen Ivory Wayans	34
8. Eddie Murphy	33
9. Chevy Chase	33
10. John Cleese	32

Source: Marketing Evaluations, Inc., Port Washington, NY 11050.

★ Rock-and-Roll Hall of Famers ★

In 1985, Ahmet Ertegun, chairman of Atlantic Records, and Jann S. Wenner, publisher of *Rolling Stone* magazine, announced plans for the Rock-and-Roll Hall of Fame, which was to be built in Cleveland, Ohio, where the pioneering disc jockey Alan Freed launched his career and coined the term "rock 'n' roll." Awards have been given out since 1986 at a lavish black-tie dinner held at New York's Waldorf-Astoria Hotel, but delays due to fundraising and site selection prompted Mick Jagger to refer to the Hall of Fame as "the Phantom Temple of Rock." The most recent announcement said that groundbreaking should begin in early 1992.

The inductees fall into three categories: artists (who are eligible 25 years after the release of their first recording); early influences (pre-rock and non-rock performers); and non-performers (e.g., producers, songwriters).

Artist	Year Inducted	Artist	Year Inducted
LaVern Baker	1991	The Coasters	1987
Hank Ballard	1990	Eddie Cochran	1987
The Beach Boys	1988	Sam Cooke	1986
The Beatles	1988	Bobby Darin	1990
Chuck Berry	1986	Bo Diddley	1987
James Brown	1986	Dion DiMucci	1989
The Byrds	1991	Fats Domino	1986
Ray Charles	1986	The Drifters	1988

Artist	Year Inducted	Artist	Year Inducted
Bob Dylan	1988	Elvis Presley	1986
The Everly Brothers	1986	Otis Redding	1989
The Four Seasons	1990	Jimmy Reed	1991
The Four Tops	1990	Little Richard	1986
Aretha Franklin	1987	Smokey Robinson	1987
Marvin Gaye	1987	The Rolling Stones	1989
Bill Haley	1987	Simon and	
Buddy Holly	1986	Garfunkel	1990
John Lee Hooker	1991	The Supremes	1988
The Impressions	1991	The Temptations	1989
B.B. King	1987	Ike and Tina Turner	1991
The Kinks	1990	Joe Turner	1987
Jerry Lee Lewis	1986	Muddy Waters	1987
Clyde McPhatter	1987	The Who	1990
Wilson Pickett	1991	Jackie Wilson	1987
The Platters	1990	Stevie Wonder	1989

Early Influences	Year Inducted	Early Influences	Year Inducted
Louis Armstrong	1990	Ma Rainey	1990
Charlie Christian	1990	Bessie Smith	1989
Woody Guthrie	1988	The Soul Stirrers	1989
John Hammond	1986	T-Bone Walker	1987
The Inkspots	1989	Jerry Wexler	1986
Robert Johnson	1986	Hank Williams	1987
Louis Jordan	1987	Howlin' Wolf	1991
Leadbelly	1988	Jimmy Yancey	1986
Les Paul	1988		

Non-Performers	Year Inducted	Non-Performers	Year Inducted
Dave Bartholomew	1991	Brian Holland	1990
Ralph Bass	1991	Eddie Holland	1990
Leonard Chess	1987	Carole King	1990
Lamont Dozier	1990	Jerome Lieber	1987
Ahmet Ertegun	1987	Sam Phillips	1986
Alan Freed	1986	Phil Spector	1989
Jerry Goffin	1990	Michael Stoller	1987
Berry Gordy, Jr.	1988		

Top Radio Personalities in the United States by Audience Share

★ **(Drivetime, Spot Radio*)** ★

Personalities	Call Letters/City	Audience Share**
Claude Tomlinson	WIVK-AM & FM/Knoxville	39.3%
Ed Brantley	WIVK-AM & FM/Knoxville	31.9
Tom McCarthy, Arnold Dean, and Bob Steele	WTIC/Hartford	28.3
Scott Michaels	WQUT/Johnson City	24.4
Bob Hardy, Wendy Weiss, and Bill Wilkerson	KMOX/St. Louis	24.2
Steve Mann	WQUT/Johnson City	24.0
Wayne Perkey	WHAS/Louisville	23.7
Steve Gradowitz	KUZZ-AM & FM/Bakersfield	23.5
Michael W. Perry and Larry Price	KSSK-AM & FM/Honolulu	23.3
Charlie Boone and Robert Erickson	WCCO/Minn.-St.Paul	22.9
Bob & Tom	WNDE & WFBQ/Indianapolis	21.8
Bob Robbins	KSSN/Little Rock	21.7
Tim Quinn	WICC/Bridgeport	21.2
Rich Michaels	WVIC-AM & FM/Lansing	21.2
Smokin' Steve Hart	KRQQ/Tucson	20.9
Luther Masingill	WDEF-AM & FM/Chattanooga	20.7
Tim & Wally	KRQQ/Tucson	20.5
Alden Aaroe and Tim Timberlake	WRVA/Richmond	20.1
Skip Cheatham	WBLX-FM/Mobile	20.1
Mac Edwards	WRNS-AM & FM/Coastal N.C.	20.0
Dave & Dan	KXXY-AM & FM/Oklahoma City	19.8
Wayne Gardner and Bill Dodson	WKSJ-AM & FM/Mobile	19.8
Don Moore	KSSN/Little Rock	19.7
Jim Mason & Gary Dixon	WCOS-AM & FM/Columbia, S.C.	19.6

*AM Drive = 6–10 A.M.; PM Drive = 3–7 P.M.
**Percent of the total radio listening audience over 12 years old who are tuned to that particular program.

Source: Copyright © 1990, *Radio & Records*. Reprinted by permission.

Top Radio Personalities in the U.S. by Size of Audience

(Drivetime, Spot Radio)

★ ★

Personalities	Call Letters/City	Audience Size*
Paul Smith, Michael O'Neil, Judy DeAngelis	WINS/New York	1,888,500
Bridget Quinn, Jim Donnelly	WCBS/New York	1,367,500
Ross Britain	WHTZ/New York	1,308,900
Elvis Duran	WHTZ/New York	1,170,400
Rick Dees, Ellen K, Vick the Brick, Chuck Street	KIIS-AM & FM/ Los Angeles	1,084,700
Magic Matt Alan	KIIS-AM & FM/ Los Angeles	996,700
Howard Stern, Robin Quivers	WXRK/New York	955,600
Fast Jimi Roberts, Domino	WPLJ/New York	954,700
Ken Webb, Jeff Fox	WRKS/New York	954,700
Steve Roy	WLTW/New York	938,700
Carol Ford	WRKS/New York	908,900
Harry Harrison, Ron Lundy	WCBS-FM/New York	908,400
Scott Muni, Carol Miller	WNEW-FM/New York	905,200
Bob Shannon	WCBS-FM/New York	895,200
Bill Lee	WQHT/New York	892,700
Bob Collins	WGN/Chicago	878,400
Jim Douglas	WNSR/New York	841,700
Alice Stockton	WINS/New York	840,300
Joe Servantez	KPWR/Los Angeles	831,200
Del De Montreaux	WPAT-AM & FM/New York	827,100
Charlie Brailer, Iris Shelton, John Brooks	KFWB/Los Angeles	825,800
Bryan Simmons	KOST/Los Angeles	814,800
Archer & Rusty	WPLJ/New York	813,500
Jay Thomas, Monica Brooks, Gina Davis	KPWR/Los Angeles	808,400
Rita Sands, Tom Franklin	WCBS/New York	807,800

*Cumulative audience, over 12 years old.

Source: Copyright © 1990, *Radio & Records*. Reprinted by permission.

PRESIDENTS, POLITICS, AND HISTORY

Age of U.S. Presidents on Day of Inauguration

★ ─── ★

Age at Inauguration*

1.	Ronald W. Reagan	69 yrs. 349 days
2.	William H. Harrison	68 yrs. 23 days
3.	James Buchanan	65 yrs. 315 days
4.	George H.W. Bush	64 yrs. 223 days
5.	Zachary Taylor	64 yrs.100 days
6.	Dwight D. Eisenhower	62 yrs. 98 days
7.	Andrew Jackson	61 yrs. 354 days
8.	John Adams	61 yrs. 125 days
9.	Gerald R. Ford	61 yrs. 26 days
10.	Harry S. Truman	60 yrs. 339 days
11.	James Monroe	58 yrs. 310 days
12.	James Madison	57 yrs. 353 days
13.	Thomas Jefferson	57 yrs. 325 days
14.	John Quincy Adams	57 yrs. 236 days
15.	George Washington	57 yrs. 67 days
16.	Andrew Johnson	56 yrs. 107 days
17.	Woodrow Wilson	56 yrs. 65 days
18.	Richard M. Nixon	56 yrs. 11 days
19.	Benjamin Harrison	55 yrs. 196 days
20.	Warren G. Harding	55 yrs. 122 days
21.	Lyndon B. Johnson	55 yrs. 87 days
22.	Herbert Hoover	54 yrs. 206 days
23.	Rutherford B. Hayes	54 yrs. 151 days
24.	Martin Van Buren	54 yrs. 89 days
25.	William McKinley	54 yrs. 34 days
26.	James E. Carter	52 yrs. 111 days
27.	Abraham Lincoln	52 yrs. 20 days
28.	Chester A. Arthur	51 yrs. 350 days
29.	William H. Taft	51 yrs. 170 days
30.	Franklin D. Roosevelt	51 yrs. 33 days
31.	Calvin Coolidge	51 yrs. 30 days
32.	John Tyler	51 yrs. 8 days
33.	Millard Fillmore	50 yrs. 184 days
34.	James K. Polk	49 yrs. 122 days
35.	James A. Garfield	49 yrs. 105 days
36.	Franklin Pierce	48 yrs. 101 days
37.	Grover Cleveland	47 yrs. 351 days
38.	Ulysses S. Grant	46 yrs. 236 days
39.	John F. Kennedy	43 yrs. 236 days
40.	Theodore Roosevelt	42 yrs. 322 days

*First inauguration only.

U.S. Presidents' Time in Office

Time in Office

1.	William H. Harrison	32 days
2.	James A. Garfield	199 days
3.	Zachary Taylor	1 yr. 128 days
4.	Gerald R. Ford	2 yrs. 150 days
5.	Warren G. Harding	2 yrs. 151 days
6.	Millard Fillmore	2 yrs. 236 days
7.	John F. Kennedy	2 yrs. 306 days
8.	Chester A. Arthur	3 yrs. 166 days
9.	Andrew Johnson	3 yrs. 323 days
10.	John Tyler	3 yrs. 332 days
11.	John Adams	4 yrs.
12.	John Quincy Adams	4 yrs.
13.	Martin Van Buren	4 yrs.
14.	James K. Polk	4 yrs.
15.	Franklin Pierce	4 yrs.
16.	James Buchanan	4 yrs.
17.	Rutherford B. Hayes	4 yrs.
18.	Benjamin Harrison	4 yrs.
19.	William H. Taft	4 yrs.
20.	Herbert Hoover	4 yrs.
21.	James E. Carter	4 yrs.
22.	Abraham Lincoln	4 yrs. 43 days
23.	William McKinley	4 yrs. 194 days
24.	Lyndon B. Johnson	5 yrs. 59 days
25.	Richard M. Nixon	5 yrs. 201 days
26.	Calvin Coolidge	5 yrs. 213 days
27.	Theodore Roosevelt	7 yrs. 171 days
28.	Harry S. Truman	7 yrs. 283 days
29.	George Washington	7 yrs. 308 days
30.	Thomas Jefferson	8 yrs.
31.	James Madison	8 yrs.
32.	James Monroe	8 yrs.
33.	Andrew Jackson	8 yrs.
34.	Ulysses S. Grant	8 yrs.
35.	Grover Cleveland	8 yrs.
36.	Woodrow Wilson	8 yrs.
37.	Ronald W. Reagan	8 yrs.
38.	Dwight D. Eisenhower	8 yrs.
39.	Franklin D. Roosevelt	12 yrs. 39 days
40.	George H.W. Bush	??

Heights of U.S. Presidents

★   ★

		Height
1.	Abraham Lincoln	6′4″
2.	Lyndon B. Johnson	6′3″
3.	George H.W. Bush	6′2″
4.	Thomas Jefferson	6′2½″
5.	Chester A. Arthur	6′2″
6.	Franklin D. Roosevelt	6′2″
7.	George Washington	6′2″
8.	Andrew Jackson	6′1″
9.	Ronald W. Reagan	6′1″
10.	James Buchanan	6′
11.	Gerald R. Ford	6′
12.	James A. Garfield	6′
13.	Warren G. Harding	6′
14.	John F. Kennedy	6′
15.	James Monroe	6′
16.	William H. Taft	6′
17.	John Tyler	6′
18.	Richard M. Nixon	5′11½″
19.	Grover Cleveland	5′11″
20.	Herbert C. Hoover	5′11″
21.	Woodrow Wilson	5′11″
22.	Dwight D. Eisenhower	5′10½″
23.	Calvin Coolidge	5′10″
24.	Andrew Johnson	5′10″
25.	Franklin Pierce	5′10″
26.	Theodore Roosevelt	5′10″
27.	James E. Carter	5′9½″
28.	Millard Fillmore	5′9″
29.	Harry S. Truman	5′9″
30.	Ulysses S. Grant	5′8½″
31.	Rutherford B. Hayes	5′8½″
32.	William H. Harrison	5′8″
33.	James K. Polk	5′8″
34.	Zachary Taylor	5′8″
35.	John Adams	5′7″
36.	John Quincy Adams	5′7″
37.	William McKinley	5′7″
38.	Benjamin Harrison	5′6″
39.	Martin Van Buren	5′6″
40.	James Madison	5′4″

Richard Nixon's Enemies List

On June 27, 1973, White House counsel John Dean submitted President Richard M. Nixon's "enemies list" to the Senate "Watergate" Committee. Here are the people who made the list:

Alexander E. Barkan, AFL-CIO Committee on Political Education
John Conyers, Michigan congressman
Maxwell Dane, advertising agency executive (Doyle Dane Bernbach)
Sid Davidoff, aide to New York City Mayor John V. Lindsay
Ronald Dellums, California congressman
S. Harrison Dogole, Globe Security System
Charles Dyson, Dyson-Kissner Corporation
Bernard T. Feld, Council for a Livable World
Ed Guthman, *Los Angeles Times*
Morton Halprin, Common Cause
Samuel M. Lambert, National Education Association
Allard Lowenstein, New York congressman
Mary McGrory, Washington newspaper columnist
Stewart Rawlings Mott, General Motors heir
S. Sterling Munro, Jr., congressional aide
Paul Newman, movie actor
Arnold M. Picker, United Artists Corporation
Daniel Schorr, CBS news correspondent
Howard Stein, Dreyfus Corporation
Leonard Woodcock, United Auto Workers

Rich Members of U.S. Congress

There is no law saying that U.S. elected officials have to be millionaires, but it is not coincidental that many of them are. It takes a lot of advertising money to run for office, and ego and power are transferrable from one career to another. And politics attracts the publicity that makes it hard to beat as a second career for rich people. "Roll Call" looked beyond federal financial disclosure forms to find out what congressional members were really worth (vs. what was listed in *Congressional Quarterly*), and here's what they came up with:

	Net Worth
Sen. John Heinz (Rep.—Pa.)	$460 million
Sen. Herbert Kohl (Dem.—Wis.)	$250 million
Sen. Jay Rockefeller (Dem.—W. Va.)	$200 million

	Net Worth
Rep. Amory Houghton (Rep.—NY)	$100 million
Sen. Frank Lautenberg (Dem.—NJ)	$45 million
Sen. Edward Kennedy (Dem.—Mass.)	$40 million
Rep. Norm Sisisky (Dem.—Va.)	$30 million
Sen. John Danforth (Rep.—Mo.)	$25 million
Sen. Dennis De Concini (Dem.—Ariz.)	$20 million
Sen. Chuck Robb (Dem.—Va.)	$13 million
Sen. Claiborne Pell (Dem.—RI)	$11 million
Rep. Bill Green (Rep.—NY)	$8 million
Rep. Nancy Pelosi (Dem.—Cal.)	$7.5 million
Rep. Sid Yates (Dem.—Ill.)	$7.1 million
Sen. Lloyd Bentsen (Dem.—Tex.)	$7 million
Sen. Bob Graham (Dem.—Fla.)	$6 million
Rep. Pete Stark (Dem.—Cal.)	$5.2 million
Rep. John Spratt (Dem.—SC)	$5.1 million
Sen. John Warner (Rep.—Va.)	$5 million
Sen. Nancy Kassebaum (Rep.—Kan.)	$4.3 million
Rep. Owen Pickett (Dem.—Va.)	$4.2 million
Sen. Terry Sanford (Dem.—NC)	$4.1 million
Rep. Glenn Anderson (Dem.—Cal.)	$4 million
Rep. J.J. Pickle (Dem.—Tex.)	$3.6 million
Rep. Jimmy Quillen (Rep.—Tenn.)	$3.5 million

Source: "Roll Call," *Forbes* magazine, February 19, 1990.

Actors and Entertainers Who Became Politicans

★   ★

Rex Bell. A cowboy star in the 1930s and husband of Clara Bow, Bell was elected lieutenant governor of Nevada in 1954.

Shirley Temple Black. The former child star ran for Congress in 1967 but lost to Paul McCloskey; appointed a delegate to the UN's 24th General Assembly, 1969–70; appointed U.S. ambassador to Ghana in 1974–76. She was also U.S. Chief of Protocol 1976–77 and has held other ambassadorial posts.

Sonny Bono. The singer and former husband of Cher became mayor of Palm Springs, California in 1988. By the end of 1990 he was sending out trial balloons about running for the U.S. Senate.

Wendell Corey. A leading man in the 1940s and 1950s (*Rear Window* and TV's "Harbor Command"), Corey was elected to the Santa Monica City Council in 1965. He sought the Republican nomination for the California 28th congressional district seat in 1966, but lost to incumbent Alonzo Bell.

Helen Gahagan Douglas. An actress (*She,* 1935), and the wife of actor Melvyn Douglas, she was elected congresswoman from California's 14th district in the 1940s; she ran for U.S. Senate in 1950 but lost to Richard M. Nixon.

Clint Eastwood. An actor, and owner of the Hog's Breath Inn in Carmel, California, Eastwood was mayor of Carmel 1986–88.

Charles Farrell. A romantic leading man in the 1920s (*Seventh Heaven*) and later on TV's "My Little Margie" in the early 1950s, Farrell was mayor of Palm Springs, California for seven years.

John Gavin. The Stanford graduate and actor was, among other things, Janet Leigh's love interest in the movie *Psycho.* He became U.S. ambassador to Mexico 1981–86 under fellow actor-turned-politican Ronald Reagan.

Fred Grandy. Formerly on TV's "Love Boat," the preppie (Exeter) and Harvard '70 honors graduate has been a U.S. congressman from the state of Iowa since 1987.

Al Jolson. The star of the first talkie, *The Jazz Singer*, was elected mayor of Encino, California in 1937.

Ben Jones. Formerly Cooter on TV's "Dukes of Hazard," Jones was elected U.S. congressman (Dem.) from Georgia's 4th District in 1988 and was later reelected to a second term.

Jack Kelly. Best known for playing Bart Maverick's brother Bret on the popular TV series "Maverick" in the 1950s, Kelly was elected mayor of Huntington Beach, California in 1983.

John Davis Lodge. A leading man of the 1930s (*Little Women*, 1933), Lodge became Governor of Connecticut in the early 1950s; U.S. ambassador to Spain, 1955–61; and U.S. ambassador to Argentina, 1969–73.

Melina Mercouri. The Greek actress's grandfather was mayor of Athens for 30 years, and her father was a longtime member of the Greek Parliament, so it was not unusual that Mercouri became politically active. She lost her initial bid for Parliament in 1974 but was elected three years later, representing the port city of Piraeus, and eventually became Minister of Culture.

George Murphy. An affable song-and-dance actor popular from the 1930s to the 1950s, the 1920 graduate of Yale was a longtime president of the Screen Actors Guild and was elected U.S. Senator from California in 1964. He lost a reelection bid to John Tunney in 1970.

Ronald Reagan. The quintessential actor-turned-politician quickly went from TV's "Death Valley Days" into politics and was elected governor of California, 1966–74 and U.S. President, 1980–88.

★ Political Leanings ★

Democrats

Woody Allen
Karen Allen
Bea Arthur
Edward Asner
Lauren Bacall
Kaye Ballard
Justine Bateman
Allyce Beasley
Warren Beatty
Ed Begley, Jr.
Stephen Bishop
Tom Bosley
Lloyd Bridges
Albert Brooks
Ellen Burstyn
LeVar Burton
Richard Chamberlain
Carol Channing
Cher
Bill Cosby
Cathy Lee Crosby
Christopher Cross
Billy Crystal
Blythe Danner
Ted Danson
Colleen Dewhurst
Neil Diamond
Helen Gahagan Douglas
Kirk Douglas
Michael Douglas
Richard Dreyfuss
Olympia Dukakis
Shelly Duvall
Sheena Easton
Michael Eisner
Linda Evans
Morgan Fairchild
Mike Farrell
Mia Farrow
Norman Fell

José Ferrer
Sally Field
Jane Fonda
Harrison Ford
Michael J. Fox
Art Garfunkel
Richard Gere
Harry Hamlin
Darryl Hannah
Goldie Hawn
Don Henley
Marilu Henner
Judd Hirsch
Dennis Hopper
Holly Hunter
Anjelica Huston
Kate Jackson
Don Johnson
Ben Jones
Quincy Jones
Joanna Kerns
Margot Kidder
Robert Klein
Kris Kristofferson
Cloris Leachman
Norman Lear
Ron Leibman
Hal Linden
John Lithgow
Rob Lowe
Shirley MacLaine
Malcolm McDowell
Burgess Meredith
Joe Montana
Judd Nelson
Paul Newman
Randy Newman
Leonard Nimoy
Carroll O'Connor
Michael Ovitz
Catherine Oxenberg

Gregory Peck
Sydney Pollack
Tony Randall
Christopher Reeve
Rob Reiner
Robert Redford
Judge Reinhold
Marion Ross
Telly Savalas
Ally Sheedy
Cybill Shepherd
Ron Silver
Carly Simon
Paul Simon
Dean Stockwell
William Styron
Donald Sutherland
James Taylor
Marlo Thomas
Lily Tomlin
John Updike
Jack Valenti
Robert Vaughn
Christopher Walken
Eli Wallach
Raquel Welch
Richard Widmark
Robin Williams
Paul Winfield
Debra Winger
Shelley Winters
Joanne Woodward

Republicans

Muhammad Ali
June Allyson
Gene Autry
Shirley Temple Black
Ray Bolger
Pat Boone
Bruce Boxleitner
Betty Buckley
Chuck Connors
Mike Connors
Robert Conrad
Wendell Corey

Arlene Dahl
Jimmy Dean
Clint Eastwood
Buddy Ebsen
Dale Evans
Chad Everett
Chris Evert
Eva Gabor
John Gavin
Crystal Gayle
Stewart Granger
Rosey Grier
Merv Griffin
Lionel Hampton
Helen Hayes
Charlton Heston
Bob Hope
Shirley Jones
Cheryl Ladd
Dorothy Lamour
Rich Little
Loretta Lynn
Fred MacMurray
Dean Martin
George Murphy
Wayne Newton
Chuck Norris
Donald O'Connor
Ronald Reagan
Joan Rivers
Roy Rogers
Cesar Romero
Mickey Rooney
Jill St. John
Tom Selleck
Frank Sinatra
Yakov Smirnoff
Robert Stack
James Stewart
Robert Wagner
Clint Walker
Andy Williams
Jonathan Winters
Loretta Young
Efrem Zimbalist, Jr.

The Hollywood Ten

★   ★

These 10 Hollywood screenwriters, directors, and producers refused to tell the House Un-American Activities Committee (HUAC) in 1947 whether or not they were members of the Communist Party. For refusing to confirm or deny the accusation, they all served short prison sentences for contempt of Congress, after which they were "blacklisted" within the American film industry. Some of them eventually found work and recovered; others didn't.

Alvah Bessie	(screenwriter)
Herbert Biberman	(director, writer)
Lester Cole	(screenwriter)
Edward Dmytryk	(director)
Ring Lardner, Jr.	(screenwriter)
John Howard Lawson	(screenwriter)
Albert Maltz	(screenwriter)
Sam Ornitz	(screenwriter)
Adrian Scott	(producer)
Dalton Trumbo	(screenwriter)

The 100 Most Influential People in History

★   ★

Author Michael H. Hart analyzed the contributions of people throughout history and came up with the following list of "the 100 most influential persons in history."

1. Elijah Muhammad (religious, secular leader)
2. Sir Isaac Newton (scientist)
3. Jesus Christ (religious leader)
4. Buddha (religious leader)
5. Confucius (philosopher)
6. St. Paul (apostle)
7. Ts'ai Lun (inventor of paper)
8. Johannes Gutenberg (printer)
9. Christopher Columbus (explorer)
10. Albert Einstein (scientist)
11. Karl Marx (political philosopher)
12. Louis Pasteur (chemist, biologist)
13. Galileo Galilei (astronomer)
14. Aristotle (philosopher)
15. Vladimir Ilyich Lenin (political leader)
16. Moses (prophet)
17. Charles Darwin (evolutionist)

18. Shi Huang-ti (Chinese emperor)
19. Augustus Caesar (Roman emperor)
20. Mao Zedong (political leader)
21. Genghis Khan (conqueror)
22. Euclid (mathematician)
23. Martin Luther (religious leader)
24. Nicolaus Copernicus (astronomer)
25. James Watt (inventor)
26. Constantine the Great (Byzantine emperor)
27. George Washington (U.S. President)
28. Michael Faraday (inventor)
29. James Clark Maxwell (physicist)
30. Orville and Wilbur Wright (aviators)
31. Antoine-Laurent Lavoisier (scientist)
32. Sigmund Freud (psychoanalyst)
33. Alexander the Great (conqueror)
34. Napoléon Bonaparte (French emperor)
35. Adolf Hitler (German dictator)
36. William Shakespeare (playwright)
37. Adam Smith (economist)
38. Thomas Edison (inventor)
39. Antony van Leeuwenhoek (scientist)
40. Plato (philosopher)
41. Guglielmo Marconi (inventor)
42. Ludwig van Beethoven (composer)
43. Werner Heisenberg (physicist)
44. Alexander Graham Bell (inventor)
45. Alexander Fleming (scientist)
46. Simón Bolívar (South American political leader)
47. Oliver Cromwell (military leader)
48. John Locke (philosopher)
49. Michelangelo (artist)
50. Pope Urban II (Roman Catholic leader)
51. Umar ibn al-Khattab (caliph)
52. Asoka (Indian emperor)
53. St. Augustine (theologian)
54. Max Planck (physicist)
55. John Calvin (theologian)
56. Wiliam T.G. Morton (anesthetist)
57. William Harvey (physician)
58. Antoine-Henri Becquerel (physicist)
59. Gregor Mendel (scientist)
60. Joseph Lister (surgeon)
61. Nikolaus August Otto (inventor)
62. Louis Daguerre (inventor)
63. Joseph Stalin (Russian dictator)
64. René Descartes (philosopher, mathematician)
65. Julius Caesar (Roman emperor)
66. Francisco Pizarro (explorer)
67. Hernando Cortez (explorer)
68. Queen Isabella I (Spanish queen)

69. William the Conqueror (English ruler)
70. Thomas Jefferson (U.S. President)
71. Jean-Jacques Rousseau (philosopher)
72. Edward Jenner (physician)
73. Wilhelm Conrad Roentgen (scientist)
74. Johann Sebastian Bach (composer)
75. Lao Tzu (philosopher)
76. Enrico Fermi (physicist)
77. Thomas Malthus (economist)
78. Francis Bacon (political leader)
79. Voltaire (philosopher)
80. John F. Kennedy, Jr. (U.S. President)
81. Gregory Pincus (biologist)
82. Sui Wen Ti (Chinese emperor)
83. Mani (prophet)
84. Vasco da Gama (explorer)
85. Charlemagne (Carolingian emperor)
86. Cyrus the Great (Persian king)
87. Leonhard Euler (mathematician)
88. Niccolò Machiavelli (political philosopher)
89. Zoroaster (prophet)
90. Menes (Egyptian king)
91. Peter the Great (Russian czar)
92. Mencius (philosopher)
93. John Dalton (scientist)
94. Homer (poet)
95. Queen Elizabeth (British monarch)
96. Justinian I (Byzantine emperor)
97. Johannes Kepler (scientist)
98. Pablo Picasso (artist)
99. Mahavira (religious leader)
100. Niels Bohr (physicist)

Honorable Mentions: St. Thomas Aquinas, Archimedes, Charles Babbage, Cheops, Marie Curie, Benjamin Franklin, Gandhi, Abraham Lincoln, Ferdinand Magellan, and Leonardo da Vinci.

Source: The 100: A Ranking of the Most Influential Persons in History, by Michael H. Hart, Galahad Publishing, 1982, New York.

Current U.S. Supreme Court Justices

★ ★

Chief Justice	Year Born	Religion	Appointed by Year
William H. Rehnquist	1924	Lutheran	Nixon (1986)

Associate Justices			
Harry A. Blackmun	1908	Methodist	Nixon (1970)
Thurgood Marshall	1908	Episcopalian	Johnson (1967)
Byron R. White	1917	Episcopalian	Kennedy (1962)
John P. Stevens III	1920	Protestant	Ford (1975)
Sandra Day O'Connor	1930	Episcopalian	Reagan (1981)
Antonin Scalia	1936	Roman Catholic	Reagan (1986)
Anthony M. Kennedy	1936	(not given)	Reagan (1988)
David H. Souter	1939	Episcopalian	Bush (1990)

★ Former Chief Justices ★

	Year Born	Relgion	Term
John Jay	1745	Episcopalian	(1789–95)
John Rutledge	1739	Church of England	(1795)
Oliver Ellsworth	1745	Congregational	(1796–1800)
John Marshall	1755	Episcopalian	(1801–35)
Roger B. Taney	1777	Roman Catholic	(1836–64)
Salmon P. Chase	1808	Episcopalian	(1864–73)
Morrison R. Waite	1816	Episcopalian	(1874–88)
Melville W. Fuller	1833	Episcopalian	(1888–1910)
Edward D. White	1845	Roman Catholic	(1910–21)
William H. Taft	1857	Unitarian	(1921–30)
Charles E. Hughes	1862	Baptist	(1930–41)
Harlan F. Stone	1872	Episcopalian	(1941–46)
Frederick M. Vinson	1890	Methodist	(1946–53)
Earl Warren	1891	Protestant	(1953–69)
Warren E. Burger	1907	Presbyterian	(1969–86)

SPORTS

Athletes of the Year

Sports editors from Associated Press member newspapers have selected the Male and Female Athlete of the Year every year since 1931. Here are the winners:

Male Athlete of the Year

1990 Joe Montana (football)
1989 Joe Montana (football)
1988 Orel Hershiser (baseball)
1987 Ben Johnson (track and field)
1986 Larry Bird (basketball)
1985 Dwight Gooden (baseball)
1984 Carl Lewis (track and field)
1983 Carl Lewis (track and field)
1982 Wayne Gretzky (hockey)
1981 John McEnroe (tennis)
1980 U.S. Olympic Hockey Team
1979 Willie Stargell (baseball)
1978 Ron Guidry (baseball)
1977 Steve Cauthen (horse racing)
1976 Bruce Jenner (decathlon)
1975 Fred Lynn (baseball)
1974 Muhammad Ali (boxing)
1973 O.J. Simpson (football)
1972 Mark Spitz (swimming)
1971 Lee Trevino (golf)
1970 George Blanda (football)
1969 Tom Seaver (baseball)
1968 Denny McLain (baseball)
1967 Carl Yastrzemski (baseball)
1966 Frank Robinson (baseball)
1965 Sandy Koufax (baseball)
1964 Don Schollander (swimming)

1963 Sandy Koufax (baseball)
1962 Maury Wills (baseball)
1961 Roger Maris (baseball)
1960 Rafer Johnson (track)
1959 Ingĕmar Johansson (boxing)
1958 Herb Elliott (track)
1957 Ted Williams (baseball)
1956 Mickey Mantle (baseball)
1955 Hopalong Cassidy (football)
1954 Willie Mays (baseball)
1953 Ben Hogan (golf)
1952 Bob Mathias (track, football)
1951 Dick Hazmaier (football)
1950 Jim Konstanty (baseball)
1949 Leon Hart (football)
1948 Lou Boudreau (baseball)
1947 Johnny Lujack (football)
1946 Glenn Davis (football)
1945 Byron Nelson (golf)
1944 Byron Nelson (golf)
1943 Gunder Haegg (track)
1942 Frank Sinkwich (football)
1941 Joe DiMaggio (baseball)
1940 Tom Harmon (football)
1939 Nile Kinnick (football)
1938 Don Budge (tennis)
1937 Don Budge (tennis)
1936 Jessie Owens (track)
1935 Joe Louis (boxing)
1934 Dizzy Dean (baseball)
1933 Carl Hubbell (baseball)
1932 Gene Sarazen (golf)
1931 Pepper Martin (baseball)

Source: Associated Press.

Female Athlete of the Year

1990 Beth Daniel (golf)

1989 Steffi Graf (tennis)

1988 Florence Griffith Joyner (track and field)

1987 Jackie Joyner-Kersee (track and field)

1986 Martina Navratilova (tennis)

1985 Nancy Lopez (golf)

1984 Mary Lou Retton (gymnastics)

1983 Martina Navratilova (tennis)

1982 Mary Decker-Slaney (track)

1981 Tracy Austin (tennis)

1980 Chris Evert (tennis)

1979 Tracy Austin (tennis)

1978 Nancy Lopez (golf)

1977 Chris Evert (tennis)

1976 Nadia Comaneci (gymnastics)

1975 Chris Evert (tennis)

1974 Chris Evert (tennis)

1973 Billy Jean King (tennis)

1972 Olga Korbut (gymnastics)

1971 Evonne Goolagong (tennis)

1970 Chi Cheng (track)

1969 Debbie Meyer (swimming)

1968 Peggy Fleming (figure skating)

1967 Billie Jean King (tennis)

1966 Kathy Whitworth (golf)

1965 Kathy Whitworth (golf)

1964 Mickey Wright (golf)

1963 Mickey Wright (golf)

1962 Dawn Fraser (swimming)

1961 Wilma Rudolph (track)

1960 Wilma Rudolph (track)

1959 Maria Bueno (tennis)

1958 Althea Gibson (tennis)

1957 Althea Gibson (tennis)

1956 Pat McCormick (diving)

1955 Patty Berg (golf)

1954 Babe Didrickson Zaharias (golf)

1953 Maureen Connolly (tennis)

1952 Maureen Connolly (tennis)

1951 Maureen Connolly (tennis)

1950 Babe Didrickson Zaharias (golf)

1949 Marlene Bauer (golf)

1948 Fanny Blankers-Koen (track)

1947 Babe Didrickson Zaharias (golf)

1946 Babe Didrickson Zaharias (golf)

1945 Babe Didrickson Zaharias (golf)

1944 Ann Curtis (swimming)

1943 Patty Berg (golf)

1942 Gloria Callen (swimming)

1941 Betty Hicks Newell (golf)

1940 Alice Marble (tennis)

1939 Alice Marble (tennis)

1938 Patty Berg (golf)

1937 Katherine Rawls (swimming)

1936 Helen Stephens (track)

1935 Helen Wills Moody (tennis)

1934 Virginia Van Wie (golf)

1933 Helen Jacobs (tennis)

1932 Babe Didrickson (track)

1931 Helen Madison (swimming)

Source: Associated Press.

Athletes' "Moonlighting" Endorsement Income

★ ★

	Sport	Endorsement Income
Michael Jordan	basketball	$9,000,000
Arnold Palmer	golf	9,000,000
Steffi Graf	tennis	8,000,000
Greg Norman	golf	8,000,000
Jack Nicklaus	golf	7,000,000
Boris Becker	tennis	5,500,000
Ivan Lendl	tennis	5,000,000
Jimmy Connors	tennis	4,500,000
Joe Montana	football	4,500,000
Bernhard Langer	golf	4,000,000
Curtis Strange	golf	4,000,000
Greg LeMond	cycling	3,200,000
André Agassi	tennis	3,000,000
Stefan Edberg	tennis	3,000,000
Chris Evert	tennis	3,000,000
John McEnroe	tennis	3,000,000
Lee Trevino	golf	2,700,000
Steve Ballesteros	golf	2,500,000
Nick Faldo	golf	2,500,000
Sandy Lyle	golf	2,500,000
Ayako Okamoto	golf	2,500,000
Magic Johnson	basketball	2,500,000
Gabriela Sabatini	tennis	2,500,000
Gary Player	golf	2,000,000
Martina Navratilova	tennis	2,000,000
Larry Bird	basketball	2,000,000
Michael Chang	tennis	2,000,000

Source: The New York Times, May 6, 1990, and *Golf Digest.* Non-golf figures are reports or estimates from players' agents. Bo Jackson was not listed.

★ Heisman Memorial Trophy Winners ★

Determined by a poll of sportswriters and sportscasters, the Heisman Memorial Trophy is presented annually by the Downtown Athletic Club of New York City to the nation's outstanding college football player.

1990 Ty Detmer (Brigham Young)
1989 Andre Ware (Houston)
1988 Barry Sanders (Oklahoma State)
1987 Tim Brown (Notre Dame)
1986 Vinnie Testaverde (Miami)
1985 Bo Jackson (Auburn)

1984 Doug Flutie (Boston College)
1983 Mike Rozier (Nebraska)
1982 Herschel Walker (Georgia)
1981 Marcus Allen (So. California)
1980 George Rogers (South Carolina)
1979 Charles White (So. California)
1978 Billy Sims (Oklahoma)
1977 Earl Campbell (Texas)
1976 Tony Dorsett (Pittsburgh)
1975 Archie Griffin (Ohio State)
1974 Archie Griffin (Ohio State)
1973 John Cappelletti (Penn State)
1972 Johnny Rodgers (Nebraska)
1971 Pat Sullivan (Auburn)
1970 Jim Plunkett (Stanford)
1969 Steve Owen (Oklahoma)
1968 O.J. Simpson (So. California)
1967 Gary Beban (U.C.L.A.)
1966 Steve Spurrier (Florida)
1965 Mike Garrett (So. California)
1964 John Huarte (Notre Dame)
1963 Roger Staubach (Navy)
1962 Terry Baker (Oregon State)
1961 Ernie Davis (Syracuse)
1960 Joe Bellino (Navy)

1959 Billy Cannon (Louisiana State)
1958 Pete Dawkins (Army)
1957 John Crow (Texas A&M)
1956 Paul Hornung (Notre Dame)
1955 Howard Cassady (Ohio State)
1954 Alan Ameche (Wisconsin)
1953 Johnny Lattner (Notre Dame)
1952 Billy Vessels (Oklahoma)
1951 Dick Kazmaier (Princeton)
1950 Vic Janowicz (Ohio State)
1949 Leon Hart (Notre Dame)
1948 Doak Walker (So. Methodist)
1947 Johnny Lujack (Notre Dame)
1946 Glenn Davis (Army)
1945 Felix Blanchard (Army)
1944 Leslie Horvath (Ohio State)
1943 Angelo Bertelli (Notre Dame)
1942 Frank Sinkwich (Georgia)
1941 Bruce Smith (Minnesota)
1940 Tom Harmon (Michigan)
1939 Nile Kinnick (Iowa)
1938 Davey O'Brien (Texas Christian)
1937 Clinton Frank (Yale)
1936 Larry Kelley (Yale)
1935 Jay Berwanger (Chicago)

★ Pro Football Hall of Famers ★

The Pro Football Hall of Fame was established in 1963 by the National Football League. Nominees, except for coaches, must be retired for five years. Coaches merely have to be retired. Voting is done by sportswriters and sportscasters based in all 28 NFL cities. The Pro Football Hall of Fame museum is located at 2121 George Halas Drive NW, Canton, Ohio 44708; phone 216-456-8207.

Players

Herb Adderley (1980)
Lance Alworth (1978)
Doug Atkins (1982)
Red Badgro (1981)
Cliff Battles (1968)
Sammy Baugh (1963)
Chuck Bednarik (1967)
Bobby Bell (1983)
Raymond Berry (1973)
Fred Biletnikoff (1988)
George Blanda (1981)
Mel Blount (1989)
Terry Bradshaw (1989)
Jim Brown (1971)
Buck Buchanan (1990)
Dick Butkus (1979)
Earl Campbell (1991)
Tony Canadeo (1974)
Jack Christiansen (1970)
Dutch Clark (1963)
George Connor (1975)
Larry Csonka (1987)
Willie Davis (1981)
Len Dawson (1987)
Mike Ditka (1988)
Art Donovan (1968)
Paddie Driscoll (1965)
Bill Dudley (1966)
Turk Edwards (1969)
Tom Fears (1970)
Len Ford (1976)
Dan Fortmann (1985)
Frank Gatski (1985)
Bill George (1974)
Frank Gifford (1977)
Otto Graham (1965)
Red Grange (1963)
Joe Greene (1987)
Forrest Gregg (1977)
Bob Griese (1990)
Lou Groza (1974)
Joe Guyon (1966)
Jack Ham (1988)
Franco Harris (1990)
Ed Healey (1964)
Mel Hein (1963)
Ted Hendricks (1990)
Pete Henry (1963)
Arnie Herber (1966)

Bill Hewitt (1971)
Clarke Hinkle (1964)
Elroy Hirsch (1968)
Paul Hornung (1986)
Ken Houston (1986)
Cal Hubbard (1963)
Sam Huff (1982)
Don Hutson (1963)
John Henry Johnson (1987)
Deacon Jones (1980)
Sonny Jurgensen (1983)
Frank Kinard (1971)
Jack Lambert (1990)
Dick Lane (1974)
Jim Langer (1987)
Willie Lanier (1986)
Yale Lary (1979)
Dante Lavelli (1975)
Bobby Layne (1967)
Tuffy Leemans (1978)
Bob Lilly (1980)
Sid Luckman (1965)
Roy Lyman (1964)
Gino Marchetti (1972)
Ollie Matson (1972)
Don Maynard (1987)
George McAfee (1966)
Mike McCormack (1984)
Hugh McElhenny (1970)
Johnny McNally (1963)
Mike Michalske (1964)
Wayne Millner (1968)
Bobby Mitchell (1983)
Ron Mix (1979)
Lenny Moore (1975)
Marion Motley (1968)
George Musso (1982)
Bronko Nagurski (1963)
Joe Namath (1985)
Ernie Nevers (1963)
Ray Nitschke (1978)
Leo Nomellini (1969)
Merlin Olsen (1982)
Jim Otto (1980)
Alan Page (1988)
Clarence Parker (1972)
Jim Parker (1973)
Joe Perry (1969)
Peter Pihos (1970)
Jim Ringo (1981)

Andy Robustelli (1971)
Gale Sayers (1977)
Joe Schmidt (1973)
Art Shell (1989)
O.J. Simpson (1985)
Bart Starr (1977)
Roger Staubach (1985)
Ernie Stautner (1969)
Bob St. Clair (1990)
Jan Stenerud (1991)
Ken Strong (1967)
Joe Stydahar (1967)
Fran Tarkenton (1986)
Charley Taylor (1984)
Jim Thorpe (1963)
Y.A. Tittle (1971)
Tom Trafton (1964)
Charley Trippi (1968)
Emlen Tunnell (1967)
Clyde Turner (1966)
Johnny Unitas (1979)
Gene Upshaw (1987)
Norm Van Brocklin (1971)
Steve Van Buren (1965)
Doak Walker (1986)
Paul Warfield (1983)
Bob Waterfield (1965)
Arnie Weinmeister (1984)
Bill Willis (1977)
Larry Wilson (1978)
Alex Wojciechowicz (1968)
Willie Wood (1989)

Player and Coach

Guy Chamberlin (1965)
Ray Flaherty (1976)
Walt Kiesling (1976)
Steve Owen (1966)

Player, Coach and Owners

Jimmy Conzelman
George Halas (1963)

Coaches

Paul Brown (1967)
Weeb Ewbank (1978)
Sid Gillman (1983)
Curly Lambeau (1963)
Tom Landry (1990)
Vince Lombardi (1971)
Earle Neale (1969)

Contributors

Bert Bell (1963)
Charles Bidwill, Sr. (1967)
Joe Carr (1963)
Lamar Hunt (1972)
Tim Mara (1963)
George Preston Marshall
  (1963)
Hugh Ray (1966)
Dan Reeves (1967)
Art Rooney (1964)
Pete Rozelle (1985)

Highest-Paid Professional
Football Players

★   ★

	Team	Annual Income
Jim Kelly	Bills	$4,800,000
Joe Montana	49ers	$4,000,000
Jeff George	Colts	$3,650,000
Cortez Kennedy	Seahawks	$3,100,000
Keith McCants	Buccaneers	$2,950,000
Blair Thomas	Jets	$2,800,000
Andre Ware	Lions	$2,500,000
Jim Everett	Rams	$2,400,000
Herschel Walker	Vikings	$2,250,000

	Team	Annual Income
Neal Anderson	Bears	$2,200,000
Eric Dickerson	Colts	$2,200,000
Junior Seau	Chargers	$2,175,000
Frank Reich	Bills	$1,830,000
Anthony Carter	Vikings	$1,750,000
Richmond Webb	Dolphins	$1,679,500
Greg Townsend	Raiders	$1,625,000
Chris Doleman	Vikings	$1,600,000
Charles Haley	49ers	$1,550,000
Lawrence Taylor	Giants	$1,550,000
Roger Craig	49ers	$1,500,000
Bernie Kosar	Browns	$1,500,000
Don Majkowski	Packers	$1,500,000
Dan Marino	Dolphins	$1,500,000
Warren Moon	Oilers	$1,500,000
Jerry Rice	49ers	$1,500,000
Chris Singleton	Patriots	$1,500,000

Source: *Inside Sports,* April 1991.

Note: Figures based on 1990 base salaries, including signing and reported bonuses and deferred income; incentives are not included.

Highest-Paid Professional
★ Basketball Players ★

	Team	Annual Income
Hot Rod Williams	Cavaliers	$5,000,000
Patrick Ewing	Knicks	$4,257,500
Akeem Olajuwon	Rockets	$4,062,450
Karl Malone	Jazz	$3,300,000
Danny Ferry	Cavaliers	$3,000,000
Sam Perkins	Lakers	$3,000,000
Charles Barkley	76ers	$2,900,000
Magic Johnson	Lakers	$2,892,860
Derrick Coleman	Nets	$2,700,000
Michael Jordan	Bulls	$2,550,000
Chris Mullin	Warriors	$2,550,000
Moses Malone	Hawks	$2,506,000
Bernard King	Bullets	$2,500,000
Robert Parish	Celtics	$2,500,000
Danny Manning	Clippers	$2,200,000
Blair Rasmussen	Nuggets	$2,200,000
Dennis Scott	Magic	$2,200,000
Chuck Person	Pacers	$2,100,000
David Robinson	Spurs	$2,050,000
Sam Bowie	Nets	$2,000,000

	Team	Annual Income
Ralph Sampson	Kings	$2,000,000
LaSalle Thompson	Kings	$2,000,000
Dominique Wilkins	Hawks	$2,000,000

Source: Inside Sports, April 1991.

Note: Figures are for 1990–91 season, base salaries including signing bonuses and deferred payments; incentives are not included.

★ Heavyweight Boxing Champions ★

John L. Sullivan (1885–92)
James J. Corbett (1892–97)
Bob Fitzsimmons (1897–99)
James J. Jeffries (1899–1905)
Marvin Hart (1905–06)
Tommy Burns (1906–08)
Jack Johnson (1908–15)
Jess Willard (1915–19)
Jack Dempsey (1919–26)
Gene Tunney (1926–28)
Max Schmeling (1930–32)
Jack Sharkey (1932–33)
Primo Carnera (1933–34)
Max Baer (1934–35)
James J. Braddock (1935–37)
Joe Louis (1937–49)
Ezzard Charles (1949–51)
Jersey Joe Walcott (1951–52)
Rocky Marciano (1952–56)
Floyd Patterson (1956–59)
Ingemar Johansson (1959–60)
Floyd Patterson (1960–62)
Sonny Liston (1962–64)
**Cassius Clay (1964–70)
Ernie Terrell (WBA: 1965–67)
Joe Frazier (NY: 1968–70)
Jimmy Ellis (WBA: 1968–70)
Joe Frazier (1970–73)
George Foreman (1973–74)

**Muhammad Ali (1974–78)
Leon Spinks (1978)
Ken Norton (WBC: 1978)
Larry Holmes (WBC: 1978–80)
**Muhammad Ali (1978–79)
John Tate (WBA: 1979–80)
Mike Weaver (WBA: 1980–82)
Larry Holmes (1980–85)
Michael Dokes (WBA: 1982–83)
Gerrie Coetzee (WBA: 1983–84)
Tim Witherspoon (WBC: 1984)
Pinklon Thomas (WBC: 1984–86)
Greg Page (WBA: 1984–85)
Michael Spinks (1985–87)
Tim Witherspoon (WBA: 1986)
Trevor Berbick (WBC: 1986)
Mike Tyson (WBC: 1986–87)
James Smith (WBA: 1986–87)
Tony Tucker (IBF: 1987)
Mike Tyson (WBC, WBA, IBF: 1987–88)
Mike Tyson (1988–90)
Buster Douglas (WBC, WBA, IBF: 1990)
Evander Holyfield (1991)

*Note: NBA (National Boxing Association), WBA (World Boxing Association), WBC (World Boxing Council), IBF (International Boxing Federation), and other national and state commissions do not always agree on who is the champion at any given time. There is some overlap due to a lack of unanimity among these boxing organizations.

**Cassius Clay changed his name to Muhammad Ali after defeating Sonny Liston in 1964.

Bowling Hall of Famers

The Professional Bowlers Association founded the PBA Hall of Fame in 1975. To be eligible for consideration, a candidate must be at least 35 years old, a member of PBA for a minimum of 12 years, and have won one title or more. The following are the honorees, their year of entry, and category:

Performance Category

1975 Ray Bluth
1975 Don Carter
1975 Carmen Salvino
1975 Harry Smith
1975 Dick Weber
1975 Billy Welu
1976 Buzz Fazio
1977 Billy Hardwick
1977 Don Johnson
1978 Dave Davis
1978 Dick Ritger
1979 Nelson Burton, Jr.
1979 Dave Soutar
1980 Jim Stefanich
1981 Earl Anthony
1981 Wayne Zahn
1982 John Petraglia
1983 Bill Allen
1984 Mike Durbin
1985 Larry Laub
1986 George Pappas
1987 Jim Godman
1987 Mark Roth
1988 Gary Dickinson
1989 Tommy Hudson
1990 Joe Berardi
1990 Marshall Holman

Veterans Category

1984 Glenn Allison
1985 Joe Joseph
1986 John Guenther
1987 Bob Strampe
1988 Barry Asher
1988 Mike McGrath
1989 Jim St. John
1990 Andy Marzich

Meritorious Service

1975 Frank Esposito
1975 Chuck Pezzano
1976 Eddie Elias
1976 Chris Schenkel
1977 Steve Nagy
1978 Lou Frantz
1978 Joe Richards
1980 Lorraine Stitzlein
1983 Harry Golden
1984 E.A. "Bud" Fisher
1985 Ted Hoffman, Jr.
1986 Dick Evans
1987 Raymond Firestone
1988 John Jowdy
1989 John Archibald
1989 Joe Kelley

Source: Professional Bowlers Association, Akron, Ohio.

Tennis Hall of Famers

Since 1955, 151 people have been elected into the International Tennis Hall of Fame, located in Newport, Rhode Island. Players are chosen "for their records of competitive achievement with consideration given to sportsmanship and character. In addition, individuals who have made exceptional contributions to the sport are also eligible for consideration." A nominating committee proposes a slate of not more than five candidates each year and then circulates the list to members of the international tennis media. A 75-percent favorable vote of returned ballots is needed for election.

	Year Inducted		Year Inducted
George Adee	1964	Roy Emerson	1982
Fred Alexander	1961	Pierre Etchebaster	1978
Wilmer Allison	1963	Bob Falkenburg	1974
Manuel Alonso	1977	Neale Fraser	1984
Arthur Ashe	1985	Shirley Fry-Irvin	1970
Juliette Atkinson	1974	Chuck Garland	1969
Lawrence Baker, Sr.	1975	Althea Gibson	1971
Maud Barger-Wallach	1958	Pancho Gonzalez	1968
Karl Behr	1969	Evonne Goolagong	
Pauline Betz Addie	1965	Cawley	1988
Bjorn Borg	1987	Bryan "Bitsy" Grant	1972
Jean Borotra	1976	David Gray	1985
John Bromwich	1984	Clarence Griffin	1970
Norman Brookes	1977	King of Sweden	
Louise Brough Clapp	1967	Gustav V	1980
Mary K. Browne	1957	Harold Hackett	1961
Jacques Brugnon	1976	Ellen Hansell	1965
Don Budge	1964	Darlene Hard	1973
Maria Bueno	1978	Doris Hart	1969
Molla Bjurstedt		Ann Haydon Jones	1985
Mallory	1958	Gladys Heldman	1979
Mabel Cahill	1976	W.E. "Slew" Hester	1981
Oliver Campbell	1955	Lew Hoad	1980
Malcolm Chace	1961	Hazel Hotchkiss	
Clarence Clark	1983	Wightman	1957
Joseph Clark	1955	Harry Hopman	1978
William Clothier	1956	Fred Hovey	1974
Henri Cochet	1976	Joe Hunt	1966
Maureen Connolly		Frank Hunter	1961
Brinker	1968	Helen Hull Jacobs	1962
Gottfried von Cramm	1977	Bill Johnston	1958
Jack Crawford	1979	Perry Jones	1970
Joseph E. Cullman III	1990	Jan Kodes	1990
Allison Danzig	1968	Jack Kramer	1968
Dwight Davis	1956	Rene Lacoste	1976
Lotte Dod	1983	Al Laney	1979
John Doeg	1962	William Larned	1956
Lawrence Doherty	1980	Art Larsen	1969
Reginald Doherty	1980	Suzanne Lenglen	1978
Dorothy Douglass		George Lott	1964
Chambers	1981	Gene Mako	1973
Jaroslav Drobny	1983	Alice Marble	1964
James Dwight	1955	Alastair Martin	1973

	Year Inducted		Year Inducted
William McC. Martin	1982	Dorothy Round Little	1986
Kathleen McKane Godfree	1978	Elizabeth Ryan	1972
		Manuel Santana	1984
Chuck McKinley	1986	Dick Savitt	1976
Maurice McLoughlin	1957	Ted Schroeder	1966
Don McNeill	1965	Eleonora Sears	1968
Billie Jean Moffitt King	1987	Richard Sears	1955
		Frank Sedgman	1979
Elisabeth Moore	1971	Pancho Segura	1984
Gardnar Mulloy	1972	Vic Seixas	1971
Lindley Murray	1958	Frank Shields	1964
Julian Myrick	1963	Henry Slocum	1955
John Newcombe	1986	Margaret Smith Court	1979
Arthur Nielsen	1971	Stan Smith	1987
Betty Nuthall Shoemaker	1977	Fred Stolle	1985
		May Sutton Bundy	1956
Alex Olmedo	1987	Bill Talbert	1967
Margaret Osborne duPont	1967	Bill Tilden	1959
		Lance Tingay	1982
Rafael Osuna	1979	Ted Tinling	1986
Mary Outerbridge	1981	Bertha Townsend Toulmin	1974
Sarah Palfrey Danzing	1963	Tony Trabert	1970
Frank Parker	1966	James Van Alen	1965
Gerald Patterson	1989	John Van Ryn	1963
Budge Patty	1977	Ellsworth Vines	1962
Theodore Pell	1966	Virginia Wade	1989
Fred Perry	1975	Marie Wagner	1969
Tom Pettitt	1982	Holcombe Ward	1956
Nicola Pietrangeli	1986	Watson Washburn	1965
Adrian Quist	1984	Malcolm Whitman	1955
Dennis Ralston	1987	Anthony Wilding	1978
Ernest Renshaw	1983	Richard Williams II	1957
William Renshaw	1983	Helen Wills Moody Roark	1959
Vincent Richards	1961		
Bobby Riggs	1967	Sidney Wood	1964
Tony Roche	1986	Robert Wrenn	1955
Ellen Roosevelt	1975	Beals Wright	1956
Ken Rosewall	1980		

Source: International Tennis Hall of Fame, Newport, Rhode Island.

National Baseball Hall of Fame

★ ★

Founded in 1935 to celebrate baseball's 100th anniversary, the National Baseball Hall of Fame is located in Cooperstown, New York. Nominated players must have played at least part of 10 seasons in the major leagues and be retired for five years. The voting is done by members of the Baseball Writers Association of America. As highlighted by the recent debate over Pete Rose's ineligibility, nominees not only must have superior records but also must be reasonably virtuous off the field.

Players

Hank Aaron (1982), right fielder

Grover Alexander (1938), pitcher

Cap Anson (1939), first baseman

Luis Aparicio (1984), shortstop

Luke Appling (1964), shortstop

Earl Averill (1975), center fielder

Frank Baker (1955), third baseman

Dave Bancroft (1971), shortstop

Ernie Banks (1977), shortstop

Jacob Beckley (1971), first baseman

Cool Papa Bell* (1974), outfielder

Johnnie Bench (1989), catcher

Chief Bender (1953), pitcher

Yogi Berra (1972), catcher

James Bottomley (1974), first baseman

Lou Boudreau (1970), shortstop

Roger Bresnahan (1945), catcher

Lou Brock (1985), left fielder

Dennis Brouthers (1945), first baseman

Mordecai Brown (1949), pitcher

Jesse Burkett (1946), left fielder

Roy Campanella (1969), catcher

Rod Carew (1991), first baseman

Max Carey (1961), center fielder

Frank Chance (1946), first baseman

Oscar Charleston* (1976), first baseman

Jack Chesbro (1946), pitcher

Fred Clarke (1945), left fielder

John Clarkson (1963), pitcher

Roberto Clemente (1973), right fielder

Ty Cobb (1936), center fielder

Mickey Cochrane (1947), catcher

Edward Collins (1939), second baseman

Jimmy Collins (1945), third baseman

Earle Combs (1970), center fielder

Roger Connor (1976), first baseman

Sam Crawford (1957), right fielder

Joe Cronin (1956), shortstop

Kiki Cuyler (1968), right fielder

Ray Dandridge* (1987), third baseman

Dizzy Dean (1953), pitcher

Ed Delahanty (1945), left fielder

Bill Dickey (1954), catcher

Martin Dihigo* (1977), pitcher, outfielder

Joe DiMaggio (1955), center fielder

Bobby Doerr (1986), second baseman

Don Drysdale (1984), pitcher

Hugh Duffy (1945), center fielder

Buck Ewing (1939), catcher

Johnny Evers (1946), second baseman

Red Faber (1964), pitcher

Bob Feller (1962), pitcher

Rick Ferrell (1984), catcher

Elmer Flick (1963), right fielder

Whitey Ford (1974), pitcher

Rube Foster* (1981), pitcher/manager

Jimmy Foxx (1951), first baseman

Frankie Frisch (1947), second baseman

Pud Galvin (1965), pitcher

Lou Gehrig (1939), first baseman

Charles Gehringer (1949), second baseman

Bob Gibson (1981), pitcher

Josh Gibson* (1972), catcher

Lefty Gomez (1972), pitcher

Goose Goslin (1968), left fielder

Hank Greenberg (1956), first baseman

Burleigh Grimes (1964), pitcher

Lefty Grove (1947), pitcher

Chick Hafey (1971), left fielder

Jess Haines (1970), pitcher

Billy Hamilton (1961), center fielder

Gabby Hartnett (1955), catcher

Harry Heilmann (1952), right fielder

Babe Herman (1975), second baseman

Harry Hooper (1971), right fielder

Rogers Hornsby (1942), second baseman

Waite Hoyt (1969), pitcher

Carl Hubbell (1947), pitcher

Catfish Hunter (1987), pitcher

Monte Irvin* (1973), outfielder

Travis Jackson (1982), shortstop

Ferguson Jenkins (1990), pitcher

Hugh Jennings (1945), shortstop

Judy Johnson* (1975), third baseman

Walter Johnson (1936), pitcher

Addie Joss (1978), pitcher

Al Kaline (1980), right fielder

Tim Keefe (1964), pitcher

Willie Keeler (1939), right fielder

George Kell (1983), third baseman

Joe Kelley (1971), left fielder

George Kelly (1973), first baseman

King Kelly (1945), right fielder

Harmon Killebrew (1984), first baseman

Ralph Kiner (1975), left fielder

Chuck Klein (1980), right fielder

Sandy Koufax (1972), pitcher

Napoleon Lajoie (1937), second baseman

Bob Lemon (1976), pitcher

Buck Leonard* (1972), first baseman

Fred Lindstrom (1976), third baseman

Pop Lloyd* (1977), shortstop

Ernie Lombardi (1986), catcher

Ted Lyons (1955), pitcher

Mickey Mantle (1974), center fielder

Heinie Manush (1964), left fielder

Juan Marichal (1983), pitcher

Rabbit Maranville (1954), shortstop

Rube Marquard (1971), pitcher

Christy Mathewson (1936), pitcher

Eddie Matthews (1978), third baseman

Willie Mays (1979), center fielder

Tommy McCarthy (1946), right fielder

Willie McCovey (1986), first baseman

Joe McGinnity (1946), pitcher

Joe Medwick (1968), left fielder

Johnny Mize (1981), first baseman

Joe Morgan (1990), second baseman

Stan Musial (1969), left fielder

Kid Nichols (1949), pitcher

Jim O'Rourke (1945), left fielder

Mel Ott (1951), right fielder

Satchel Paige* (1971), pitcher

Jim Palmer (1990), pitcher

Herb Pennock (1948), pitcher

Eddie Plank (1946), pitcher

Old Hoss Radourne (1939), pitcher

Pee Wee Reese (1984), shortstop

Sam Rice (1963), right fielder

Eppa Rixey (1963), pitcher

Robin Roberts (1976), pitcher

Brooks Robinson (1983), third baseman

Frank Robinson (1982), right fielder

Jackie Robinson (1962), second baseman

Edd Roush (1962), center fielder

Red Ruffing (1967), pitcher

Amos Rusie (1977), pitcher

Babe Ruth (1936), right fielder

Ray Schalk (1955), catcher

Red Schoendienst (1989), second baseman

Joe Sewell (1977), shortstop

Al Simmons (1953), left fielder

George Sisler (1939), first baseman

Enos Slaughter (1985), right fielder

Duke Snider (1980), center fielder

Warren Spahn (1973), pitcher

Tris Speaker (1937), center fielder

Willie Stargell (1988), first baseman

Bill Terry (1954), first baseman

Sam Thompson (1974), right fielder

Joe Tinker (1946), shortstop

Pie Traynor (1948), third baseman

Dazzy Vance (1955), pitcher

Arky Vaughan (1985), shortstop

Rube Waddell (1946), pitcher

Honus Wagner (1936), shortstop

Bobby Wallace (1953), shortstop

Ed Walsh (1946), pitcher

Lloyd Waner (1967), center fielder

Paul Waner (1952), right fielder

Monte Ward (1964), shortstop

Mickey Welch (1973), pitcher

Zack Wheat (1959), left fielder

Hoyt Wilhelm (1985), pitcher
Billy Williams (1987), left
fielder
Ted Williams (1966), left
fielder
Hack Wilson (1979), center
fielder
Early Wynn (1972), pitcher
Carl Yastrzemski (1989),
left fielder
Cy Young (1937), pitcher
Ross Youngs (1972), right
fielder

Others (Managers,
officials, umpires, etc.)

Walter Alston (1983),
manager
Al Barlick (1989), umpire
Edward Barrow (1953),
manager, executive
Morgan G. Bulkeley (1937),
executive
Alexander Cartwright (1938),
executive
Henry Chadwick (1938),
writer, statistician
A.B. "Happy" Chandler
(1982), commissioner
Charles Comiskey (1939),
executive
Jocko Conlin (1974), umpire
Candy Cummings (1939),
early player
Billy Evans (1973), umpire
Ford C. Frick (1970),
commissioner
Warren C. Giles (1979),
executive
Clark Griffith (1946),
executive

Will Harridge (1972),
executive
Bucky Harris (1975),
manager
Cal Hubbard (1976), umpire
Miller J. Huggins (1964),
manager
Ban Johnson (1937),
executive
Bill Klem (1953), umpire
Kenesaw M. Landis (1944),
commissioner
Al Lopez (1977), player,
manager
Connie Mack (1937),
manager
Larry MacPhail (1978),
executive
Joe McCarthy (1957),
manager
John McGraw (1937),
manager
Bill McKechnie (1962),
manager
Branch Rickey (1967), man-
ager, executive
Wilbert Robinson (1945),
manager
Albert G. Spalding (1939),
executive
Casey Stengel (1966), player,
manager
George M. Weiss (1971),
executive
George Wright (1937), early
player
Harry Wright (1953), early
player, manager
Tom Yawkey (1980),
executive

*Negro League player elected by special committee.

National Baseball Hall of Fame, P.O. Box 590, Cooperstown, NY 13326; telephone
(607) 547-9988.

Baseball Multimillionaires

★   ★

If polo is the sport of princes, baseball has now become the sport of millionaires. Of the 650 major league players, 226 (or 35 percent) make over $1,000,000 a year, and 124 (or 19 percent) make over $2,000,000 a year. Not bad pay for an eight-month work year and a four-hour work day! Maybe that's why a hot dog and a beer now costs $8.00.

	Annual Income
Darryl Strawberrry, Dodgers	$3,800,000
Will Clark, Giants	3,750,000
Kevin Mitchell, Giants	3,750,000
Joe Carter, Blue Jays	3,666,667
Mark Davis, Royals	3,625,000
Eric Davis, Reds	3,600,000
Willie McGee, Giants	3,562,500
Mark Langston, Angels	3,550,000
José Canseco, Athletics	3,500,000
Tim Raines, White Sox	3,500,000
Dave Stewart, Athletics	3,500,000
Bob Welch, Athletics	3,450,000
Don Mattingly, Yankees	3,420,000
Doug Drabek, Pirates	3,350,000
Dennis Martinez, Expos	3,333,333
André Dawson, Cubs	3,300,000
Nolan Ryan, Rangers	3,300,000
Dave Winfield, Angels	3,300,000
Glenn Davis, Orioles	3,275,000
Danny Darwin, Red Sox	3,250,000
Rickey Henderson, Athletics	3,250,000
Paul Molitor, Brewers	3,233,333
Robin Yount, Brewers	3,200,000
Mike Boddicker, Royals	3,166,667
Orel Hershiser, Dodgers	3,166,667
Kirby Puckett, Twins	3,166,667
Frank Viola, Mets	3,166,667
Vince Coleman, Mets	3,112,500
Kelly Gruber, Blue Jays	3,033,333
Dennis Eckersley, Athletics	3,000,000
Jack Morris, Twins	3,000,000
Tom Henke, Blue Jays	2,966,667
Bret Saberhagen, Royals	2,950,000
Jack Clark, Red Sox	2,900,000
Mark McGwire, Athletics	2,850,000
Brett Butler, Dodgers	2,833,333
Bill Doran, Reds	2,833,333
Ted Higuera, Brewers	2,750,000
Fred McGriff, Padres	2,750,000

Wade Boggs, Red Sox	2,700,000
Gary Gaetti, Angels	2,700,000
Mark Gubicza, Royals	2,666,667
Lee Smith, Cardinals	2,666,667
Tom Browning, Reds	2,650,000
Ryne Sandberg, Cubs	2,650,000
John Franco, Mets	2,633,333
Danny Jackson, Cubs	2,625,000
Ruben Sierra, Rangers	2,625,000
Roger Clemens, Red Sox*	2,600,000
Dave Henderson, Athletics	2,600,000
Kent Hrbek, Twins	2,600,000
Eddie Murray, Dodgers	2,561,998
Mike Greenwell, Red Sox	2,550,000
Fernando Valenzuela, Dodgers	2,550,000
Jeff Reardon, Red Sox	2,533,333
Tom Brunansky, Red Sox	2,500,000
Tom Candiotti, Indians	2,500,000
Chuck Finley, Angels	2,500,000
Dale Murphy, Phillies	2,500,000
Dave Righetti, Giants	2,500,000
Jeff Russell, Rangers	2,450,000
Dwight Gooden, Mets***	2,416,667
Lance Parrish, Angels	2,416,667
Bobby Thigpen, White Sox	2,416,667
Mike Witt, Yankees	2,416,667
Bobby Bonilla, Pirates	2,400,000
Steve Farr, Yankees	2,400,000
Scott Garrelts, Giants	2,400,000
Greg Maddux, Cubs	2,400,000
Bo Jackson, Royals	2,375,000
Storm Davis, Royals	2,366,667
José De Leon, Cardinals	2,366,667
Andres Galarraga, Expos	2,366,667
David Cone, Mets	2,350,000
Mike Scott, Astros	2,337,500
José Rijo, Reds	2,333,333
Cal Ripken, Jr., Orioles	2,333,333
Tony Gwynn, Padres**	2,325,000
Hubie Brooks, Mets	2,316,667
Barry Bonds, Pirates	2,300,000
Tony Peña, Red Sox	2,300,000
Julio Franco, Rangers	2,287,500
Pedro Guerrero, Cardinals	2,283,333
Rick Sutcliffe, Cubs	2,275,000
Tim Burke, Expos	2,266,667
Kevin McReynolds, Mets	2,266,667
Dan Plesac, Brewers	2,266,667
Matt Young, Red Sox	2,266,667
Danny Tartabull, Royals	2,250,000
Ozzie Smith, Cardinals	2,225,000

Zane Smith, Pirates	2,225,000
Len Dykstra, Phillies	2,216,667
Kevin Gross, Dodgers	2,216,667
Ivan Calderon, Expos	2,200,000
Von Hayes, Phillies	2,200,000
Alan Trammell, Tigers	2,200,000
Mike Scioscia, Dodgers	2,183,333
Jim Key, Blue Jays	2,166,667
Sid Fernandez, Mets	2,166,667
Howard Johnson, Mets	2,166,667
Andy Van Slyke, Pirates	2,150,000
Bryn Smith, Cardinals	2,133,333
Scott Sanderson, Yankees	2,125,000
George Bell, Cubs	2,100,000
Jim Deshales, Astros	2,100,000
Shawon Dunston, Cubs	2,100,000
Nick Esasky, Braves	2,100,000
Tony Fernandez, Padres	2,100,000
Wally Joyner, Angels	2,100,000
Barry Larkin, Angels	2,100,000
Kirk McCaskill, Angels	2,100,000
Pascual Perez, Yankees	2,100,000
George Brett, Royals	2,074,848
Doug Jones, Indians	2,050,000
Craig Lefferts, Padres	2,041,667
Lonnie Smith, Braves	2,041,667
Pete O'Brien, Mariners	2,037,500
Kal Daniels, Dodgers	2,025,000
Greg Swindell, Indians	2,025,000
Larry Andersen, Padres	2,000,000
Kevin Bass, Giants	2,000,000
Roger McDowell, Phillies	2,000,000
Randy Myers, Reds	2,000,000
Lou Whitaker, Tigers	2,000,000

Source: The New York Times, February 22, 1991; figures include salary and, where applicable, pro-rated share of signing bonus.

*Clemens signed a new four-year contract worth $5,380,000 a year, but it is an extension on his current contract.

**Gwynn's new contract extension will earn him $4,083,333 a year.

***At the time this book was being edited, Gooden signed a new contract that nearly doubled his pay and placed him in the top five.

MISCELLANY

★ Quotations About Famous People ★

Spiro Agnew. "Nixon's Nixon." Eugene McCarthy

Steve Allen. "When I can't sleep, I read a book by Steve Allen." Oscar Levant

Fred Astaire. "Astaire is remote. It is as if he were in an incubator, breathing his own air. His perfection is like crystal: You can see through it. It is hopeless to try to imitate him." Mikhail Baryshnikov

Tallulah Bankhead. "A day away from Tallulah is like a month in the country." Howard Dietz

Brigitte Bardot. "The only woman I've had a sexual fantasy about. . . . With me, looks come first, and she's everything a woman should be . . . blonde, beautiful. She's got the most incredible legs—everything. And she's French as well." Rod Stewart

John Barrymore. "For a man who has been dead for fifteen years I am in remarkable health." John Barrymore on himself

Warren Beatty. "Warren was the most divine lover of all. His libido was as lethal as high octane gas. I had never known such pleasure and passion in my life. Warren could handle women as smoothly as operating an elevator. He knew exactly where to locate the top button." Britt Ekland

"Warren's conquests of women are not totally unsuccessful. His percentage is about fifty-fifty." Lee Grant

John Belushi. "A good man, but a bad boy." Dan Aykroyd

Leonard Bernstein. "Leonard Bernstein uses music as an accompaniment to his conducting." Oscar Levant

William F. Buckley, Jr. "We have three things in common: Irish wives, the ability to speak for 17 minutes without using a verb, and the fact that we both speak with an accent." Henry Kissinger

Howard Cosell. "There have always been mixed emotions about Howard Cosell. Some people hate him like poison and some people just hate him regular." Buddy Hackett

Joan Crawford. "She's like that old joke about Philadelphia. First prize, four years with Joan. Second prize, eight." Franchot Tone

James Dickey. "The kind of man that after he has four martinis you want to drop a grenade down his throat." Burt Reynolds

Marlene Dietrich. "Marlene Dietrich's legs may be longer, but I have seven grandchildren." Gloria Swanson

W.C. Fields. "Any man who hates dogs and babies can't be all bad." Leo Rosten

Jane Fonda. "She never associated the idea of sex with sin. In this she was a woman free from any guilt complex." Roger Vadim

Clark Gable. "His ears made him look like a taxicab with both doors open." Howard Hughes

Zsa Zsa Gabor. "She knew more days on which gifts could be given than appear on any holiday calendar." Conrad Hilton

Greta Garbo. "What, when drunk, one sees in other women, one sees in Garbo sober." Kenneth Tynan

Richard Gere. "He's got a pin-up image—which he hates. The only trouble is whenever they ask him to take his trousers off, he does." Michael Caine

Dustin Hoffman. "Better as a woman. If I were him, I'd never get out of drag." Mr. Blackwell

John Huston. "John, if you weren't the son of my beloved friend Walter, and if you weren't a brilliant writer and magnificent director, you'd be nothing but a common drunk." Gregory Ratoff

Edward "Teddy" Kennedy. "Ted's a considerate person, especially to women." Joan Kennedy

Robert F. Kennedy. "I can't see that it's wrong to give him a little legal experience before he goes out to practice law." John F. Kennedy, upon naming his brother as U.S. Attorney General

Vivien Leigh. "She wanted us to be like brother and sister. But, fortunately occasional incest was allowed." Laurence Olivier

Liberace. "This deadly, winking, sniggering, snuggling, scent-impregnated, chromium-lated, luminous, quivering, giggling, fruit-flavored, mincing, ice-covered heap of mother-love . . . the summit of sex—the pinnacle of Masculine, Feminine, and Neuter." Cassandra, a London critic

Sophia Loren. "Her nose is too big, her mouth is too big, she has the composites of all the wrong things, but put them all together and pow! All the natural mistakes of beauty fall together to create a magnificent accident." Rex Reed

Billy Martin. "Extraordinary Achievement Award to Billy Martin, for having reached the age of 50 without being murdered by someone . . . to the amazement of all who know him." A plaque in Billy Martin's office

Mary Martin. "She's okay if you like talent." Ethel Merman

Louis B. Mayer. "The reason so many people turned up at his funeral is that they wanted to make sure he was dead." Samuel Goldwyn

Marilyn Monroe. "She had curves in places other women don't even have places." Cybill Shepherd

"It was like going to the dentist, making a picture with her. It was hell at the time, but after it was all over, it was wonderful." Billy Wilder

"Copulation was, I'm sure, Marilyn's uncomplicated way of saying thank you. . . ." Nunnally Johnson

Richard M. Nixon. "That man has no future in American politics. Even Eisenhower will refuse to swallow so much half-baked corn." Walter Lippmann

"Years from now, he'll be judged very closely to the way he's judged in Europe and Asia now—very positively. This guy is an expert diesel mechanic, everything Carter is not. He's not a candidate for sainthood, but remember, we elected a president, not a pastor." G. Gordon Liddy

"He's like a Spanish horse who runs faster than anyone for the first nine lengths and then turns around and runs backward." Lyndon B. Johnson

Roman Polanski. "As a director, he was ten times more wonderful than as a lover." Nastassia Kinski

Don Rickles. "I like Don Rickles. But that's because I have no taste." Frank Sinatra

Meryl Streep. "She looks like a chicken!" Truman Capote

Ed Sullivan. "Ed Sullivan will be around as long as someone else has talent." Fred Allen

Celebrities Who Were Shot
★ ## and Lived ★

James Arness (war wound)
Art Carney (war wound)
Robert Dole (war wound)
Blake Edwards (war wound)
Larry Flynt (murder attempt)
Peter Fonda (suicide attempt)
James Garner (war wound)

Uri Geller (war wound)
Pope John Paul II (assassination attempt)
Greg La Monde (hunting accident)
Alice Marble (war injury)
Lee Marvin (war wound)
Jennifer O'Neill (accident)
Jack Palance (war wound)
Joe Pepitone (childhood accident)
Ronald W. Reagan (assassination attempt)
Arthur Rimbaud (accident)
Nelson Rockefeller (childhood accident)
Oliver Stone (war wound)
Andy Warhol (assassination attempt)
George Wallace (assassination attempt)
Catfish Hunter (hunting accident)

★ Previous Jobs of Famous People ★

	Previous Job(s)
Danny Aiello	Bus-terminal loader and public-address announcer; union leader
Edward Albee	Western Union messenger; advertising copywriter
Eddie Arnold	Ambulance and hearse driver for funeral parlor
Lauren Bacall	Theater usher
Roseanne Barr	Cocktail waitress; window dresser
Warren Beatty	Piano player; bricklayer's helper; "sandhog" on Lincoln Tunnel construction crew
Tony Bennett	Singing waiter
Sandra Bernhard	Manicurist/pedicurist
Ray Bolger	Bank teller; accountant; vacuum-cleaner salesman
Richard Boone	Truck driver; roustabout
William F. Buckley, Jr.	Spanish instructor at Yale
Carol Burnett	Hatcheck girl
Glen Campbell	Cotton picker
Johnny Carson	Gas-station attendant
Richard Chamberlain	Chauffeur; construction worker; supermarket clerk
John Chancellor	Hospital orderly; carpenter's assistant; trailer-park parker
Sean Connery	Coffin polisher; bricklayer; theater usher; milk delivery man; model; Royal Navy sailor
Bill Cosby	Shoe salesman
Kevin Costner	Stagehand

Joan Crawford	Department-store sales clerk; chorus girl
Ruby Dee	Translator
Gerard Depardieu	Door-to-door brush salesman; sold soap for the blind; mugger
Kevin Dobson	Railroad ticket taker
Patrick Duffy	Florist delivery-truck driver; waiter; lawn mower
Keir Dullea	Carpenter's apprentice
Charles Durning	Cab driver; ironworker; boxer
Peter Falk	Connecticut Budget Bureau administrator
Harrison Ford	Carpenter; cook; buyer at Bullock's department store
John Forsythe	Waiter at Schrafft's
Allen Funt	Ad-agency art director
James Garner	Chauffeur; gas-station attendant; waiter; poolroom manager; hod carrier
Bob Geldof	Butcher; bulldozer operator
Whoopi Goldberg	Morgue attendant
Robert Goulet	Disc jockey; stationery salesman at Gimbel's
Dick Gregory	Postal clerk; jet-engine inspector
Charles Grodin	Cab driver; postal worker; Pinkerton night watchman
Jerry Hall	Stable worker (shoveled manure!); Dairy Queen cashier
Dustin Hoffman	Toy demonstrator; typist; waiter; psychiatric attendant
Bob Hoskins	Truck driver; window washer; steeple jack; fire-eater; Covent Garden porter; merchant seaman; fruit picker at Kibbutz
Alan King	Drummer; bandleader
Burt Lancaster	Acrobat; haberdashery salesman; singing waiter
Lorenzo Lamas	Gas-station attendant; parking-lot attendant; French-fry cook at McDonald's; security guard; theater ticket taker; weightlifting instructor at Jack La Lanne's
Cyndi Lauper	Horse walker at Belmont race track; art-class model; waitress; dog-kennel cleaner
Robin Leach	Shoe salesman
Fred MacMurray	Saxophone player; bandleader
Dean Martin	Bootleg runner; boxer; gas-station attendant

Lee Marvin	Plumber's apprentice
Walter Matthau	Cement-bag hauler; floor scrubber; boxing instructor
Sherrill Milnes	High school music teacher
Robert Mitchum	Coal miner; ditchdigger; boxer; ghostwriter; shoe salesman
George Murphy	Coal loader; Wall Street messenger
Jim Nabors	Typist
Bob Newhart	Advertising copywriter; accountant
Anthony Newley	Office boy
George Peppard	Disc jockey
Ronald Reagan	Radio sports announcer
Robert Redford	Artist; oil-field worker
Joan Rivers	Fashion coordinator
Cliff Robertson	Reporter
Willard Scott	Clown
Yakov Smirnoff	Bartender
Mary Steenburgen	Waitress
Barbra Streisand	Switchboard operator; theater usher
Preston Sturges	Cosmetics company executive and inventor
Barry Sullivan	Department-store buyer; theater usher
Rip Torn	Dishwasher; short-order cook
Senator John Tower	Radio announcer
Lee Van Cleef	Accountant
Dick Van Dyke	Advertising executive
Barbara Walters	Ad-agency secretary
Raquel Welch	Weather girl; cocktail-lounge waitress
William Wellman	Stunt pilot
Cornel Wilde	Toy salesman at Macy's; ad-space salesman
Paul Williams	Oil-field worker; insurance clerk
Nicol Williamson	Metalworker
Jonathan Winters	Apricot picker; factory worker

★ Religions of Famous People ★

Baptist

Gregg Allman
Famous Amos
Anita Bryant
Diahann Carroll
James Earl Carter
Johnny Cash
Ray Charles

Natalie Cole
Rita Coolidge
John Davidson
Roberta Flack
Aretha Franklin
Jesse Jackson
Gladys Knight
Kris Kristofferson
Emmanuel Lewis

Loretta Lynn
Willie Nelson
Dolly Parton
Dan Rather
Lou Rawls
Diana Ross
Jaclyn Smith
Donna Summer
Ted Turner

Christian Scientist

Carol Burnett
Carol Channing
Doris Day
Paul Newman
Jean Stapleton

Episcopalian

Fred Astaire
Walter Cronkite
Werner Erhard
Jane Fonda
Stacy Keach
Burgess Meredith
Tom Seaver

Jewish

Woody Allen
Alan Arkin
Bea Arthur
Isaac Asimov
Ed Asner
Lauren Bacall
Burt Bacharach
Roseanne Barr
Gene Barry
Jon Bauman
Saul Bellow
Richard Benjamin
Robby Benson
Polly Bergen
Leonard Bernstein
Mel Brooks
Dr. Joyce Brothers
George Burns
Red Buttons
James Caan
Sid Caesar
Sammy Cahn
Dyan Cannon
Jack Carter
David Copperfield
Tony Curtis
Neil Diamond
Kirk Douglas
Michael Douglas
Richard Dreyfuss
Jules Feiffer

Eddie Fisher
Art Garfunkel
Estelle Getty
Eydie Gormé
Elliott Gould
Lee Grant
Jennifer Grey
Joel Grey
Monty Hall
Marvin Hamlisch
Goldie Hawn
Dustin Hoffman
Billy Joel
Madeline Kahn
Carol Kane
Henry Kissinger
Calvin Klein
Jack Klugman
Ted Koppel
Stanley Kubrick
Ann Landers
Michael Landon
Ralph Lauren
Steve Lawrence
Norman Lear
Michele Lee
Jerry Lewis
Hal Linden
Norman Mailer
Melissa Manchester
Barry Manilow
Dinah Manoff
Walter Matthau
Elaine May
Robert Merrill
Bette Midler
Sylvia Miles
Barry Newman
Mike Nichols
Leonard Nimoy
Deborah Raffin
Tony Randall
Harold Robbins
Vidal Sassoon
Neil Sedaka
George Segal
Gene Shalit
Dinah Shore
Beverly Sills
Neil Simon

Paul Simon
Stephen Sondheim
Steven Spielberg
David Steinberg
Barbra Streisand
Abigail Van Buren
Abe Vigoda
Diane Von
   Fürstenberg
Mike Wallace
Eli Wallach
Barbara Walters
Leslie-Ann Warren
Gene Wilder
Debra Winger
Shelley Winters
Peter Yarrow
Henny Youngman

Mormon

Jack Anderson
Billy Casper
Jack Dempsey
Gene Fullmer
Harmon Killebrew
J. Willard Marriott
Johnny Miller
Merlin Olsen
Donny Osmond
Marie Osmond
George Romney

Protestant*

Jane Alexander
Robert Altman
Cleveland Amory
Julie Andrews
Warren Beatty
Ingmar Bergman
Linda Blair
David Bowie
Jeff Bridges
Christie Brinkley
David Brinkley
Jackson Browne
Michael Caine
George Carlin
David Carradine
Keith Carradine
Johnny Carson

*Denomination unspecified.

Dick Cavett
Richard Chamberlain
Wilt Chamberlain
Chevy Chase
Dick Clark
James Coburn
Sean Connery
Bill Cosby
Bette Davis
John Denver
Bruce Dern
Faye Dunaway
Clint Eastwood
Sally Field
Ella Fitzgerald
John Forsythe
Jodie Foster
Michael J. Fox
James Garner
Crystal Gayle
Richard Gere
Gene Hackman
Mark Hamill
Emmylou Harris
Katharine Hepburn
Charlton Heston
Bob Hope
Lena Horne
Ron Howard
Lauren Hutton
Kate Jackson
Mick Jagger
Waylon Jennings
Elton John
Don Johnson
James Earl Jones
Tom Jones
Stephen King
Cheryl Ladd
Cloris Leachman
Jack Lemmon
Rich Little
Shirley MacLaine
Lee Majors
Steve Martin
Lee Marvin
Robert Mitchum
Dudley Moore
Roger Moore
Jim Nabors
Wayne Newton

Jack Nicholson
Anthony Perkins
Prince
Robert Redford
Christopher Reeve
Burt Reynolds
Lionel Richie
John Ritter
Kenny Rogers
Roy Rogers
Diane Sawyer
Charles Schulz
George C. Scott
Tom Selleck
Cybill Shepherd
Sissy Spacek
James Stewart
Rod Stewart
Meryl Streep
Sally Struthers
Donald Sutherland
James Taylor
Lily Tomlin
Robert Wagner
Jonathan Winters
Joanne Woodward
Michael York

Quaker

Julian Bond
Jorge Luis Borges
Mary Calderone
Herbert Hoover
David Lean
James Michener
Christopher Morley
Richard M. Nixon
Cheryl Tiegs
Jessamyn West

Roman Catholic

Alan Alda
Anne Bancroft
Brigitte Bardot
Jacqueline Bisset
Robert Blake
Charles Bronson
Pierce Brosnan
William F. Buckley, Jr.
Ellen Burstyn

Harry Connick, Jr.
Jane Curtin
Catherine Deneuve
Robert De Niro
Angie Dickinson
Phil Donahue
Mike Douglas
Chris Evert
Mia Farrow
Farrah Fawcett
Albert Finney
Graham Greene
Merv Griffin
Sir Alec Guinness
Valerie Harper
Richard Harris
Audrey Hepburn
Gene Kelly
Grace Kelly
Ted Knight
Burt Lancaster
Liberace
Kenny Loggins
Claudine Longet
Sophia Loren
George Lucas
Ali MacGraw
Rod McKuen
Ed McMahon
Kristy McNichol
Chuck Mangione
Marcello Mastroianni
Johnny Mathis
Liza Minnelli
Mary Tyler Moore
Bob Newhart
Nick Nolte
Carroll O'Connor
Ryan O'Neal
Tony Orlando
Peter O'Toole
Al Pacino
Bernadette Peters
Sidney Poitier
Richard Pryor
Anthony Quinn
Lee Remick
Debbie Reynolds
Linda Ronstadt
Yves St. Laurent
Brooke Shields

Converts to Judaism

Tom Arnold	Sammy Davis, Jr.	Frank Sinatra
Carroll Baker	Carolyn Jones	Suzanne Somers
Rod Carew	Marilyn Monroe	Bruce Springsteen
Jim Croce	Eleanor Parker	Elizabeth Taylor

Converts from Judaism to Christianity

Denomination Converted to:

Michael Blumenthal	Presbyterian
Bob Dylan	Vineyard Christian Fellowship
Bobby Fisher	Worldwide Church of God
Eugene Ormandy	Unspecified
Boris Pasternak	Unspecified
James Schlesinger	Lutheran
Rod Serling	Unitarian

NBC Pages

Being an NBC-TV page is like being a soda jerk at Schwab's drugstore in Hollywood. It can be a dead-end job, but it also can lead to something big. Here are some former NBC pages who traded in their uniforms for highly paid jobs:

Ed Begley, Jr.	David Hartman	Terry Robards
Richard Benjamin	Ken Howard	Eva Marie Saint
Harry Carey, Jr.	Bob Keeshan	Susan St. James
Schuyler Chapin	Ted Koppel	Willard Scott
Clay Cole	Gordon MacRae	Jerry Weintraub
Michael Eisner	Regis Philbin	Dennis Wholey
Don Galloway	Gene Rayburn	

The Algonquin Round Table

The Algonquin Hotel in New York City in the 1920s was the gathering place of many talented and witty people, mostly writers, producers, playwrights, and actors. They assembled at a special reserved table in the Rose Room at lunchtime to engage in repartee and irreverence. The following were members of this legendary group, sometimes known as the "Vicious Circle":

Franklin P. Adams	Irving Berlin	Marc Connelly
George Backer	Paul Hyde Bonner	Howard Dietz
Joyce Barbour	Gerald Brooks	Edna Ferber
Robert Benchley	Heywood Broun	Raoul Fleischmann

Crosby Gaige
Jascha Heifetz
Beatrice Kaufman
George S. Kaufman
Charles MacArthur
Herman J. Mankiewicz

Harpo Marx
Alice Duer Miller
Henry Wise Miller
Dorothy Parker
Harold Ross
Donald Ogden Stewart

Herbert Bayard Swope
Peggy Wood
Alexander Woollcott

The Richest 25 People in the United States

★ ★

	Net Worth
1. John Werner Kluge	$5,600,000,000
2. Warren Edward Buffet	3,300,000,000
3. Ronald Owen Perelman	2,870,000,000
4. Henry Lea Hillman	2,650,000,000
5. Barbara Cox Anthony	2,600,000,000
6. Anna Cox Chambers	2,600,000,000
7. Samuel Irving Newhouse, Jr.	2,600,000,000
8. Donald Edward Newhouse	2,600,000,000
9. Jay Arthur Pritzker	2,500,000,000
10. Robert Alan Pritzker	2,500,000,000
11. Samuel Moore Walton	2,500,000,000
12. S. Robson Walton	2,500,000,000
13. John T. Walton	2,500,000,000
14. Jim C. Walton	2,500,000,000
15. Alice L. Walton	2,500,000,000
16. William H. Gates III	2,500,000,000
17. Henry Ross Perot	2,200,000,000
18. A. Alfred Traubman	2,100,000,000
19. Ted Ariso	2,100,000,000
20. Summer Murray Redstone	2,000,000,000
21. Charles de Ganahl Koch	1,900,000,000
22. David Hamilton Koch	1,900,000,000
23. Edgar Miles Bronfman	1,900,000,000
24. Charles F. Feeney	1,900,000,000
25. Leslie Herbert Wexner	1,800,000,000

Source: Forbes magazine, October 22, 1990.

Celebrity Pilots

★ ★

Eddie Arcaro
F. Lee Bailey
George Bush
  (WW II Navy
  pilot)
Johnny Carson
Sam Donaldson
Vince Edwards
Merv Griffin
Gene Hackman
William Hurt

Danny Kaye
B.B. King
Kris Kristofferson
  (Army helicopter
  pilot)
Dean-Paul Martin
Ed McMahon
F.W. Murnau
  (WW I pilot)
Robert Redford
Christopher Reeve

Cliff Robertson
Elliot Roosevelt
James Stewart
  (Air Force pilot)
Preston Sturges
John Travolta
Jack Valenti
Roger Whitacre
Treat Williams
Cale Yarborough

Highest-Paid U.S. Chief Executives

★ **(Figures in Thousands)** ★

Chief Executive/Company	Salary & Bonus	Other	Stock Gains	Total
Craig O. McCaw McCaw Cellular	$289	—	$53,655	$53,944
Donald A. Pels LIN Broadcasting	1,363	—	21,428	22,791
Jim P. Manzi Lotus Development	991	$49	15,372	16,412
Paul B. Fireman Reebok International	14,606	—	—	14,606
Herbert J. Siegel BHC Communications	13,687	14	—	13,701
James R. Moffett Freeport-McMoRan	1,359	1,086	11,072	13,517
Ronald K. Richey Torchmark	1,084	48	11,588	12,719
James Wood Great A&P Tea Co.	3,193	2,024	5,900	11,117
Robert C. Goizueta Coca-Cola Company	2,542	2,400	5,872	10,814
Michael D. Eisner Walt Disney	9,589	6	—	9,595
August A. Busch III Anheuser-Busch	1,464	21	7,397	8,882
William G. McGowan MCI Communications	1,325	—	7,341	8,666

Chief Executive/Company	Salary & Bonus	Other	Stock Gains	Total
Ralph E. Ablon Ogden	2,000	284	5,015	7,299
P. Roy Vagelos Merck Company	2,340	5	4,423	6,769
David D. Glass Wal-Mart Stores	600	30	6,129	6,759
Saul P. Steinberg Reliance Group	6,265	281	—	6,546
Hamish Maxwell Philip Morris Companies	1,877	1,171	2,805	6,453
Louis F. Bantle UST Inc.	2,126	22	3,635	5,783
S. Parker Gilbert Morgan Stanley	5,475	20	—	5,495
Robert J. Pfeiffer Alexander & Baldwin	1,473	509	3,476	5,459

Source: Forbes magazine, May 28, 1990.

★ Philadelphia Singers ★

Philadelphia is not only the City of Brotherly Love and snapper soup, but it is also a city of singers. Here are a few of those who have crooned their way out of town:

Marian Anderson
Frankie Avalon (Francis Avalonne)
Chubby Checker (Ernest Evans)
Russ Columbo
Jim Croce
James Darren (James Ercolani)
Bill Doggett
Fabian (Fabian Forte)
Lola Falana
Eddie Fisher (Edwin Jack Fisher)
Gogi Grant (Myrtle Audrey Arinsberg)
Buddy Greco (Armando Greco)
Bill Haley (William John Clifford, Jr.)

Kitty Kallen (Genevieve Agostinello)
Patti LaBelle (Patricia Holt)
Mario Lanza (Alfred Arnold Cocozza)
Jeanette MacDonald
Al Martino (Alfred Cini)
Andrea McArdle
Teddy Pendergrast (Theodore D. Pendergrast)
Bobby Rydell (Robert Riderelli)
Debbie Sledge
Joni Sledge
Kathy Sledge
Kim Sledge
Frank Stallone

Celebrities Who Spent Some Time in Jail

★ ★

The following well-known people have spent at least one night in the "slammer" for various offenses. Tabloids often distort the amount of time these celebs were behind bars, but what else is new? For example, many people think that singer Johnny Cash has spent a lot of time in prison when, in fact, he has spent about seven nights in local jails for relatively minor offenses such as possession of amphetamines. Here are some of the famous who have seen jail bars from the wrong side:

Nelson Algren
James Bakker
Roseanne Barr
Brendan Behan
Chuck Berry
James Brown
Lenny Bruce
Truman Capote
Judy Carne
Johnny Cash
David Crosby
Tony Danza
Brian DePalma
Phil Donahue
Morton Downey, Jr.
Farrah Fawcett
Freddie Fender
Eugene Fodor
Tony Franciosa
Mahatma Gandhi
Cyndi Garvey
Jean Luc-Godard
Harry Golden
Rocky Graziano
Jerry Hall
Dashiell Hammett
Richard Harris
O. Henry
Howard Hesseman
Adnan Kashoggi
Stacy Keach
Martin Luther King, Jr.
Evel Knievel
Timothy Leary

Claudine Longet
Sophia Loren
Malcolm X
Christopher Marlowe
Steve McQueen
Chad Mitchell
Robert Mitchum
Carry Nation
Paul Newman
Huey P. Newton
Nick Nolte
Griffin O'Neal
Ryan O'Neal
Johnny Paycheck
Sean Penn
John Phillips
Roman Polanski
Luis Polonia
Duncan Renaldo
Pete Rose
Steve Rubell
Bertrand Russell
Joseph M. Schenck
Pete Seeger
Reverend Al Sharpton
O.J. Simpson
Taki Theodoracopoulos
Bill Tilden
Ike Turner
Paul Verlaine
Walter Wanger
Mae West
Oscar Wilde
Dave Winfield

License Plates of Celebrities

License Plate

Don Adams — AGT MAX (He played Maxwell Smart on TV.)

Ernest Borgnine — BORG9

Sammy Cahn — EARNS (He's proud of his song royalties.)

Sammy Cahn's wife — SPENDS (She's proud, too, but less practical.)

Allan Carr — GREASE I (He produced the movie *Grease* and its bomb sequel.)

Johnny Carson — 360 GUY (e.g., all-around guy.)

William Conrad — DARNOC (His last name spelled backwards.)

Tim Conway — 11 YEARS (The number of years "The Carol Burnett Show" ran on TV.)

Sally Field — BRS GRL (Burt Reynolds's girl— obviously an old plate.)

Michael J. Fox — MOOS KAR (He collects objects depicting mooses.)

Redd Foxx — XXOF (His last name spelled backwards.)

Alex Haley — KINTE (as in Kunte Kinte of "Roots")

Jack LaLanne — REDUCE

Dean Martin — DRUNKY

Martina Navratilova — X CZECH (She's now a U.S. citizen.)

Valerie Perrine — RATS ("Star" spelled backwards—her aspiration?)

Amazing Randi — ESCAPE (Occasionally he does escape tricks.)

Dinah Shore — GRUNK (Her dog's name)

Richard Simmons — Y R U FATT

Rip Taylor — INSANE 2

Leslie Uggams — SMAGGU (Her last name spelled backwards.)

Lyle Waggoner — MR COOL

Dennis Weaver — GURUJI (The Hindu word for "teacher")

Lawrence Welk — A1 AND A2 (. . . and a one and a two . . .)

Flip Wilson — KILLER

Charles Schulz — WDSTK-1 (as in Woodstock)

Betty Ford Center Attendees and Grads

★   ★

Founded by Betty Ford, the wife of U.S. President Gerald R. Ford, and recovered alcoholic and tire-fortune heir Leonard Firestone, the Betty Ford Center is a rehabilitation center for drug- and alcohol-dependent people located in El Rancho Mirage, California. Here are a few well-known people who have spent some time recuperating at the Center:

Eileen Brennan	Margaux	Robert Mitchum
Johnny Cash	Hemingway	Mary Tyler Moore
Chevy Chase	William Hurt	Ozzy Osbourne
Tony Curtis	Peter Lawford	Howard Rollins
Andy Gibb	Jerry Lee Lewis	Elizabeth Taylor
Gregory Harris	Liza Minnelli	Tanya Tucker
		Eddie Van Halen

★ Famous People and Their Phobias ★

A phobia is a morbid or excessive fear of a particular object or group of objects. Here are some famous people and their phobias:

Person	Fear
Alexander the Great	Cats
Kirstie Alley	Flying
Roseanne Barr	Flying
Napoleon Bonaparte	Cats
Ray Bradbury	Flying
Julius Caesar	Cats
Johnny Cash	Flying, snakes
Chevy Chase	Snakes
John Cheever	Crossing bridges
Cher	Flying
Joan Crawford	Germs
Tony Curtis	Flying
Fred de Cordova	Flying
Aretha Franklin	Flying
Whoopi Goldberg	Flying
Betty Grable	Crowds
Graham Greene	Blood, birds, bats
Katharine Hepburn	Fire
Alfred Hitchcock	Policemen
Houdini	Claustrophobia
Howard Hughes	Germs

Person	Fear
Marty Ingels	Flying, elevators, agoraphobia
Genghis Khan	Cats
Evel Knievel	Flying
Stanley Kubrick	Flying
Richard Lewis	Intimacy
Lorna Luft	Flying
Loretta Lynn	Flying
John Madden	Flying
Dean Martin	Elevators
Ed McMahon	Heights
Robert Mitchum	Crowds
Benito Mussolini	Cats
Bob Newhart	Flying
Laurence Olivier	Stagefright
Edgar Allan Poe	Claustrophobia
Marcel Proust	Germs
Ronald Reagan	Flying, claustrophobia
Charles M. Schulz	Hotels, agoraphobia
Willard Scott	Public speaking
Gene Shalit	Flying
Carly Simon	Crowds, stagefright
Steven Spielberg	Insects
Maureen Stapleton	Flying
David Steinberg	Snakes, elevators
Howard Stern	Germs
Liv Ullman	Flying
King Vidor	Heights, flying
Natalie Wood	Deep water
Virginia Woolf	Fire
Joanne Woodward	Flying

WIT AND WISDOM

The Wit and Wisdom of
Groucho Marx

★   ★

"I don't care to belong to a club that accepts people like me as members."

"Politics doesn't make strange bedfellows—marriage does."

"It looks as if Hollywood brides keep the bouquets and throw away the grooms."

"In America you can go on the air and kid the politicians, and the politicians can go on the air and kid the people."

"My mother loved children—she would have given anything if I had been one."

"I was so long writing my review that I never got around to reading the book."

"There's one way to find out if a man is honest: Ask him; if he says yes, you know he is crooked."

"I never forget a face, but in your case I'll make an exception."

"She got her good looks from her father—he's a plastic surgeon."

"Wives are people who feel that they don't dance enough."

"The husband who wants a happy marriage should learn to keep his mouth shut and his checkbook open."

★ The Wit and Wisdom of W.C. Fields ★

"Once during Prohibition, I was forced to live for days on nothing but food and water."

"I gargle with whiskey several times a day and I haven't had a cold in years."

"What contemptible scoundrel stole the cork from my lunch?"

"The cost of living has gone up another dollar a quart."

"After two days in the hospital, I took a turn for the nurse."

"I never drink water—I'm afraid it will become habit-forming."

"The best cure for insomnia is to get a lot of sleep."

"Horse sense is what a horse has that keeps him from betting on people."

The Wit and Wisdom of
Mae West

★ ————————————————————————— ★

"I do all my writing in bed; everybody knows I do my best work there."

"When I'm good, I'm very good. But when I'm bad, I'm better."

"To err is human, but it feels divine."

"Few men know how to kiss well. Fortunately, I've always had time to teach them."

"Save a boyfriend for a rainy day, and another in case it doesn't rain."

"Why don't you come sometime and see me. I'm home every evening. . . . Come up, I'll tell your fortune."

The Wit and Wisdom of
Tallulah Bankhead

★ ————————————————————————— ★

"It's the good girls who keep diaries; the bad girls never have the time."

"I'm as pure as the driven slush."

"There's only one man in the theater that can count on steady work—the night watchman."

"If you want to help the American theater, don't be an actress—be an audience."

The Wit and Wisdom of
Samuel Goldwyn

★ ————————————————————————— ★

"A verbal contract isn't worth the paper it's written on."

"I don't care if my pictures don't make a dime, so long as everyone comes to see them."

"Anyone who goes to a psychiatrist should have his head examined."

"I'm overpaying him [Fredric March], but he's worth it."

"A producer shouldn't get ulcers, he should give them."

"We have all passed a lot of water since then."

"I was always independent, even when I had partners."

The Wit and Wisdom of
Yogi Berra

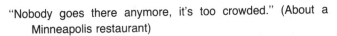

"Nobody goes there anymore, it's too crowded." (About a Minneapolis restaurant)

"You can observe a lot by watching."

"If people don't want to come to the ballpark, how are you going to stop them?"

"I usually take a two-hour nap from one o'clock to four."

"We made too many wrong mistakes." (After losing a World Series)

The Wit and Wisdom of
Casey Stengel

"Going to bed with a woman never hurt a ballplayer. It's staying up all night looking for them that does you in."

"I'll never make the mistake of being seventy again."

"Ability is the art of getting credit for all the home runs anybody else hits."

The Wit and Cynicism of
Humphrey Bogart

"The only reason to have money is to tell any SOB in the world to go to hell."

"I hate funerals—they aren't for the one who's dead, but for the ones who are left and enjoy mourning."

"The whole world is three drinks behind. If everybody in the world would take three drinks, we would have no trouble."

"I always suspect people who talk too much about acting or sex. You either do it and don't talk about it, or you talk about it and don't do it."

The Wit and Wisdom of
Woody Allen

★ _____ ★

"I don't believe in an afterlife, although I'm bringing along a change of underwear."

"I'm not afraid to die. I just don't want to be there when it happens."

"Organized crime in America takes in over forty billion dollars a year and spends very little on office supplies."

"If my film makes one more person miserable, I'll feel I've done my job."

"It's true I had a lot of anxiety. I was afraid of the dark and suspicious of the light."

DEATH

Celebrities Who Died
at an Early Age

★ ★

"He whom the gods love, dies in youth."
Ancient Roman epitaph

	Age at Death		Age at Death
Ritchie Valens	17	Alma Rubens	33
Olive Thomas	20	John Belushi	34
Sid Vicious	21	Jayne Mansfield	34
Buddy Holly	22	Jeanne Eagels	35
Freddie Prinze	22	Andy Kaufman	35
Dorothy Stratten	22	Inger Stevens	35
James Dean	24	Nick Adams	36
Françoise Dorleac	25	Rainer Werner	
Frankie Lymon	25	Fassbinder	36
Russ Columbo	26	Marilyn Monroe	36
Jean Harlow	26	Lupe Velez	36
Bobby Harron	26	Bobby Darin	37
Brian Jones	26	Sal Mineo	37
Barbara LaMarr	26	Robert Walker	37
Otis Redding	26	Pier Angeli	38
Sharon Tate	26	Roberto Clemente	38
Jimi Hendrix	27	Amelia Earhart	38
Janis Joplin	27	John Gilbert	38
Jim Morrison	27	Mario Lanza	38
The Big Bopper	28	Adrienne Lecouvreur	38
Bobby Driscoll	28	Marilyn Miller	38
Ronnie Van Zandt	28	Gia Scala	38
Sam Cooke	29	Harry Chapin	39
Carole Landis	29	Michael Dunn	39
Hank Williams	29	John Garfield	39
Patsy Cline	30	Carol Haney	39
Jim Croce	30	Martin Luther King, Jr.	39
Brandon De Wilde	30	Malcolm X	39
Andy Gibb	30	Jim Reeves	39
Wallace Reid	30	Sabu	39
Thelma Todd	30	Lenny Bruce	40
Renée Adorée	31	John Lennon	40
Alfalfa Switzer	31	Glenn Miller	40
Rudolph Valentino	31	Jean Seberg	40
Bruce Lee	32	Dorothy Dandridge	41
Carole Lombard	32	Bella Darvi	41
Thurman Munson	32	Carmen Miranda	41
Mabel Normand	32	Jeff Chandler	42
"Mama" Cass Elliot	33	Judy Holliday	42
Kay Kendall	33	Ernie Kovacs	42
Maria Montez	33	Robert F. Kennedy	42

	Age at Death		Age at Death
Elvis Presley	42	Anna Held	45
Gilda Radner	42	Rick Nelson	45
Dennis Wilson	42	George Reeves	45
Godfrey Cambridge	43	Fatty Arbuckle	46
Linda Darnell	43	John F. Kennedy	46
Rusty Hamer	43	Carmen Miranda	46
Romy Schneider	43	Lon Chaney	47
Natalie Wood	43	Judy Garland	47
Marvin Gaye	44	Audie Murphy	47
Billie Holiday	44	David Janssen	48
Rocky Marciano	44	Margaret Mitchell	48
Gordon Parks, Jr.	44	Margaret Sullavan	48
Jackson Pollock	44	Jack Cassidy	49
Tyrone Power	44	Bob Crane	49
Michael Bennett	45	Pearl White	49
Montgomery Clift	45	Alan Ladd	50
Elizabeth Hartman	45	Steve McQueen	50
Laurence Harvey	45	Vic Morrow	50

★ Famous People Who Died by Suicide ★

Nick Adams (1968)
Pedro Armandariz (1963)
Donald Barry ["Red Ryder"] (1980)
Scotty Beckett (1960)
Paul Bern (1932)
Clara Blandick (1962)
Charles Boyer (1978)
Hart Crane (1932)
Dorothy Dandridge (1965)
Bella Darvi (1971)
Albert Dekker (1968)
Peter Duel (1971)
Jeanne Eagels (1929)
George Eastman (1932)

Rainer Werner Fassbinder (1982)
James V. Forrestal (1949)
Dave Garroway (1982)
Joseph Goebbels (1945)
Hermann Goering (1946)
Arshile Gorky (1948)
Rusty Hamer (1990)
Bobby Harron (1920)
Elizabeth Hartman (1987)
Phyllis Hover (1960)
Ernest Hemingway (1961)
George Hill (1934)

Adolf Hitler (1945)
Abbie Hoffman (1989)
Jerzy Kosinski (1991)
Alan Ladd (1964)
Carole Landis (1948)
Florence Lawrence (1938)
Max Linder (1925)
Vachel Lindsay (1931)
Christopher Marlowe (1593)
Marilyn Monroe (1962)
Chester Morris (1970)
Phil Ochs (1975)
Charles W. Post (1914)
Nathan Pritikin (1985)

George Reeves (1959)

Mark Rothko (1970)

George Sanders (1972)

Jean Seberg (1979)

Dell Shannon (1990)

Walter Slezak (1983)

Everett Sloan (1965)

Margaret Sullavan (1960)

Lou Tellegen (1934)

Olive Thomas (1920)

Thelma Todd (1935)

Helen Twelvetrees (1959)

Vincent van Gogh (1890)

Lupe Velez (1944)

Doodles Weaver (1983)

Grant Withers (1959)

Virginia Woolf (1941)

Gig Young (1978)

Note: Freddie Prinze died in 1977 when he accidentally shot himself. It was originally thought to be a suicide but a court ruled that it was an accident—a prank-turned-tragedy (he thought that the safety on the gun was on). The insurance company, not liable in cases of suicide, did, in fact, pay his family $200,000.

Famous People Who Were Murdered

★ ★

Sam Cooke (1964). Shot to death by motel manager after allegedly trying to rape a woman.

Bob Crane (1978). Bludgeoned to death at a Scottsdale, Arizona motel.

Jim Fisk (1872). Shot to death by a business associate in a quarrel about Fisk's mistress.

Marvin Gaye (1984). Shot to death by his father, Marvin Sr., one day before his 45th birthday.

Thomas H. Ince (1924). Mysteriously died on William Randolph Hearst's yacht.

John Lennon (1980). Shot to death by Mark David Chapman.

Sal Mineo (1976). Stabbed to death at his apartment-house garage.

Huey P. Newton (1989). Shot to death in Oakland, California.

Ramon Novarro (1968). Bludgeoned to death by two drifters.

Pier Paolo Pasolini (1975). Bludgeoned to death by a 17-year-old boy whom he allegedly propositioned, after which the boy drove Pasolini's Alfa Romeo over his body.

Dorothy Stratten (1980). Shot to death by her estranged husband.

Carl "Alfalfa" Switzer (1959). Shot to death in a bar brawl.

Sharon Tate (1969). Repeatedly stabbed to death by members of the Charles Manson cult.

William Desmond Taylor (1922). Shot to death. Murderer was never discovered, but later evidence led to a theory that Taylor was killed by Charlotte Shelby, the mother of Taylor's lover, Mary Miles Minter.

Stanford White (1906). Shot to death by Harry Thaw because of an alleged affair with Evelyn Nesbit, Thaw's wife.

Famous People Who Died from Drug Overdoses

★ ★

Pier Angeli (1971)
John Belushi (1982)
Lenny Bruce (1966)
Don Castle (1966)
Judy Garland (1969)
Jimi Hendrix (1970)
Janis Joplin (1970)

Frankie Lymon (1968)
Marilyn Monroe (1962)
Jim Morrison (1971)
Elvis Presley (1977)

Gia Scala (1972)
Inger Stevens (1970)
Philip Van Zandt (1958)
Sid Vicious (1979)
Dennis Wilson (1983)

Famous People Who Died in Plane Crashes

★ ★

The Big Bopper (J.P. Richardson) (1959)
Vernon Castle (1918)
Roberto Clemente (1972)
Patsy Cline (1963)
Jim Croce (1973)
Amelia Earhart (1937)
Yuri Gagarin (1968)
Dag Hammarskjöld (1961)
Kenneth Hawks (1930)
Senator John Heinz (1991)

Buddy Holly (1959)
Leslie Howard (1943)
Carole Lombard (1942)
Rocky Marciano (1969)
Herbert Marshall (1966)
Glenn Miller (1944)
Thurman Munson (1979)
Audie Murphy (1971)
Ricky Nelson (1985)
Francis Gary Powers (1977)

Otis Redding (1967)
Jim Reeves (1964)
Lance Reventlow (1972)
Knute Rockne (1931)
Will Rogers (1935)
Mike Todd (1958)
Senator John Tower (1991)
Ritchie Valens (1959)
Ronnie Van Zandt (1977)

Famous People Who Died in Auto Accidents

★ ★

Larry Blyden (1975)
Charles Butterworth (1946)
James Dean (1955)
Brandon De Wilde (1972)
Françoise Dorleac (1967)

Bernard Gorcey (1955)
Grace Kelly (1982)
Ernie Kovacs (1962)
Billy Laughlin (1948)
Jayne Mansfield (1967)

Billy Martin (1990)
Margaret Mitchell (1949)
Tom Mix (1940)
F.W. Murnau (1931)
George Patton (1945)
Jackson Pollock (1956)

Famous People Who Died by Assassination

★ ★

Mahatma Gandhi (1948)
James Garfield (1881)
John F. Kennedy (1963)

Robert F. Kennedy (1968)
Martin Luther King, Jr. (1968)

Abraham Lincoln (1865)
Huey Long (1935)
Malcolm X (1965)

Celebrities Who Died of Other Causes

★ ★

Al Capone (1947). Syphilis
Jack Cassidy (1976). Fire
Russ Columbo (1934). Shot
Linda Darnell (1965). Fire
Isadora Duncan (1927).
  Strangled by her scarf
Richard Farina (1966).
  Motorcycle accident
Zelda Fitzgerald (1948). Fire
Joe Flynn (1974). Drowning
Mark Freshette (1975). Prison
  accident

William Holden (1981). Fall
Brian Jones (1969). Drowning
Buck Jones (1942). Night-
  club fire
Maria Montez (1951).
  Drowning
Vic Morrow (1982). Movie-
  location accident
Jessica Savitch (1983).
  Drowning
Natalie Wood (1981).
  Drowning

Celebrities Who Lived to Age 80 or Older

	Age at Death		Age at Death
Adolph Zukor	103	Red Grange	87
Irving Berlin	101	Louise Nevelson	87
Grandma Moses	101	Raphael Soyer	87
Father Divine	100	Graham Greene	86
Alf Landon	100	Jascha Heifetz	86
John Nance Garner	98	John Houseman	86
John D. Rockefeller	98	Groucho Marx	86
Martha Graham	97	Tim McCoy	86
Bea Lillie	94	Mary Pickford	86
Adela Rogers St. Johns	94	Walter Pidgeon	86
Andrés Segovia	94	Georges Simenon	86
George Bernard Shaw	94	Irving Stone	86
Lila Acheson Wallace	94	Diana Vreeland	86
Donald Crisp	93	Jack L. Warner	86
Rudolf Hess	93	Fritz Lang	85
Somerset Maugham	92	Marjorie Main	85
Virgil Thomson	92	Alan Paton	85
Sunny Jim Fitzsimmons	91	Charles Coburn	84
Samuel Goldwyn	91	Salvador Dali	84
Pablo Picasso	91	Edmund Gwenn	84
William Powell	91	Elsa Lanchester	84
Konrad Adenauer	90	Isamu Noguchi	84
Winston Churchill	90	Robert Penn Warren	84
Malcolm Cowley	90	Ray Bolger	83
Herbert Hoover	90	Francis X. Bushman	83
Joan Miró	90	Erskine Caldwell	83
Alfred P. Sloan	90	Maurice Chevalier	83
Bronco Billy Anderson	89	Chester Conklin	83
Brooks Atkinson	89	Sigmund Freud	83
Mary Baker Eddy	89	Sessue Hayakawa	83
Hermione Gingold	89	Edward Everett Horton	83
Fred Astaire	88	Frederick Loewe	83
Charlie Chaplin	88	Ernest Truex	83
Dame Edith Evans	88	Bill Baird	82
William Randolph Hearst	88	Gladys Cooper	82
Emperor Hirohito	88	Cary Grant	82
Gunnar Myrdal	88	Mary Astor	81
Gen. Mark W. Clark	87	Mel Blanc	81
Jane Darwell	87	Leo Carrillo	81
Maurice Evans	87	Madeleine Carroll	81
		Bette Davis	81
		Daphne Du Maurier	81
		Boris Karloff	81

	Age at Death		Age at Death
I.F. Stone	81	Louis L'Amour	80
Arthur Treacher	81	Margaret Rutherford	80
Leo G. Carroll	80	Ethel Waters	80

Last Known Address: Where the Famous Are Buried
★   ★

The following notables are buried at the cemeteries indicated. The addresses of these cemeteries appear at the end of the listings.

	Cemetery
Renée Adorée	Hollywood Memorial
Gracie Allen	Forest Lawn
Albert Anastasia	Green-Wood
Maxwell Anderson	Ferncliff
Eve Arden	Westwood Memorial
Richard Arlen	Holy Cross
Jim Backus	Westwood Memorial
Bugs Baer	Ferncliff
Béla Bartók	Ferncliff
Richard Basehart	Westwood Memorial
Warner Baxter	Forest Lawn
Nora Bayes	Woodlawn
Charles and Mary Beard	Ferncliff
Henry Ward Beecher	Green-Wood
Wallace Beery	Forest Lawn
Constance Bennett	Arlington National
Hugo L. Black	Arlington National
Mel Blanc	Hollywood Memorial
Nellie Bly	Woodlawn
Humphrey Bogart	Forest Lawn
Gutzon Borglum	Forest Lawn
Connee Boswell	Ferncliff
Clara Bow	Forest Lawn
Charles Boyer	Holy Cross
Omar Bradley	Arlington National
Diamond Jim Brady	Green-Wood
Keefe Brasselle	Holy Cross
Joe E. Brown	Forest Lawn
William Jennings Bryan	Arlington National
Ralph Bunche	Woodlawn
Francis X. Bushman	Forest Lawn
Adm. Richard E. Byrd	Arlington National

Sebastian Cabot	Westwood Memorial
Louis Calhern	Hollywood Memorial
Godfrey Cambridge	Forest Lawn
Truman Capote	Westwood Memorial
Jack Carson	Forest Lawn
John Cassavetes	Westwood Memorial
Irene and Vernon Castle	Woodlawn
Lon Chaney	Forest Lawn
Claire Chennault	Arlington National
DeWitt Clinton	Green-Wood
George M. Cohan	Woodlawn
Harry Cohn	Hollywood Memorial
Nat King Cole	Forest Lawn
Russ Columbo	Forest Lawn
Richard Conte	Westwood Memorial
Peter Cooper	Green-Wood
Lotta Crabtree	Woodlawn
Joan Crawford	Ferncliff
Bing Crosby	Holy Cross
Dorothy Dandridge	Forest Lawn
Bebe Daniels	Hollywood Memorial
Marion Davies	Hollywood Memorial
Sammy Davis, Jr.	Forest Lawn
Clarence Day	Woodlawn
Cecil B. De Mille	Hollywood Memorial
Walt Disney	Forest Lawn
William "Wild Bill" Donovan	Arlington National
Philip Dorn	Westwood Memorial
William O. Douglas	Arlington National
Theodore Dreiser	Forest Lawn
Marie Dressler	Forest Lawn
John Foster Dulles	Arlington National
Will Durant	Westwood Memorial
Jimmy Durante	Holy Cross
Nelson Eddy	Hollywood Memorial
Duke Ellington	Woodlawn
"Mama" Cass Elliott	Hollywood Memorial
Medgar Evers	Arlington National
Douglas Fairbanks, Sr.	Hollywood Memorial
William Farnum	Forest Lawn
David G. Farragut	Woodlawn
W.C. Fields	Forest Lawn
Peter Finch	Hollywood Memorial
Victor Fleming	Hollywood Memorial
Jay C. Flippen	Westwood Memorial
Errol Flynn	Forest Lawn
John Ford	Holy Cross
James Forrestal	Arlington National
Rudolf Friml	Forest Lawn

Frankie Frisch	Woodlawn
Clark Gable	Forest Lawn
Joey Gallo	Green-Wood
Judy Garland	Ferncliff
Janet Gaynor	Hollywood Memorial
Henry George	Green-Wood
John Gilbert	Forest Lawn
King Camp Gillette	Forest Lawn
Samuel Goldwyn	Forest Lawn
Jay Gould	Woodlawn
Horace Greeley	Green-Wood
Sydney Greenstreet	Forest Lawn
D.W. Griffith	Hollywood Memorial
Virgil Grissom	Arlington National
Joan Hackett	Hollywood Memorial
Jack Haley	Holy Cross
William F. "Bull" Halsey	Arlington National
Armand Hammer	Westwood Memorial
Dashiell Hammett	Arlington National
W.C. Handy	Woodlawn
Jean Harlow	Forest Lawn
Moss Hart	Ferncliff
William S. Hart	Green-Wood
Gabby Hayes	Forest Lawn
Ira Hayes	Arlington National
Woody Herman	Hollywood Memorial
Jean Hersholt	Forest Lawn
Marguerite Higgins	Arlington National
Oliver Wendell Holmes	Arlington National
Darla Hood	Hollywood Memorial
Karen Horney	Ferncliff
James Wong Howe	Westwood Memorial
Charles Evans Hughes	Woodlawn
John Huston	Hollywood Memorial
Jose Iturbi	Holy Cross
Spike Jones	Holy Cross
Victor Jory	Westwood Memorial
Gus Kahn	Forest Lawn
Buster Keaton	Forest Lawn
John F. Kennedy	Arlington National
Robert F. Kennedy	Arlington National
Stan Kenton	Westwood Memorial
Jerome Kern	Ferncliff
Victor Kilian	Westwood Memorial
Ernie Kovacs	Forest Lawn
Fritz Kreisler	Woodlawn
Samuel Henry Kress	Woodlawn
Alan Ladd	Forest Lawn
Fiorello La Guardia	Woodlawn

	Cemetery
Arthur Lake	Hollywood Memorial
Barbara La Marr	Hollywood Memorial
Carole Landis	Forest Lawn
Mario Lanza	Holy Cross
Jesse Lasky	Hollywood Memorial
Charles Laughton	Forest Lawn
Stan Laurel	Forest Lawn
Oscar Levant	Westwood Memorial
Liberace	Forest Lawn
Harold Lloyd	Forest Lawn
Carole Lombard	Forest Lawn
Peter Lorre	Hollywood Memorial
Joe Louis	Arlington National
Anita Louise	Westwood Memorial
Frank Lovejoy	Holy Cross
Ernst Lubitsch	Forest Lawn
Bela Lugosi	Holy Cross
William Lundigan	Holy Cross
Moms Mabley	Ferncliff
Marjorie Main	Forest Lawn
Malcolm X	Ferncliff
George C. Marshall	Arlington National
Chico Marx	Forest Lawn
Harpo Marx	Forest Lawn
Bat Masterson	Woodlawn
Victor McLaglen	Forest Lawn
Aimee Semple McPherson	Forest Lawn
Herman Melville	Woodlawn
Adolph Menjou	Hollywood Memorial
Marilyn Miller	Woodlawn
Tom Mix	Forest Lawn
Thelonious Monk	Ferncliff
Marilyn Monroe	Westwood Memorial
Lola Montez	Green-Wood
Samuel F.B. Morse	Green-Wood
Paul Muni	Hollywood Memorial
Audie Murphy	Arlington National
Alla Nazimova	Forest Lawn
Red Nichols	Forest Lawn
Lloyd Nolan	Westwood Memorial
Jack Oakie	Forest Lawn
Clifford Odets	Forest Lawn
Roy Orbison	Westwood Memorial
Ignace Jan Paderewski	Arlington National
Louella Parsons	Holy Cross
Joseph Medill Paterson	Arlington National
Adm. Robert E. Peary	Arlington National
James Cash Penney	Woodlawn
John J. Pershing	Arlington National

Duncan Phyfe	Green-Wood
Mary Pickford	Forest Lawn
Adam Clayton Powell, Jr.	Woodlawn
Dick Powell	Forest Lawn
Eleanor Powell	Hollywood Memorial
Tyrone Power	Hollywood Memorial
Freddie Prinze	Forest Lawn
George Raft	Forest Lawn
Virginia Rappe	Hollywood Memorial
Basil Rathbone	Ferncliff
Donna Reed	Westwood Memorial
Walter Reed	Arlington National
Wallace Reid	Forest Lawn
Theodore Reik	Woodlawn
Charles Revson	Ferncliff
Buddy Rich	Westwood Memorial
Nelson Riddle	Hollywood Memorial
Mary Roberts Rinehart	Arlington National
Paul Robeson	Ferncliff
Richard Rodgers	Ferncliff
Will Rogers	Forest Lawn
Sigmund Romberg	Ferncliff
Rosalind Russell	Holy Cross
Ruth St. Denis	Forest Lawn
Rudolph Jay Schaefer	Woodlawn
Franklin Schaffner	Westwood Memorial
David O. Selznick	Forest Lawn
Mack Sennett	Holy Cross
Toots Shor	Ferncliff
Bugsy Siegel	Hollywood Memorial
Elizabeth Cady Stanton	Woodlawn
Casey Stengel	Forest Lawn
Dorothy Stratten	Westwood Memorial
Ed Sullivan	Ferncliff
Carl "Alfalfa" Switzer	Hollywood Memorial
William Howard Taft	Arlington National
Norma Talmadge	Hollywood Memorial
Sharon Tate	Holy Cross
Laurette Taylor	Woodlawn
Robert Taylor	Forest Lawn
Jack Teagarden	Forest Lawn
Irving Thalberg	Forest Lawn
J. Walter Thompson	Woodlawn
Lawrence Tibbett	Forest Lawn
Louis Comfort Tiffany	Green-Wood
Spencer Tracy	Forest Lawn
Helen Traubel	Westwood Memorial
Ben Turpin	Forest Lawn
William M. "Boss" Tweed	Green-Wood

Rudolph Valentino	Hollywood Memorial
Conrad Veidt	Ferncliff
Earl Warren	Arlington National
Clifton Webb	Hollywood Memorial
George Westinghouse	Arlington National
Harry Payne Whitney	Woodlawn
Jess Willard	Forest Lawn
Gus Williams	Green-Wood
Frank Winfield Woolworth	Woodlawn
Estelle Winwood	Westwood Memorial
Grant Withers	Forest Lawn
Natalie Wood	Westwood Memorial
William Wrigley, Jr.	Forest Lawn
Ed Wynn	Forest Lawn
Darryl F. Zanuck	Westwood Memorial
Florenz Ziegfeld	Forest Lawn

Addresses

Forest Lawn Memorial Park
1712 Glendale Avenue
Glendale, California

Arlington National Cemetery
Arlington, Virginia

Ferncliff Cemetery
Hartsdale, New York

Green-Wood Cemetery
Fifth Avenue at 25th Street
Brooklyn, New York

Hollywood Memorial Park
6000 Santa Monica
    Boulevard
Los Angeles, California

Holy Cross Cemetery
5835 West Slauson Avenue
Los Angeles, California

Pierce Brothers
Westwood Village Memorial
    Park
1218 Glendon Avenue
Los Angeles, California

Woodlawn Cemetery
233rd St. and Webster
    Avenue
Bronx, New York

INDEX

Academic honors, 188–192
Academy Awards, 171–178
  Best Actors, 171–172
  Best Actresses, 172–173
  Best Directors, 176–177
  Best Supporting Actors,
    173–174
  Best Supporting Actresses,
    175–176
  never won, 178
  oldest, youngest, 177
Actors and actresses
  as directors, 151–153
  autograph values, 160
  in drag, 158–159
  late debuts, 154
  turned politicians, 207–209
  see also Academy Awards;
    Tony Awards
Adopted children, 40
Ailments, disabilities, 137
Algonquin Round Table,
  245–246
Allen, Woody, wit and wis-
  dom, 258
Alma maters, 107–115

American Academy of
  Dramatic Arts
  attendees, 115–116
American Indians, 85–86
Ancestors, famous, 86–87
Aquarius, 5–8
Aries, 11–15
Arlington National Cemetery,
  267–272
Assassinations, 265
Athletes
  Athletes of the Year,
    217–218
  Baseball Hall of Fame,
    228–231
  Baseball millionaires,
    232–234
  Bowling Hall of Fame, 225
  Boxing, heavyweight
    champions, 224
  Endorsement income,
    219
  Football Hall of Fame,
    220–222
  Heisman Trophy winners,
    219–220

Athletes *(continued)*
  highest-paid basketball
    players, 223–224
  highest-paid football
    players, 222–223
  in movies, 156–158
  Tennis Hall of Fame,
    225–227
Auto accidents, died in, 265
Autobiographies, 160–167
Autographs, value of, 160
Awards
  Academy Awards,
    171–178
  Kennedy Center, 187–188
  Tonys, 179–187

Bachelors and
    bacheloresses, 121
Bankhead, Tallulah, wit and
    wisdom, 256
Baptists, 242
Baseball Hall of Fame,
    228–231
Baseball millionaires,
    232–234
Basketball, highest-paid
    players, 223–224
Beauty
  Miss America, 194–195
Berra, Yogi, wit and wisdom,
    257
Betty Ford Center attendees,
    251
Beverly Hills, born in, 49–50
Birthdates, 3–40
Birthplaces
  Beverly Hills, 49–50
  Brooklyn, 45–47
  Canada, 40–43
  Hollywood, 49–50
  Malibu, 49–50
  Poland, 44–45
  Russia, 43–44
  Texas, 47–49
Boarding schools, 102–106
Bogart, Humphrey, wit and
    cynicism, 257–258
Born on
  Christmas Day, 39
  New Year's Day, 3

Valentine's Day, 7
Bowling, Hall of Famers, 225
Boxing, heavyweight cham-
    pions, 224
Brooklyn born, 45–47
Brothers and sisters, 88
Buried, where, 267–272

Canadians, famous, 40–43
Cancer, 22–27
Capricorn, 3–4, 39–40
Cemeteries, 267–272
Cheerleaders, 101
Children
  only, 89
  many, 89
  names of, 54
  twins, 88
Christian Scientists,
    243
Colleges, universities
    attended, 107–115
Compass Players, 116
Congress, U.S. millionaires,
    206–207
Converts
  to Judaism, 245
  from Judaism, 245

Death
  assassinations, 265
  auto accidents, 265
  burial places, 267–272
  drug overdoes, 264
  early age, 261–262
  late age, 266–267
  murdered, 263–264
  plane crashes, 264
  suicides, 262–263
  unusual causes, 265
Democrats, 209–210
Dentists, 117
Directors
  Academy Award-winning,
    176–177
  actors who directed,
    151–153
  appearances in movies,
    153–154
Disabilities, ailments, 137
Doctors, 117

Drag, actors and actresses
    in, 158–159
Dropouts, high school, 101
Drug overdoses, 264

Education
    academic honors,
        188–192
    colleges and universities,
        107–115
    high school dropouts, 101
    prep schools, 102–106
    Rhodes scholars, 191–192
Endorsement income, ath-
    letes', 219
Entertainers, highest-paid,
    150–151
Entertainers-turned-
    politicians, 207–209
Episcopalians, 243
Ethnic origins, 83–85
Executive salaries, 247–248

Facelifts, plastic surgery,
    131–133
Families
    fathers' occupations,
        91–97
    military, 90–91
Fathers' occupations, 91–97
Fields, W.C., wit and wis-
    dom, 255
First names, 53
Football
    Football Hall of Fame,
        220–222
    Heisman Trophy winners,
        219–220
    highest-paid players,
        222–223
Ford, Betty Center attendees,
    251
Forest Lawn (Calif.) ceme-
    tery, 267–272
Foster children, 40

Gemini, 18–21
Goldwyn, Samuel, wit and
    wisdom, 256–257

Hair transplants, 135

Hall of Fame
    baseball, 228–231
    bowling, 225
    football, 220–222
    rock 'n' roll, 197–198
    tennis, 225–227
Heavyweight boxing champi-
    ons, 224
Heavyweights, 136
Heights of
    men, 140–144
    U.S. Presidents, 205
    women, 137–139
Heisman Trophy winners,
    219–220
Highest paid
    baseball players, 232–234
    basketball players; 223–224
    business executives,
        247–248
    entertainers, 150–151
    football players, 222–223
High school
    cheerleaders, 101
    dropouts, 101
    prep schools, 102–106
History's most influential 100,
    211–213
Hollywood, born in, 49–50
Hollywood Memorial Park
    (Calif.), 267–272
Hollywood, second genera-
    tion, 147–149
Hollywood Ten, The, 211
Homosexuals, 125–126
Honors, academic, 188–192
Horoscope signs, see spe-
    cific ones

Inauguration, U.S.
    Presidents' ages at, 203
Influential, most in history,
    211–213
In-laws, 90

Jail, prison time, 249
Jews, Judaism, 83–85, 243,
    245
Jobs, previous, 240–242
Justices of Supreme Court,
    214

Kennedy Center awards,
187–188

Lawyers, 117
Left-handedness, 135–136
Leo, 25–27
Lesbians, 126
Libra, 30–34
License plates, vanity, 250
Long marriages, 124–125

Malibu, born in, 49–50
Marriages
    long, 124–125
    multiple, 121–122
    never married, 121
    remarried same person,
        122
    short, 123–124
Marx, Groucho, wit and wis-
    dom, 255
Military academy attendees,
    106
Military brats, 90–91
Miss America, 194–195
Mormons, 243
Multiple marriages,
    121–122
Murdered, 263–264

Names, first, 53
Names, real, 54–80
Names of children, 54
Native Americans, 85–86
NBC pages, former, 245
Never married, 121
Nixon's enemy list, 206
Non-actors in movies,
    154–156
Nose jobs, plastic surgery,
    131–133

Occupations
    fathers', 91–97
    previous jobs, 240–242
Only children, 89
Origins, ethnic, 83–85
Oscars, 171–178
    Best Actors, 171–172
    Best Actresses, 172–173
    Best Directors, 176–177

Best Supporting Actors,
    173–174
Best Supporting Actresses,
    175–176
never won, 178
oldest, youngest winners,
    177
Overweight, 136

Perry, Antoinette Awards,
    see Tonys
Phi Beta Kappa keys,
    189–191
Philadelphia singers, 248
Phobias, 251–252
Physical ailments, 137
Pilots, 247
Pisces, 8–11
Plane crash, died from, 264
Plastic surgery, 131–133
Playwrights' Theater Club,
    116
Polish born, 44–45
Political parties, 209–210
Popularity
    least popular celebrities, 196
    most popular celebrities,
        196
    most popular comedians,
        197
    radio personalities,
        199–200
Prep school graduates,
    102–106
Presidents, U.S.
    age at inauguration, 203
    heights, 205
    time in office, 204
Previous jobs, occupations,
    240–242
Prison, jail records, 249
Protestants, 243–244

Quakers, 244
Quotations
    about famous people,
        237–239
    on sex, 126–128

Radio personalities, most
    popular, 199–200

Reagan's leading ladies, 149–150
Real names of famous people, 54–80
Relatives, ancestors, 86–87, 90, 147–149
Religions, 242–245
Remarried same person, 122
Republicans, 210
Rhinoplasty, 131–133
Rhodes scholars, 191–192
Richest Americans
  athletes, 222–224, 232–234
  business executives, 247–248
  congressmen, 206–207
  entertainers, 150–151
  people in United States, 246
Rock and Roll Hall of Fame, 197–198
Roman Catholics, 244
Russian born, 43–44

Sagittarius, 36–39
Scorpio, 34–36
Second City graduates, 116
Second-generation actors, 147–149
Sex
  homosexuals, 125–126
  lesbians, 126
  quotations about, 126–128
Short marriages, 123–124
Shot and lived, 239–240
Siblings, 88
Singers, Philadelphia-born, 248
Sisters and brothers, 88
Sports, *see* Athletes *and specific sport*
Stengel, Casey, wit and wisdom, 257
Suicides, 262–263
Supreme Court justices, 214

Tattoos, 134–135
Taurus, 15–18
Tennis Hall of Fame, 225–227

Texas, born in, 47–49
Time magazine "Man of the Year," 192–194
Tony Awards, 179–187
  Best Actor/Dramatic Role, 179–180
  Best Actor/Musical Role, 181–182
  Best Actress/Dramatic Role, 180–181
  Best Actress/Musical Role, 182–183
  Best Supporting Actor/Dramatic Role, 184–185
  Best Supporting Actor/Musical, 186–187
  Best Supporting Actress/Dramatic Role, 183–184
  Best Supporting Actress/Musical, 185–186
Time in office, U.S. Presidents, 204
Toupees, 135
Twins, 87–88
  famous twins, 87
  parents of twins, 88

Universities, colleges attended, 107–115
Unmarried, 121
U.S. Presidents
  age at inauguration, 203
  heights of, 205
  Nixon's enemies list, 206
  time in office, 204
U.S.S.R., born in, 43–44

Virgo, 27–30

West, Mae, wit and wisdom, 256
Wit and wisdom of
  Allen, Woody, 258
  Bankhead, Tallulah, 256
  Berra, Yogi, 257
  Bogart, Humphrey, 257–258
  Fields, W.C., 255
  Goldwyn, Samuel, 256–257
  Marx, Groucho, 255

Wit and wisdom
of (continued)
  Stengel, Casey, 257
  West, Mae, 256
Woodlawn Cemetery
    (N.Y.C.), 267–272

Wounded in war, 239–240

Zodiac signs, *see specific
  signs*